CONTESTED LANDS

Conflict and Compromise in
New Jersey's Pine Barrens

In the series
CONFLICTS IN URBAN AND
REGIONAL DEVELOPMENT
edited by
John R. Logan and Todd Swanstrom

Contested Lands

Conflict and Compromise in New Jersey's Pine Barrens

ROBERT J. MASON

Temple University Press

PHILADELPHIA

Temple University Press, Philadelphia 19122
Copyright © 1992 by Temple University. All rights reserved
Published 1992
Printed in the United States of America

The paper used in this publication meets the minimum requirements of
American National Standard for Information Sciences—Permanence of
Paper for Printed Library Materials, ANSI Z39.48-1984 ∞

Library of Congress Cataloging-in-Publication Data
Mason, Robert J., 1955–
    Contested lands : conflict and compromise in New Jersey's Pine Barrens /
Robert J. Mason.
        p.   cm. — (Conflicts in urban and regional development)
    Includes bibliographical references and index.
    ISBN 0-87722-925-2
    1. Land use—Government policy—New Jersey—Pine Barrens.
I. Title.   II. Series.
HD266.N52P565 1992   91-29633
333.75′09749′6—dc20   CIP

Contents

Maps and Tables

Acknowledgments

Though they no longer may recognize large parts of it, I want to acknowledge those who oversaw this work in its first incarnation as a dissertation: Ken Mitchell, Frank Popper, Briavel Holcomb, and Phil Burch of Rutgers University. They are wonderful colleagues and supportive friends. Frank Popper's pearls of land use planning wisdom, regularly dispensed, have helped me enormously in the various stages of writing and rewriting.

Early support for the dissertation came in the form of a grant from the Rutgers University Office of Community Affairs. For that assistance, I am most grateful to John Cooney, director of that office.

Howard Green, research director for the New Jersey Historical Commission, has been enormously helpful from the outset. He provided important critical insights and encouraged me to apply for a grant-in-aid from the New Jersey Historical Commission. I received the grant and am most grateful to the commission for its help.

B. Budd Chavooshian, of the Department of Environmental Resources at Rutgers University, also helped in the early stages. He gave generously of his time and helped me secure research funds from Rutgers University. Budd's insights as a Pinelands commissioner and former New Jersey planning director have been invaluable.

Acknowledgments

In transforming the manuscript from dissertation into its current form, I have been adeptly guided by Michael Ames, editor-in-chief at Temple University Press, and Todd Swanstrom, co-editor of the Conflicts in Urban and Regional Development series. They have been extraordinarily patient, encouraging, and constructive in their respective roles. Mary Capouya, production editor at Temple University Press, eased me through the final, tedious stages with competence and good humor. Connie Mason and Mary Wilson helped me proofread the typescript.

Many others helped shape and reshape this manuscript; I will mention just a few. Jim Mertes of Texas Tech University is a veritable fountain of information about greenline parks and greenways. Janet Jackson, education director at the Philadelphia Zoo and a long-time friend of the Pine Barrens, has been supportive throughout. Shira Birnbaum shared with me many of her thoughts about planning and politics in the Pines.

Pinelands Commission staff have been more than helpful in answering queries, providing materials and maps, offering access to files, and accommodating me at many meetings. I want to thank Executive Director Terry Moore, Public Programs Manager Bob Bembridge, planners Mike Bolan and Alice D'Arcy, cartographer Fred Douthitt, and public liaison Pat Murphy.

Many residents and local officials throughout the Pines gave generously of their time and knowledge. Business aside, it is always a pleasure to visit them. The list of names is much too long to produce here; instead, I offer my heartfelt thanks to all.

Steve Shore capably produced the maps for this book. Johns Hopkins University Press is acknowledged for permission to reprint, in Map 2, Jonathan Berger and John Sinton's Pine Barrens subregion boundaries.

All who assisted deserve much credit. Responsibility for any errors or omissions is, of course, entirely mine.

Finally, special thanks to family and friends for helping me through this long process. You have made it all worthwhile.

Abbreviations

ANJEC   Association of New Jersey Environmental Commissions
APA   Adirondack Park Agency
BLSJ   Builders League of South Jersey
CAFRA   Coastal Area Facilities Review Act (New Jersey)
CCES   Center for Coastal and Environmental Studies
        (Rutgers University)
CMP   Comprehensive Management Plan (Pinelands)
CZMP   Coastal Zone Management Program
DCR   Division of Coastal Resources (New Jersey)
DEP   Department of Environmental Protection (New Jersey)
DRI   Development of Regional Impact program
EDF   Environmental Defense Fund
FOCUS   Federation of Conservationists United Societies, Inc.
LCDC   Land Control and Development Commission (Oregon)
LULU   Locally unwanted land uses
NEPA   National Environmental Policy Act
NIMBY   "Not in my backyard"
NJAS   New Jersey Audubon Society
NJBA   New Jersey Builders Association
NJCF   New Jersey Conservation Foundation
NJPC   New Jersey Pinelands Commission
PCS   Pinelands Cultural Society
PDC   Pinelands Development Credit program
PEC   Pinelands Environmental Council
PRC   Pinelands Review Committee
PURD   Planned unit residential development

RPA	Regional Plan Association (New York)
RPAA	Regional Plan Association of America
STOP	Stop Tax Oppression Promptly
TDR	Transfer of development rights
ULI	Urban Land Institute

CONTESTED LANDS

Conflict and Compromise in
New Jersey's Pine Barrens

1

Introduction

Just four days before Ronald Reagan's 1981 inauguration, outgoing Secretary of the Interior Cecil D. Andrus approved a comprehensive zoning and regulatory plan for New Jersey's Pine Barrens. Marking as it did the accelerated culmination of several years of state and federal efforts, the timing of Andrus's act does not seem especially surprising. Yet, when viewed in a longer-term context, it makes less sense. The Pinelands plan, as it is known in bureaucratic parlance, came on line as the nation was sliding into a recession—an unlikely time for measures that threatened to restrict economic development even further. Moreover, nearly a decade had elapsed since the nation's interest in land use and environmental planning had peaked, and almost another decade would pass before comparable environmental fervor was rekindled.

Indeed, the scope and authority of the Pinelands effort stand in stark contrast to the antiregulatory climate and subdued environmental enthusiasm of the early to mid 1980s. Pinelands planning more closely resembles its predecessors of the early 1970s than it portends things to come; current national interest leans heavily toward issues of waste disposal, toxic and hazardous threats, and global

issues such as greenhouse warming, ozone depletion, tropical defor-
estation, and habitat destruction (Adams et al. 1985; Conservation
Foundation 1987; Council on Environmental Quality 1990; Hays
1987; Maize 1988; Portney 1990; Renew America 1990). Regional
land use initiatives may of course flow from these concerns, but they
are not the bread-and-butter issues of today's environmentalism.

Why, then, did comprehensive land use regulation take root in
the Pine Barrens in such an unlikely era? And what does this imply
for other regions contemplating similar programs? Chapter 4 offers
insights, focusing on the critical roles of local and regional politics.
Socially and politically, the differences between the Pine Barrens
and other rural or quasi-urban regions are more in the way of detail
than general form. What does distinguish the Pines is location: They
constitute the largest tract of sparsely settled land in the northeastern megalopolitan corridor (Map 1). Although the Pines lack the
rugged mountains, swift streams, or spectacular coastlines typical of
many national and state parks, they possess vast quantities of pure
groundwater, distinct flora and fauna, and a rich and fascinating
history of human occupance and resource exploitation. And they
are virtually in the backyard of nearly 25 million people.

Two years before Andrus signed off on the Pinelands comprehensive plan, federal legislation had established the Pinelands as the
nation's first, and to this date only, national reserve. Unlike most
national parks, the Pines are settled and are substantially in private
ownership. Day-to-day management of this newly created preserve
would be largely a state responsibility. In 1979, the New Jersey
Legislature passed the Pinelands Protection Act, which explicitly
defined a regional planning scheme, ostensibly to be shared among
federal, state, and local governments.

More than a million acres are included in the national reserve, and
934,000 of them are regulated by the Comprehensive Management
Plan (CMP). The Pinelands are divided into two major subregions:
a core preservation area, where very little new development is permitted, and an outer protection area, where development is allowed
at different densities in several kinds of zones (Map 4). Thus residential and commercial growth are to be accommodated but are to
be directed toward areas of least ecological vulnerability.

Pinelands land uses are managed by a fifteen-member commission
consisting of seven gubernatorial appointees, one representative
from each of the seven counties with land in the Pinelands, and one

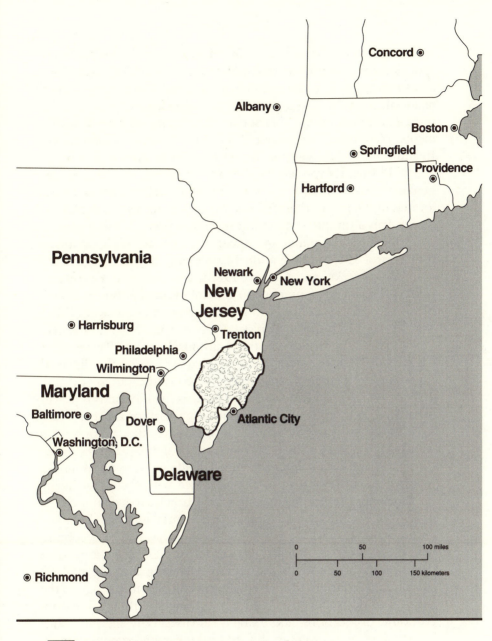

New Jersey Pinelands

Source: New Jersey Pinelands Commission, *Comprehensive Management Plan for the Pinelands National Reserve and Pinelands Area* (New Lisbon, N.J.: State of New Jersey Pinelands Commission, 1980), xvi.

MAP 1. LOCATION OF NEW JERSEY PINE BARRENS

federal representative. The commission developed the CMP and is responsible for its implementation. Although the federal role in Pinelands management is, for the most part, limited to the provision of financial, research, and logistical support, federal law does require the Department of the Interior to review proposed CMP amendments. New Jersey's governor also must review proposed changes. In addition, he has veto power over the actions of the commission.

The Pinelands experience represents an attempt to accommodate personal, institutional, economic, and ecological interests in an area located in the most urbanized state, as well as region, of the United States. It is a unique situation in several respects. Yet it also serves as a model for the public management of private lands on a large scale (Carol 1987). The National Conference of State Legislatures (Morandi, Meeks, and Sacarto 1983), Conservation Foundation (1985), President's Commission on Americans Outdoors (1987), National Wetlands Policy Forum (Conservation Foundation 1988), Task Force on Northern Forest Lands (Harper, Falk, and Rankin 1990), and Commission on the Adirondacks in the Twenty-First Century (1990) are among those who have drawn on the Pinelands experience in their efforts to protect valued landscapes.

The case for protecting areas as valued as the Pinelands is powerful indeed, and regional planning, in some form or another, seems to be the best way to go about it. The waters are muddied only when we begin to consider the particulars. In the initial planning for the Pinelands, important interests and individuals were vastly underrepresented; little or no power was shared with them. Yet during the Pinelands plan's implementation, the balance to a degree shifted in favor of community and rural entrepreneurial interests. Simply to ensure its own survival, Pinelands planning has had to accommodate these interests. At best, this crudely represents a move in the direction of more socially just regional planning. But the goal of a socially and economically just environmental planning program that actually works is indeed an elusive one, fraught with political traps, economic dislocations, and moral quandaries. Why and how, then, did the Pinelands program shift toward greater accommodation of local interests? What are the consequences of that shift, and what lessons are offered for other land use planning programs?

In seeking to understand the Pinelands program better, and as a consequence learn how to manage valued natural and cultural landscapes better, four closely related themes emerge: the Pinelands as a place, the emergence of centralized planning in the Pines, equity in regional management, and the politics of the plan's implementation. The very essence of the place is being altered by regional planning—the area is redefined, its sociopolitical character is changed, and it is perceived in new and different ways. My central concern is with the first five to ten years of the regional plan's implementation. Within this critical time span, I seek to understand the changing politics of place and the associated conflicts of interest and their resolution. More specific questions are raised within this general framework.

The Pine Barrens as a Place

For any endeavor that seeks to protect ecological and cultural resources, the question of regional definition is basic: It sets the stage for planning; it can both constrain and enhance the levels of protection afforded the resources in question; it determines, usually in no small part, the legal and administrative arrangements that will be necessary; and it plays an important part in defining the nature of the resultant conflicts. Federal and state Pinelands definitions are based almost entirely on physical criteria, with only minor adjustments made for social, economic, or political reasons. Only the coastal region might be considered an exception (Map 4).

But Pinelands planning involves much more than physical landscapes. Indeed, the Pinelands story is one of conflicting values—values that differ deeply, but not so deeply as to be beyond reconciliation at least on some level. As currently practiced, Pinelands planning represents, on the one hand, a rational, central ordering of a regional landscape based on a set of ecological principles; on the other, it is a negotiated settlement, with various exactions and concessions made in rough proportion to the political influence of the key players. This planning process, controlled largely by interests based outside the Pines, in essence defines the region and shapes its future.

It is imperative, therefore, that the area being planned for be understood—physically, socially, politically, and historically—by those whose hands might guide its fate. All these attributes give meaning to space, transforming a green section of the map into a place—perhaps into many places. In the Pinelands, scientists and planners have produced regional definitions based on geology, soils, and vegetation (see Chapter 3). Associated debate has rarely questioned the existence of a discrete physical region; instead, it has focused on the selection and application of criteria for delineating precise regional boundaries (McCormick and Forman 1979).

More elusive is the extent to which the Pine Barrens constitute a cultural or political region—or, more aptly, many such regions. The Pinelands Commission addresses the question of "cultural resources" through a set of policies that seeks to "maintain opportunities for traditional lifestyles . . . maintain the social and cultural integrity of traditional Pinelands communities . . . [and] maintain and enhance historic and archeological areas and sites of national, state, and local importance" (New Jersey Pinelands Commission 1980, 194). These criteria imply that there may be a culture region as well as natural region. In further support of the notion that the Pinelands are considered something more than a physical region is the way in which the CMP manages growth. Physical criteria are not uniformly applied throughout; instead, growth is directed away from those areas least ecologically suitable to those more suitable. The guiding assumption is that the entire region can and should accommodate a certain amount of development, an amount that is to be apportioned among the region's municipalities. Thus, even though ecological considerations are paramount in Pinelands management, the Pinelands nonetheless are treated as a political region.

But is there a Pinelands culture region? To what degree, past and present, are local economies, political interests, and folkways congruent with physical Pine Barrens boundaries? As presented in Chapter 3, the historical evidence regarding socioeconomic integration at the regional scale is not very compelling. Yet it is possible— and, I would argue, far more appropriate—to view the Pines as a series of subregions. This is precisely what Berger and Sinton (1985) have attempted to do (Map 2). Their efforts have been largely ignored by Pinelands planners.

Historical evidence notwithstanding, today's New Jerseyans and residents of neighboring states are likely to think of the Pinelands— or Pine Barrens—as a region. Over the past twenty years or so, both scholarly and popular recognition of the Pines have grown enormously. Pinelands planning, along with the attention that preceded and accompanies it, has bolstered regional identity both within and outside the region. Indeed, it has helped "create" a region where none was recognized or understood before. At the same time, it has tended to obscure subregional distinctions. Perhaps inadvertently, it has also helped nurture a highly romanticized concept of a region whose few remaining inhabitants are engaged in a valiant struggle against the forces of modern society that alienate people from the land. This contemporary restructuring of the region carries implications for our present view as well as our historical understanding of the Pines. These implications are considered through the course of this book.

Emergence of Centralized Planning

Time, as well as place, is fundamental to regional planning. When, and under what circumstances, is it appropriate to initiate a particular planning scheme? The Pinelands case is intriguing. If one considers only national trends, the plan's timing seems wrong. If we are to make sense of the Pinelands effort, we need to consider a variety of geographical scales, ranging from international to local. Three scales are especially important:

1. The local scale. This refers to the immediate Pinelands, or Pine Barrens, area. This is where most agricultural, housebuilding, and other rural entrepreneurial interests are active, and where opposition to regional planning has been most vocal.
2. The state–megalopolitan scale. This is the stage for most Pinelands planning activity—in the state legislature, through the state-level Pinelands Commission, and through the activities of interest groups based largely in New Jersey (but with a significant presence from the nearby megalopolitan centers of New York and Philadelphia).
3. The national scale. Congressional and interest-group activity inspired designation of the Pinelands National Reserve. The Pinelands program is widely viewed as a land use experiment of national significance.

Why did local, state, and national concerns culminate in a comprehensive plan for the Pinelands when they did? Why did a strong, centralized regulatory program similar to the "Quiet Revolution" initiatives of the 1970s emerge in the antiregulatory climate of the Reagan era? Three possible explanations may be offered:

1. Discrete or cumulative threats to the physical environment of the Pinelands became so severe as to provoke a strong regulatory response.
2. Pinelands planning is the culmination of years of local, regional, state, and federal efforts to protect the region; in other words, the CMP is part of an evolutionary process that has been moving toward ever-stricter control over local land use.
3. Pinelands planning is the result of some coincidental combination of circumstances—a series of idiosyncratic events or processes that might be difficult or impossible to have foreseen, let alone replicate elsewhere.

These six propositions of scale and circumstance are not mutually exclusive; in fact, each of them is of some importance in explaining events in the Pinelands. But the local and the idiosyncratic seem best suited to the task of explanation.

Although the Pinelands planning program is widely cited nationally, principal impetus did not come from Congress or the national-level environmental lobby. Although it is true that significant institutional and political support was present at the federal level, the Pinelands plan was largely an outcome of local (i.e., the regional megalopolis surrounding the Pines) events. The following factors were of principal importance:

1. The commitment of Brendan Byrne, governor of New Jersey from 1973 to 1979, to Pinelands planning. Byrne did not consider himself an environmentalist, but he was strongly influenced on the Pinelands issue by the writings of John McPhee (1967, 1974). Byrne's personal commitment went well beyond short-term political opportunism; indeed, he viewed Pinelands protection not simply as a legislative victory, but as a legacy to New Jersey.
2. In the late 1970s, New Jersey legalized casino gambling in Atlantic City, prompting concern about the impacts of associated growth on the nearby Pinelands.
3. The anticipated development of offshore oil and gas (which in fact never materialized) likewise generated concern about environmental impacts on the Pinelands.
4. Strong congressional support for the idea of a Pinelands National Reserve came from Representative James Florio (who became

New Jersey's governor in 1989) and Senators Clifford Case and Harrison Williams. Strong support from local environmentalists and politicians, combined with the area's unique physical and cultural characteristics that inspired that sentiment, made the Pines fertile ground for testing the greenline concept of planning, that is, the management of private lands for public purposes.

5. The greenline concept also enjoyed support within the U.S. Department of the Interior. The now defunct Heritage Conservation and Recreation Service, and later the National Park Service, provided impetus and technical assistance.

6. Environmental interest groups—mostly in the New Jersey–New York–Philadelphia area, but some national organizations as well —strongly supported Pinelands preservation efforts. The environmental groups did not, however, provide the spark that brought the Pinelands plan into being. Indeed, a less-than-center-stage role for environmental organizations was the norm for most land use regulatory programs of the 1970s (Popper 1981), with the notable exception of the California Coastal Commissions. Still, the significance of their supporting role should not be understated; without their support, the Pinelands plan would probably have been weaker or nonexistent.

7. In New Jersey, the critical supporting role of environmental organizations was facilitated by the state's size, population, economy, and political culture. Some of the same circumstances that produce so many environmental problems in New Jersey also give rise to concerted responses. New Jersey ranks high in the nation for its environmental programs, as well as the voting records of its congressional representatives (Alexander 1990; League of Conservation Voters 1990; Renew America 1990). Not only does New Jersey government have a comparatively strong commitment to environmental protection; it also is accessible to interest groups. Trenton, the state capital, is no more than a couple of hours away from the farthest corner of the state, and lies within the densely populated megalopolitan corridor that bisects New Jersey. New Jersey's population geography makes the corridors of power physically accessible, and this helps explain the numbers and effectiveness of environmental organizations in the state.

In sum, a strong Pinelands plan might not have materialized had any one of the above ingredients been absent. It was very much a combination of factors that gave birth to the comprehensive plan. Greenline parks proponent Charles Little, working as a private consultant when interviewed in 1985, looked back on the process as the metaphorical "stone soup." And indeed, that brew was sufficiently formidable to counter the hastening national retreat from comprehensive, centralized land use regulation.

Equity in Regional Management

America's native inhabitants were at first perplexed when Europeans introduced the notion of land as a commodity. They believed that humans could hold rights to things on the land (Cronan 1983; Petulla 1988), but could not own the land itself. Over the succeeding few centuries, the "land as a commodity" view has generally prevailed. Yet, even since early colonial times, we have also demonstrated the capacity to treat land as a resource, to nurture it so that it can in turn continue to nurture us in economic and spiritual ways. More recently, we have virtually perfected our ability to use the ownership and control of land as means of exclusion, allowing us to sort ourselves spatially on the basis of race and class.

Though never very deeply suppressed in our collective thinking, these controversies surface when governments single out valued environments for special protection. Indeed, regional land use controversies often are viewed as debates between the "land as a resource" and "land as a commodity" camps; or between conservationists ("wise use" of land) and preservationists (set aside maximum possible acreages). Environmentalists tend to see their opponents as rapists of the land; local residents, in turn, view many environmentalists as misguided extremists. The truth, of course, lies contentiously in between.

The Pinelands—the contested physical space as well as the bureaucratic power centers that govern their fate—form an arena for conflict among environmental, rural entrepreneurial, agricultural, and community concerns. But in the Pines, as elsewhere, the terms of debate are all too often drawn narrowly (see Collins and Russell 1988; Goldstein 1981). Indeed, the relationship between regional organization and distribution of a whole host of costs and benefits is pervasive and complex. Pinelands planning has the intraregional effect of reapportioning economic as well as noneconomic values.

It potentially affects property values, taxes, employment opportunities, and environmental quality generally. Effects can vary widely from individual to individual and from community to community. At a broader, more abstract level of analysis, we might attempt to compare costs and benefits for the region's residents with those accruing to surrounding regions, states, and the nation.

Friedmann and Weaver (1979) characterize regional planning generally as an "instrument of urban-industrial expansion." The Pinelands program—in seeking to maintain open space, protect amenities, and preserve ecosystems—conforms in some degree to this characterization. It enlarges the megalopolitan region, transforming what was once deemed "empty space" (Klimm 1953) into an integral part of that system. Although, as argued in Chapter 3, the Pine Barrens have long been tied into the surrounding urban fabric, the relationship has changed in recent years. The revised spatial definition of New Jersey's critical planning area arises largely from increased, and often conflicting, demands for accessible open space, ecological protection, and suburban housing and commercial services.

One of the outcomes of Pinelands planning has been the protection of a large scientific laboratory. Not only does the Pinelands effort help maintain the physical resource that constitutes the laboratory, it also provides funding and institutional support for specific research endeavors. But more significant than the obvious benefits to ecologists and biologists may be those to the larger population of northern New Jersey and the nearby Philadelphia and New York areas. The recreational opportunities and the basic assurance that there are still relatively unspoiled areas nearby constitute important benefits. The spiritual comfort provided by the latter may indeed be valuable, even to those who rarely or never visit the region. Environmental protection also benefits residents of the region—in tangible ways (tourism revenues) and intangible ways (peace of mind). But it also brings significant costs: foregone development opportunities, impacts from increased recreational use, and tax increases needed to offset lost revenues and finance new services. The benefits and costs of Pinelands planning are distributed unevenly both within and outside the Pinelands. Because so many of them are intangible, and therefore difficult to describe in even the most general terms, the resultant conflicts of interest are likewise elusive. Indeed, some may result more from misunderstanding than differences in basic values.

Radical political economists (Geisler 1980; Heiman 1983, 1988, 1989; Markusen 1981; Plotkin 1987; Walker and Heiman 1981), none of whom have considered the Pinelands program specifically, might be inclined to view it as a response to the needs of monopoly capitalism. But this argument is difficult to support either empirically or theoretically—unless perhaps the role of environmentalism and the importance of small, rural entrepreneurial interests are clearly understood (Birnbaum 1991; Bryant 1989). By and large, interest-group and individual actions have defined and guided the Pinelands effort, and the Pinelands plan owes its existence principally to a coincidence of events at a particular time. Monopolistic or oligopolistic forces did not attempt to obstruct the Pinelands efforts, nor did they tend to support them. While a few specific exceptions might be cited, the larger picture has been one of indifference.

Although the visions of regional futures expressed by communities and interest groups often clash with those prescribed by Pinelands planning, all parties have had to accept and adjust to the changes imposed by Pinelands planning. As it turns out, all key players—"losers" as well as "winners"—have adapted and indeed have informed and influenced in their own ways the region's changing political economy. Because Pinelands planning creates and maintains a large nature–culture preserve, its principal constituency is made up of urban-based interests. And to the degree that such preserves are vital over the long term to maintaining the balance between expansion of production and the integrity of consumption amenities (Heiman 1988), it may eventually become apparent that the Pinelands National Reserve serves the needs of big capital interests as well.

The Politics of Regional Plan Implementation

The first several years of Pinelands planning, particularly the first half of the 1980s, were the most crucial. As a new and untested concept, the Pinelands National Reserve faced several challenges—legislative, administrative, and judicial—to its legitimacy. It survived these tests and today enjoys a comfortable base of political support. The Pinelands program travels with confidence along the basic course set during its early years.

Pinelands planning, guided by the gospel of Quiet Revolution prophets (see Babcock 1966; Babcock and Siemon 1985; Bosselman and Callies 1971; Reilly 1973), perpetuates the status quo in critical-area planning and management of the 1970s. Like many of those earlier regional planning endeavors, the Pinelands process has been one of brokering among interests; of finding the right equilibrium among the various groups that have stakes in the process and are active politically. Thus, and probably unavoidably, a few major interests have dominated. The Pinelands Commission's and National Park Service's institutional biases toward the "ecocentric" persisted through a period of growing environmental conservatism. Although these views were more strongly supported in the early days of Pinelands planning, bureaucratic inertia has sustained them so that they are still well represented at the working level. In large part, the ecocentric philosophy endured because its proponents have been flexible; the commission, staff, and most environmental supporters have adapted to changing political circumstances with considerable dexterity.

During the first decade of Pinelands planning, all the key players —not just the commission and its environmental supporters— adapted amicably and efficiently to changing political circumstances. Although the Pinelands effort was initially framed in preservationist terms, the Pinelands Commission prospered as a bureaucratic entity not by remaining in the public embrace of particular environmental interest groups but by attempting to satisfy a range of key interests. On numerous occasions, the commission took comfort from the adage to which so many bureaucracies subscribe: "If everyone is yelling at us, we must be doing something right."

In large part, the Pinelands program has been sustained by legislative and gubernatorial support, combined with an absence of persistent, well-organized public opposition. Except for the housebuilding interests, and to a lesser extent agricultural concerns, local opposition to Pinelands planning has been vocal but not nearly so effective as it might have been. Indeed, the municipal conformance process (Chapter 7) was a valuable tool for blunting local opposition. The commission's practice of negotiating with one township or county at a time was in essence a divide-and-conquer strategy— and a rather effective one at that. Moreover, locally based interests were placated in several ways: Governor Thomas Kean's appointment of Pinelands commissioners who were highly receptive to local concerns, the streamlining of development application requirements, a tax-reimbursement program for townships, infrastructure funds provided by a state bond issue, commission funding for local planning activities, and the improvement of working relations between commission staff and local officials (see Chapter 7). What opposition there was in the Pinelands had decreased enormously by the mid 1980s (Chapter 5). And this provided the commission with new opportunities to enhance its image, allowing it to redirect energies initially consumed by the municipal conformance process toward other concerns, including research, education, and public awareness.

The municipal and county conformance program cannot be viewed as entirely smooth sailing for the Pinelands Commission. But the initial rapidity and overall rate of conformance of local plans and ordinances with regional mandates is without parallel in the country. On this basis alone, the program's administrators have deemed it a success (see Moore 1986). But, as Fischer (1985) points out with respect to California's coastal program, these are rather narrowly defined measures of success. Other indicators might include actual changes in local land uses, numbers and kinds of development approvals and denials, degree of interest-group participation in and support for Pinelands planning, and patterns of electoral support or approval. Beyond this, we need to consider broader questions, outlined earlier, about the fundamental validity of planning and management assumptions, intra- and interregional equity, and community and individual perceptions of environmental quality.

Because the Pinelands are not unpopulated wilderness, local communities have played a critical role in plan implementation. In order to convey some sense of the social, political, and economic "texture" of the Pines—and the implications for regional planning—three communities are examined in depth. They were chosen to illustrate, but by no means exhaustively cover, the range of local issues and concerns encountered in Pinelands management. The three townships are:

1. Woodland Township, dubbed the traditional "capital of the Pines" and located entirely within the preservation area of the Pinelands National Reserve (where the CMP most strictly limits development).

2. Hamilton Township, which has been slated to absorb a dispro-
   portionate share of regional growth. It owes this distinction to
   its proximity to Atlantic City and the environmental suitability
   (according to the Pinelands Commission) of parts of its land base
   for growth.
3. Manchester Township, which is made up largely of retirement-
   home developments. Despite the curtailment of additional projects, Manchester officials conformed quite amicably with the
   provisions of the CMP.

While the experiences of these townships point to the inadequate
attention Pinelands planning has given to local concerns, they also
attest to the creativity and competence of the Pinelands program
in ultimately securing local compliance with its broader objectives.
But it is not only the Pinelands Commission that has been creative;
townships, counties, and key interest groups and individuals also
have adapted with aplomb to the economic, political, and social
changes brought about by Pinelands planning. Many of them have
been instrumental not only in guiding but also benefiting from those
changes.

Larger Planning Contexts

The Pine Barrens' location near the heart of megalopolis (Map 1)
is critically important in bringing to bear an array of pressures and
influences in ways more immediate and intense than might be the
case for more remote regions. While the Pines are valued for recreation, they are not a playground on the order of such places as the
Adirondacks, Lake Tahoe, or Cape Cod. Still, these and many other
places are comparable in varying degree with the Pine Barrens in
terms of natural and cultural characteristics, as well as location fairly
close to large population concentrations. Although only the Pinelands have thus far been granted national reserve status, many other
valued areas are afforded some sort of special federal, state, or local
protection. The Pinelands experience, therefore, offers a valuable
model for the management of valued places across the nation.

In certain quarters, both the Adirondack Park and Pinelands
National Reserve are seen as premier examples of greenline parks.
The Pinelands, because of their size, proximity to urban popula-

tions, and involvement of multiple levels of government in their management, are the top contender. Greenline planning may be broadly defined as an intergovernmental planning partnership that relies on a variety of land-management techniques to protect a regional landscape. Conservation easements, tax incentives, lease-back schemes, local and regional zoning, and fee-simple ownership are among the tools typically used. In contrast with most of our national and state parks, people live in greenline parks; towns, farms, and other material expressions of human occupance belong in greenline parks. Cultural landscape protection is foremost in the minds of greenline park planners, who frequently invoke eloquent images of what they call the "living landscape" (Corbett 1983; Fogleman et al. 1985; Hirner 1985; Little 1983; Mitchell 1978; Morrison 1983). Inspired by the trim, tidy, agriculturally produc-tive British countryside (Lowenthal and Prince 1964, 1965), where the land is overwhelmingly in private hands but development is strictly controlled through a rigorous combination of legislative and administrative arrangements (Blacksell and Gilg 1981; Fogleman et al. 1985; Green 1981; Hirner 1985; MacEwen and MacEwen 1982; Simmons 1978), greenline proponents tend to gloss over the political, economic, and cultural differences that would strain their hopeful national comparisons (Fogleman et al. 1985).

The greenline idea was spawned in the 1970s, a time of rapidly escalating demand for park and recreation space, but decreasing funds for its acquisition. Charles E. Little, who coined the term and developed the greenline concept, put principal emphasis on the pro-vision of recreational opportunities near urban areas (U.S. Congress, Senate, 1975). Local economies and cultures would remain intact in coexistence with expanded public access and use. No generic green-line legislation ever emerged, but as noted in Chapter 4, there was a failed attempt in 1977. Although the Carter administration did not strongly endorse the concept, officials apparently expected to pro-mote it during Carter's second term of office (Little 1983). Today, no formal system of greenline parks exists, nor does the term surface on many legislative agendas. Yet a variety of parks and recreation areas are believed by greenline proponents to fit the conceptual mold in varying degree (see Corbett 1983; Fogleman et al. 1985; Hirner 1985). Besides the Adirondacks and Pinelands, notable ex-amples include the Santa Monica Mountains National Recreation Area (California), the Columbia River Gorge National Scenic Area

(Washington–Oregon), the Cuyahoga Valley National Recreation Area (Ohio), the Upper Delaware River (New York–Pennsylvania), Fire Island National Seashore (New York), and Indiana Dunes National Lakeshore (Indiana).

Where greenline planning actually has taken place, much of it is afflicted with a confusion of goals: The preservation of open space and scenery—basically aesthetic concerns—are transformed into ecological imperatives. Fire Island National Seashore, Indiana Dunes National Lakeshore, Santa Monica Mountains National Recreation Area, and Cuyahoga Valley National Recreation Area all are examples of this (Foresta 1984, 1986; Hirner 1985; Mitchell 1978; U.S. Congress, Senate, 1975). To a much greater degree than was the case in the Pinelands, recreation was a central rationale for their designation. But in the actual management of these places, strict environmental preservation policies have prevailed—sometimes benefiting the few at the expense of the many (Foresta 1984). In other words, these greenline parks function largely as preserves for the enjoyment of those already living there, plus small numbers of visitors. Some of preservation's most ardent supporters see no irony in subscribing to an ecological ethic that offers them so much direct personal benefit. Indeed, even those residents and consumers of the Pinelands (different as it is from the cases previously cited) who have much to gain by "shutting the door" have become some of the most knowledgeable and sincere ecological preservationists. There is a fundamental inequity here, and it is evident in the Pinelands, other greenline parks, and much of the no-growth sentiment that proliferated in the 1970s and remains strong in many places today.

These critical observations notwithstanding, the Pinelands experience still provides a worthy model for greenline park planning. Does the Pinelands program's success in achieving its basic goals imply that it is a harbinger of other, similar greenline planning programs? While some greenline enthusiasts would like to think so, their arguments are not very persuasive. Pinelands planning has largely been a state-level activity, with minimal input from both local and federal levels. Formal local participation has been mostly of a token nature; the federal role is primarily one of providing funding. This is not the intergovernmental partnership that some advocates of greenline planning would envision (Eugster, 1985 interview). Of course, the Pinelands have not generated the same sort of national concern as have Florida's Everglades and Big Cypress Swamp (Carter 1974); there the federal government has taken a more active role. In the Pinelands, it may well be that federal funding is, in fact, the most appropriate role. But one then needs to ask greenline advocates just what they mean when they speak enthusiastically of intergovernmental partnerships.

I have argued that the Pinelands should be treated as a group of subregions, rather than a single physiographic region. And indeed this approach receives some affirmation in the recent direction taken by what I shall loosely term the "green spaces movement." The report of the President's Commission on Americans Outdoors (1987) calls for a network of private, state, and local "greenways" to link America's open spaces. Greenways are linear spaces, often defined by such features as stream valleys, ridgelines, rail rights-of-way, and canal towpaths (Didato 1990; Little 1990). Larger greenline parks are not specifically advocated in the commission's report, though the Pinelands receive brief mention in the Appendix. The report—trying in the words of one of its authors to "appeal to a western President who likes to chop wood"—places great emphasis on the private and the local. Despite this, it evoked scant response from Ronald Reagan, presumably because of its recommendation that a trust fund be created to dispense $1 billion per year to assist in the provision of open space and recreation opportunities. As of 1991, the American Heritage Trust Act had not progressed beyond the congressional subcommittee level.

Greenways are distinct from greenline parks in that they usually are much smaller. And while their blanket characterization as "community-based, democratic" efforts (Little 1990, xi) may overstate the case, they do not tend to provoke anything like the level of insider–outsider conflict evident in the Pinelands, Adirondacks, and other such places. Greenways are smaller, more manageable, and often more identifiable places than their greenline brethren—though indeed there is no reason that greenways cannot be important elements within greenline parks. While greenways can protect critical ecological corridors, they generally do not offer the same potential for ecosystem protection as do greenline parks. But it is easier to rally constituencies around greenways, and opponents are more readily isolated; they often appear petty and mean spirited.

Some ardent supporters of the greenway concept might have us believe that it is well on its way to becoming a guiding tenet of the green spaces movement (Grove 1990; Hiss 1988; Little 1990), perhaps winning over those who only a few years ago were calling for a national system of greenline parks. Charles Little, a pioneer advocate of both concepts, does not even mention greenline parks in his book about greenways (Little 1990). This downscaling of green sentiment seems in keeping with Popper's (1988) revisionist view of land use regulation; that is, there is a great deal of regulation today, but it is more spatially specific than that of the 1970s. Although the Pinelands experience is no analog for greenways, it does, I believe, point to the importance of making the planning scheme responsive at the appropriate spatial scale.

Finally, Pinelands planning serves as a model for the international system of biosphere reserves. These reserves, designated by the UN Educational, Scientific, and Cultural Organization, constitute a global network of symbolic and scientific value. Within reserves, national governments are expected to promote ecosystem protection in conjunction with sustainable resource use. Because the reserves vary so dramatically in their particular purposes and cultural contexts, it is difficult to make broad comparisons among them. But one thing common to the entire system is the advocacy by the UN Man and the Biosphere Program of a "core–buffer" spatial planning concept (Batisse 1982, 1985; U.S. Man and the Biosphere Program 1989). The Pinelands, with their preservation and protection areas, offer an ideal application. As a consequence, they also provide valuable lessons about the human problems that must be confronted when trying to reconcile an ecologically driven planning scheme with human settlement patterns, political subdivisions, and economic systems.

Prospect

The Pinelands program has succeeded in achieving its basic goals, emerging virtually unscathed from an era that was not very hospitable to centralized land use planning. Yet its success does not portend a reversal of these hostile sentiments; indeed, a resurgence of the Quiet Revolution seems an unlikely prospect, at least for the near future. But some specific impulses reflected in the Pinelands, including some of those of the CMP's strongest opponents, may be representative of emerging directions in land use regulation.

Very powerful local protectionist concerns gave rise to vehement opposition to Pinelands planning and continue to be wellsprings of discontent. Yet these same concerns may translate into support for certain kinds of land use controls—especially those that seek to exclude specific activities or facilities.

In contrast to Quiet Revolution regulations, these controls are locally inspired and locally based—and there is evidence that increasing numbers of communities are adopting such controls (Boyte 1980; Plotkin 1987; Popper 1988). In the Pinelands—as discussed in Chapter 7—opposition to such unwanted facilities as solid and hazardous waste landfills, sand and gravel mines, utility lines, airport expansions, and radio towers has caused some former detractors of Pinelands planning to become supporters. But the larger lesson here is that general citizen support for centralized regulatory programs is not likely to be bolstered any time soon. Indeed, just the opposite. When, for example, such programs use their preemptive powers to seek sites for locally unwanted land uses, or LULUs (Popper 1985), they provoke strong opposition. Conversely, the use of their powers to block LULUs does not necessarily endear them permanently to local constituencies. While communities and residents might befriend the agency when in need, few of them are prepared to relinquish all locational decision-making authority to any supralocal entity, no matter how seemingly well intentioned its efforts.

America is entering yet another era of heightened environmental awareness and concern, and this might lead us to believe that a discouraged public is ready for greater government intervention in environmental affairs. There is considerable truth to this assumption. Still, when it comes to environmental protection—and especially public health—few citizens are prepared to trust their governments wholeheartedly. Government's role is essential, but in New Jersey, as elsewhere, it is treated with much skepticism and caution. Central to the Pinelands program, and my analysis of it, are precisely these sorts of critical questions about the governance of valued resources and those who would use them or benefit from their protection.

2

Regional and Environmental Planning in the United States

Physical regions have been immensely important in shaping human history, and many an environmentalist would argue that they should continue to be a principal basis for organizing human activities. In other words, we should fully respect a river basin's carrying capacity, the habitat requirements of native species, the fertility of a region's soils, and other such natural limits (see Parsons 1985; Sale 1985). We should plan our activities in harmony with, rather than in spite of, nature's spatial patterns (McHarg 1969). This is not a concept discovered by environmental planners of recent vintage. Around the turn of the century, the planner and sociologist Patrick Geddes (Glikson 1971; Stalley 1972), as well as contemporary and predecessor utopians, anarchists, regional geographers, and sociologists, were promoting the notion of physical region as an organizing concept for planning (Weaver 1984).

This chapter reviews the historical and contemporary contexts within which Pinelands planning has emerged and continues to evolve. While the nature and timing of the Pinelands program are the product of political, economic, and social circumstances specific to the mid to late twentieth century, these conditions are not

21

without precedent. Indeed, I argue that recent Pinelands conflicts invoke issues that have been prominent at various times over the past hundred years.

Pre-1960s

American environmentalism, at least since the late nineteenth century, has progressed through a series of stages, each to some degree building on the accomplishments of the one before (see Nash 1990; Petulla 1988). But regionalism and regional land use planning, at least beyond the bounds of the major metropolitan regions, have evolved in a rather less coherent fashion. Even so, tenuous linkages are evident between the various bursts of interest and activity that punctuate our planning history.

It is an interesting history, marked by a strange duality: deep reverence for private property rights in juxtaposition with government ownership of a large portion of the nation's land base. Clearly, America's veneration of private property rights has been an instrumental force in its spatial and economic development (Wolf 1981). Yet, contrary to a good deal of popular current thinking, examples of land use and natural resource planning can be found as early as the colonial period (Cronan 1983; Linowes and Allensworth 1975; Nash 1990). Moreover, fully four-fifths of today's land base has at one time or another been in federal hands. Still, during our first century as a nation, privatization and private gain—with land regarded as a commodity rather than a resource—were the impulses that guided our management of the vast federal estate. Explicit public expressions of concern about land and resource conservation were few and far between.

Appreciation of the value of America's wilderness began to take root early in the nineteenth century and achieved fuller expression by mid to late century (Nash 1982, 1990). But it was not this emerging concern for wilderness preservation that prompted designation of the first national parks so much as it was a concern for filling the cultural void left by the country's comparatively short architectural, artistic, and literary heritage. "Scenic monumentalism" inspired the early national parks movement; only later did the idea of wilderness as a public resource come into its own (Runte 1979).

In 1893, Frederick Jackson Turner (1920) proclaimed the end

of the American frontier. Around the same time, the notion that our forests were without limits was coming under serious challenge. The first federal forest reserves were established under the Forest Reserve Act of 1891; this was the beginning of today's national forest system. In 1885, New York State created the Adirondack and Catskill Forest Preserves, and the 2.8-million-acre Adirondack Park was established in 1892. The state at one time owned all of what would become the initial Adirondack Park, but large acreages were sold in the 1780s. After the park was created, destructive logging practices continued on state as well as private lands—and in 1885 the constitution was amended, calling for state lands in the Adirondacks to be kept in a "forever wild" state. The principal reason for these state actions was to conserve watershed and timber for future downstate commercial uses; recreation was a secondary rationale. Even then, local opposition to state intervention was considerable; independent loggers, in particular, resisted the idea. In the Pine Barrens, where Joseph Wharton had hoped to implement his scheme to divert Pine Barrens water to Philadelphia, the legislature in 1884 passed a law prohibiting conveyance of water out of state.

The great debate involving the preservation of wilderness versus the conservation and wise use of resources took form around the turn of the century. It pitted John Muir, founder of the Sierra Club, against his one-time associate and chief of the Federal Division of Forestry (subsequently the U.S. Forest Service), Gifford Pinchot (Nash 1990; Petulla 1988). Muir is preservation's icon; Pinchot represented progressive conservation (Hays 1959). The Muir–Pinchot rift signaled the beginning of the separate evolution of the preservation movement, which gradually gained momentum and strength in succeeding years. While the semantic boundaries between preservation and conservation have become blurred almost beyond identification (Dunlap 1980; Norton 1986), the underlying arguments about use versus preservation of resources remain very relevant today. Many current debates, including those in the Pine Barrens, Adirondacks, and other valued regions, are fundamentally similar to those that raged nearly a century ago.

At the local level, formal land use management has been with us at least since 1916, when New York City passed the country's first zoning law (Platt 1991). Today, despite strong resistance in many rural regions, local zoning is the most pervasive and accepted land use regulatory instrument in America. Yet local zoning alone—in the absence of a larger regional, state, or national vision—falls short as a means of comprehensive land use management. The first explicit thrust toward national land use planning came in the years following World War I. Large agricultural surpluses and a declining farm dollar prompted calls for federal and state action to help agriculture adjust to reduced demand. Among other things, the proposed agricultural "readjustment" would have eliminated submarginal farming enterprises through land classification and rural zoning (Guttenberg 1973). Indeed, Guttenberg viewed agricultural readjustment as the second phase of the conservation movement spearheaded by Gifford Pinchot. But the readjustment view, because it granted legitimacy to the idea of recreation as a land use in its own right, posed a significant challenge to the prevailing work ethic (Guttenberg 1973). This same ethical challenge, along with its thorny economic and political contradictions, is not lost on today's farmers, loggers, and rural entrepreneurs in the Pine Barrens, Adirondacks, and other rural regions.

A committee report published in the 1923 *Yearbook of Agriculture* concluded that America had entered an era of land scarcity (Gray et al. 1924). It called for a national land use policy that would guide expansion of agriculture, forestry, and other land uses based on a scientific classification of land jointly undertaken by the federal and state governments. Noteworthy is the report's recognition of forests as homes for birds and other animals, marshes and shallow lakes as breeding places, and wild lands as economically productive recreation havens. Although the committee's recommendations were "virtually codified" at a 1931 national land use conference (Guttenberg 1973, 10), no such federal policy was forthcoming.

But several states acted during the 1920s. New York, Michigan, and Wisconsin began classifying, and in some cases developing and regulating, their lands. Wisconsin's 1929 law was the first that actually regulated and restricted the location of broad categories of land uses as well as public and private facilities. Guttenberg states: "Although the intent of this legislation was to interdict the use of submarginal land for agricultural purposes and to divert it to alternative uses such as forestry and recreation, the implications for local community organization were momentous . . . county boards might lay out schools, roads, and even new towns to fit conditions in the new agricultural, forest, and recreational districts" (1973, 14–15).

Another significant event of the 1920s was the issuance, under

Secretary of Commerce Herbert Hoover in 1924, of the model State Zoning Enabling Act. This act still serves as a basis for state land use control instruments (Boschken 1982). Because the U.S. Constitution reserves land use regulatory powers to the states, they must enact special legislation if they wish to pass these powers on to localities. Although state enabling legislation became common during the 1920s (Boschken 1982), adoption of zoning ordinances or acceptance of comprehensive planning did not automatically become the norm in rural areas. Indeed, quite the opposite. Rural planning was most often spurred by statewide comprehensive planning—and the examples cited here notwithstanding, a real push for statewide planning did not come until after the 1932 election (Linowes and Allensworth 1975).

Another important development of the 1920s was the founding in 1923 of the Regional Plan Association of America (RPAA). The RPAA was an expression of a particular form of regionalism that has intellectual linkages with, but differs very significantly from, nineteenth-century anarchist and utopian thinking, as well as progressive planning theory and practice (see Weaver 1984). Led by a group of prominent architects and planners that included such luminaries as Benton MacKaye and Lewis Mumford, the RPAA championed progressive reforms aimed at achieving a balance between city and country. Its germination came between two fertile periods for government reform: the Progressive era and the New Deal. Perhaps this was the appropriate time quietly to develop grand schemes for the future; opportunities to put some of the ideas into practice would come a bit later.

American regionalists of the 1920s envisioned a landscape somewhat like a quilt; regions were the patches within that quilt. The RPAA's notion of balanced regions—drawing heavily on the earlier work of Paul Vidal de la Blache (see Buttimer 1978) and Patrick Geddes (Glikson 1971; Stalley 1972)—was one of decentralized, yet integrated, entities made up of city, countryside, natural resources, and wilderness (Friedmann and Weaver 1979). Planning regions were to be created not simply by drawing boundaries on maps; instead, they were to be based on "natural" regions (Dickinson 1964; Friedmann and Weaver 1979; Glikson 1971; MacKaye 1928). To RPAA members, the folk arts indigenous to specific regions expressed and symbolized local culture; the regions were organic, evolving entities created by people interacting with their physical environments (Friedmann and Weaver 1979; Sussman 1976). RPAA members not only promoted the enhancement of existing regional culture; they also called for a planned regionalization—a "fourth migration"—as the appropriate accommodation of metropolitan expansion. Garden cities, townless highways, rural electrification, economic planning, and affordable housing were all part of the regionalists' visions (Sussman 1976). Though nature was an integral part of this vision, the city's countryside was to be more than a mere nature preserve.

But, say Friedmann and Weaver (1979), the regionalists rarely escaped elitist frames of reference. When it came to a serious confrontation of such issues as widespread rural poverty and metropolitan financial dominance, the regionalists came up short. Interest in indigenous local culture, according to Friedmann and Weaver (1979, 35) was a "jumping-off point for pluralism in the arts." The southern regionalists—Howard Odum prominent among them—were an exception; they sought to protect southern rural values from northern metropolitan onslaughts, and to alleviate rural poverty and racism (Friedmann and Weaver 1979; Weaver 1984). Like the RPAA, the southern regionalists stressed regional balance and development, but they put greater emphasis on regional social attributes than physical character.

Regionalism prospered during the 1930s, finding expression not only among intellectuals but also in various manifestations of popular thinking and culture (Steiner 1983). The New Deal set the stage for the implementation of some of the regionalists' theories of appropriate regional development. Creation in 1933 of the National Planning Board (which later became the National Resources Committee) and a 1934 congressional resolution requesting the President to undertake comprehensive river basin planning were instrumental in advancing the cause of regional planning.

The 1933 passage of the Tennessee Valley Authority Act inaugurated the grandest venture ever into integrated river basin development. To be sure, there were other examples of basinwide planning—the New England Regional Commission, Colorado River Basin Compact, and Northwest Regional Planning Commission (Friedmann and Weaver 1979)—but these were principally single-purpose entities, despite rhetoric to the contrary. The TVA act authorized the agency to consider the economic and social welfare of those residing in the basin (Friedmann and Weaver 1979; Selznick 1953; White 1969). But, alas, the TVA did not devote itself to regional planning; the bulk of its energies instead were directed to selling power and fertilizer (Friedmann and Weaver 1979; Selznick 1953; Sussman 1976). In the words of Friedmann and Weaver (1979, 78) it had become "a powerful instrument of urban industrial expansion."

More generally, the concept of comprehensive river basin planning became disengaged from early ideals of linking economic development, water resources planning, and land use planning at the regional (drainage basin) level. Nonetheless, the idea persisted until the 1960s and beyond, finding increased application in the developing countries. In the American context, at least, its main successes seem to reside in improved engineering practices at the basinwide scale. The high ideals with which the concept was introduced may have gained it wide political support, but that support was not very deeply grounded (Westcoat 1984). Although the New Deal years were marked by a higher valuation of nature within explicitly human and regional contexts than was the case during the Progressive era, neither the New Deal nor succeeding decades allowed for full development of regional planning's social welfare function (Friedmann and Weaver 1979; Sussman 1976).

By the late 1930s, with the nation again being propelled toward war, New Deal regional planning initiatives retreated into relative insignificance. After the war, state comprehensive planning agencies were either eliminated or turned into economic development units (Linowes and Allensworth 1975). In 1943, the federal government disbanded the National Resources Planning Board (1939 successor to the National Resources Committee). Shortly thereafter, state and national energies were directed toward stimulating industry and employment in a peacetime economy.

Although there was little explicit public policy emphasis on planning during the expansionist postwar era, one cannot discount the enormous effects on local, regional, and national spatial organization and development of the Housing Acts of 1949 and 1954, the G.I. Housing Bill, and the Public Highway Act of 1956—which established the Highway Trust Fund (see Davies 1983; Platt 1991). These federal actions encouraged suburbanization and helped make rural areas more accessible and affordable than ever before. They also helped spur many of the land use controversies of recent decades. In the Adirondacks, for example, completion of the limited-access

Adirondack Northway greatly cut travel time from northeastern metropolitan areas—and as a result increased the region's attractiveness as a vacation and second-home mecca for the middle class. New Jersey's Garden State Parkway made southern New Jersey more accessible. The northern Pine Barrens became a desirable retirement destination, and Atlantic City's newfound accessibility would later become an argument in support of legalized gambling.

The Modern Environmental Era

The 1960s witnessed a reemergence of national concern for regional social welfare. In 1961 Congress passed the Area Redevelopment Act, and in 1965 the Appalachian Regional Commission was established (House 1983; Weaver 1984). Ten more Title V regional commissions were to follow during the 1960s and 1970s, ultimately covering much of the country. Title II River Basin Commissions were also established during this period, along with a host of mostly single-purpose regional interstate compacts and ten "federal regional councils." In terms of coordinated regional planning and economic development, expectations tended greatly to exceed accomplishments of these programs (House 1983).

Ecology, amenity, and recreation all are important values in the management of river basins and other federally designated regions (House 1983). Yet, as these values found increased expression during the 1960s and 1970s, clear manifestations of regionalism tended to become less conspicuous. Regions were viewed more as convenient administrative units than as basic constructs for the organization of society. Still, regionalism has its adherents, and elements of their thinking surface frequently within the modern environmental movement—most recently, perhaps, in the calls for a "bioregional" organization of society.

The term *environmental movement*, commonly equated with the groundswell of the late 1960s and 1970s, gives the impression that this was the only period in America's history to witness a strong show of environmentalism (Nash 1982, 1990; Schnaiberg 1977). Clearly, this is not the case. But the 1970s movement was indeed distinct from its predecessors. Morrison, Hornback, and Warner (1972) argue that it was unique in both scope and intensity; none before it was so intensely concerned about human relationships with environmental systems, nor was there such a sense of imminent crisis. None captured as much public attention or so convinced political and economic elites of the gravity of the situation (Schnaiberg 1977). Indeed, I maintain that the environmental fervor of the early 1970s was a prerequisite to the strong Pinelands preservation program that finally came on line in 1980.

But why all the interest and activity surfaced around 1970 is enigmatic. Perhaps the earlier civil rights and antiwar movements had a role in setting the stage (Gale 1972; Schnaiberg 1977). Liberalization of requirements for standing to sue (Andrews 1980) also played a part, aiding environmentalists in their legal quests. And specific events—perhaps to a degree greater than environmental deterioration generally—played key roles. Nuclear tests of the early 1960s (Sills 1975), the publication of Rachel Carson's *Silent Spring* (Carson 1962), the Santa Barbara oil spill of 1969, and ecological decimation in Vietnam (Andrews 1980) all prompted public outrage.

The Quiet Revolution

Many of the environmental concerns that guided land use policy debates of the early and mid 1970s were central to the Pinelands program. But it would be a mistake to conclude that the "Quiet Revolution in land use control" of the early 1970s (Bosselman and Callies 1971), which broke important early ground for the Pinelands program, was nothing more than an outgrowth or extension of the environmental movement. Land use planning involves more than, or at least differs from, the establishment of water- and air-quality standards or consideration of environmental impacts of specific projects. Granted, some land use programs are little more than a collection of environmental regulations. More commonly, though, land use plans strive to be comprehensive and prescriptive (see Smith 1979). The intent is to organize the use of space to protect certain values and to promote others—to make preservation "compatible" with development. This may be accomplished by developing sets of criteria based on such things as distance to water table and soil capabilities. *Design with Nature*, by Ian McHarg (1969), is perhaps the best-known exposition of the environmental criteria approach. But most environmental planning entails more than the straightforward application of criteria. It attempts to order the landscape, often in a way that goes well beyond the most stringent definitions of public health or welfare.

Land use regulation may be rooted in the desire to protect a way of life; to preserve something of a simpler, rural past; or to maintain or develop pleasing vistas (see Bosselman and Callies 1971, 318). Local land use planning seeks to do all these things, with the most immediate impetus coming from residents' desires to maintain their property values and insulate themselves from those of a different race or economic class. State-level land use planning, whether comprehensive or directed toward specific critical areas, tends to be more clearly linked with such technical and regulable aspects of the environment as air and water quality. But the Quiet Revolution in land use control of the 1970s had a broader agenda than pure air and water.

In 1961, Hawaii enacted what was in effect a state zoning plan; it was a forerunner of the Quiet Revolution. Facing rapid urbanization and tourism growth, the state sought to protect its valued agricultural base (Bosselman 1986; Callies 1984; Myers 1976). Not until some years later would protection of the physical environment be explicitly articulated as an objective. Bosselman and Callies (1971), in building their case for the Quiet Revolution, view several other initiatives of the mid 1960s as important early efforts: Massachusetts' wetland protection legislation (the Jones Act and the Coastal Wetlands Act of the 1960s), Wisconsin's shoreland protection program (the Water Resources Act of 1966 and subsequent regulations), and the New England River Basins Commission, which was created by federal executive order in 1967 (see Foster 1984). Though there is considerable variation, these programs tend generally to be limited in geographic scope (they focus on critical areas), regulatory authority, or both. Indeed, no regulatory powers at all were granted to the New England River Basins Commission.

More comprehensive and stringent programs began to come on line in the late 1960s and early 1970s. Among the more prominent individual programs—all of them important prologues to the Pinelands program—were Vermont's Environmental Control Act (1970), California's Coastal Commissions (approved by voter referendum, 1972), New York State's Adirondack Park Agency Private Land Use and Development Plan (1973), Oregon's Land Conservation and Development Act (1973), and Colorado's Land Use Act

(1974). These programs and others have been described in considerable detail (see Advisory Commission on Intergovernmental Relations 1973; Bosselman and Callies 1971; Carol 1987; DeGrove 1984, 1986, 1989; Healy and Rosenberg 1979; Hess 1983; Jackson 1981; Linowes and Allensworth 1975; Mandelker 1976; Morandi et al. 1983; Pelham 1979; Platt 1991; Popper 1981). Suffice it to say that they represent a considerable centralization of land use regulatory power, and all have evoked heated opposition from the principally rural areas over whose fates they have secured greater control. One such area, New York State's Adirondack Park, deserves to be singled out here.

The Adirondack Park

In 1973, the Private Land Use and Development Plan for the Adirondack Park went into effect (see Booth 1987; Commission on the Adirondacks in the Twenty-First Century 1990; Graham 1978; Heiman 1983, 1988; Liroff and Davis 1981; Popper 1981; Terrie 1985). Comparisons between the Adirondack Park and Pinelands National Reserve are inevitable (see Booth 1987; Porter 1986; Salomon 1982). Both places are accessible to large metropolitan populations, both have extensive undeveloped areas (though the Adirondack Park's total acreage is 6 million, compared with the Pinelands' 1.1 million acres), both have valued natural resources, both offer recreational and scenic amenities, and both are regulated by comprehensive land use plans. But, unlike the Pines, the Adirondacks have seen a long history of recreational use by the privileged classes of the East, as well as a long history of aggressive state intervention to protect natural resources and amenities.

During the late 1960s and 1970s, the concept of Adirondack regional planning was a subject of heated debate. In 1967, Laurance Rockefeller commissioned a study that yielded a proposal for an Adirondacks national park (Wirth, Thompson, and Thompson 1967). The Rockefeller report encountered virtually unanimous hostility, failing even to gain the support of environmental preservationists (Graham 1978; Liroff and Davis 1981). Governor Nelson Rockefeller's response was to appoint a Temporary Study Commission on the Future of the Adirondacks, and this distinguished group's recommendations gave birth to the idea of a state agency to plan and regulate land use. The legislative and other struggles leading to the 1971 creation of the Adirondack Park Agency (APA) are reviewed in detail by Graham (1978), Heiman (1983, 1988), Liroff and Davis (1981), Nelson and Hahn (1980), and Popper (1981).

Only sparse support for regional planning was evident in the Adirondacks, but the concept enjoyed considerable support through much of the rest of New York State (Hahn and Dyballa 1981; Heiman 1983). In large measure, the idea was sold to legislators and the general public by making the same argument that justified most other Quiet Revolution actions; that is, local governments were ill equipped to deal with proposed large-scale residential development. Indeed, in 1970 three massive proposals were on the drawing boards in the Adirondacks (Liroff and Davis 1981), and collectively they constituted precisely the kind of crisis that Hahn and Dyballa (1981) identify as a precondition for state action.

Immediately after its creation, the eleven-member APA hurriedly set about drafting a land use plan. Completed in 1973, it may have been the most stringent land use plan of its time (Popper 1981). The plan designates six categories of land use: industrial, hamlet (2 percent of park), moderate intensity (3 percent), low intensity (8 percent), rural use (34 percent), and resource management (53 percent). Restrictions are most stringent in the resource management areas, which are zoned for one principal building per 42.7 acres; the most intense development is directed toward the hamlets. About 62 percent of the Adirondack Park is in private ownership.

To the extent that the APA enjoyed early support in the Adirondacks, it was mostly with the understanding that the agency would be true to its avowed intent to be a partner in planning with local governments, not just a regulator (Liroff and Davis 1981). But the agency blundered badly in its early dealings with Adirondackers (D'Elia 1979; Graham 1978; Liroff and Davis 1981; Popper 1981). Partly because of this, and partly as a result of general disenchantment with regional planning, the agency faced some rather tough sledding in its early years. Opposition remained adamant through the 1970s; even by late 1991, only 13 of 105 Adirondack communities had APA-approved plans.

The Quiet Revolution in Perspective

The Quiet Revolution represents a partial "taking back" of land use regulatory authority by the states. Because the U.S. Constitution reserves police powers to the states, and because the courts have affirmed that states have wide latitude to act in the public interest, the states wield potentially vast power over virtually all land use decisions. But, in practice, those powers are greatly circumscribed, or at least delegated to localities (see Platt 1991). When states reaffirm their authority over critical areas, they are reclaiming some of their reserved power, and because this is done selectively, it often prompts protests from residents of the targeted areas. They feel that the state government is acting in a discriminatory, unfair fashion. As a result, state governments are inclined to temper their enthusiasm when reclaiming land use regulatory powers, especially when it comes to negotiating critical-area boundaries and imposing restrictions on property owners.

The real "revolution," such as it was, should probably be placed in about the same few years of ascendancy as—or perhaps very slightly after—those for the environmental movement. By 1977, ten states had statewide land use laws of some sort, eleven had coastal or shoreland management statutes, and there were four regional land use agencies (Hess 1983). Between 1965 and 1977, state legislatures adopted ninety-four statutes promulgating minimum development-control standards for sensitive areas (Kusler 1983). A Council on Environmental Quality (1979) summary of state critical-area protection laws revealed that by 1979, the great majority of states had in place at least some statutory protection for wetlands, floodplains, coastal areas, agricultural lands, and endangered species. Fred Callies and David Bosselman, who in 1971 named the newborn movement the Quiet Revolution, saw unity of purpose in all this legislative activity. The revolution's twin goals were accommodation of large-scale development and state or regional oversight, rather than local control, over matters of regional concern (Bosselman and Callies 1971; Walker and Heiman 1981).

But Quiet Revolution fervor was not limited to the country's statehouses. Between 1970 and 1975, Congress sought to shift some control over land use decisions toward the federal level, but various attempts to pass a "National Land Use Policy Act" met with failure (Lyday 1976). Some very large corporations—among them Westinghouse, General Electric, and Alcoa—were investing in real estate around this time (Plotkin 1980). Unlike smaller housebuilders, most of whom built in their own areas and were fairly comfortable with (and sometimes in control of) local planning and zoning boards, these large firms needed to know the rules of the game so they could plan and build with a minimum of uncertainty and delay. Indeed, developers were frustrated by the no-growth sentiment that took root in many communities in the early 1970s. Even locally based developers were adversely affected by municipal efforts to channel, restrict, and sometimes stop growth—but not to the same degree (potentially, at least) as the big developers.

A rather odd alliance of interests, including large developers and environmentalists, coalesced in favor of more centralized land use controls. In 1972 and 1973, the Senate passed land use bills. But intense intergovernmental wrangling, described by Lyday (1976) and Plotkin (1980), reduced the bills to "little more than a request by the national government that the states voluntarily review local land-use decisions having a regional impact" (Plotkin 1980, 433). The act lacked clear standards and enforcement authority.

Despite this weakening in the Senate, the real demise came in the House. Plotkin (1980) identifies several reasons for the erosion of support, among them personnel and policy changes in a beleaguered Nixon administration. Perhaps more fateful was the onset of the 1973–1974 economic recession. In general, economic downturns bode ill for land use regulation at any level of government. In the early to mid 1970s, many corporations and banks faced large losses on their real estate ventures, and the environmental movement was more on the defensive than it had been a year or two earlier. As a result, pressure to pass national land use legislation subsided. As Plotkin (1980) points out, though, corporate support never was very vocal or direct; instead, it was concealed in various "objective" governmental and intergovernmental reports.

The time was thus right for locally based entrepreneurial interests, hesitant about the bill from the start but willing to bargain on the assumption that it probably would become law, to mobilize in opposition. The National Association of Home Builders became a leading opponent—just as the New Jersey Builders Association would later become an opposition leader in the Pinelands struggle. The House of Representatives, with its shorter terms of office and greater susceptibility than the Senate to the influence of local elites, defeated the bill by a narrow margin, 204–211. Representative Morris Udall's attempt to reintroduce the bill in 1975 failed, and there has been no subsequent action on a national land use policy.

During the years that a national land use policy was being debated, other legislation and regulations with significant land use implications were enacted. Among them were the Department of Housing and Urban Development's 701 Program, which provided guidance and funding for regional planning; the A-95 review process, which required multijurisdictional notification and encouraged regional coordination on federally assisted projects; and laws creating air- and water-quality management areas, river basin commissions, and resource conservation and development councils to encourage areawide land use planning (Moss 1977; Platt 1991; Platt, Macinko, and Hammond 1983; South Jersey Resource Conservation and Development Council 1979). But the Natural Resources Defense Council (Moss 1977) concludes that most such programs were limited in effectiveness by the fact that their statutory authority was derived from the states.

Perhaps the closest thing we have to a national land use policy is the Coastal Zone Management Act. The Coastal Zone Management Program (CZMP), meant to provide a balance between the environment and development (Healy and Zinn 1985), sets forth broad national policy and provides grants to states for program administration. Participating states (only six eligible states are nonparticipants) must meet certain basic requirements regarding coastal zone delineation and land use planning. New Jersey is a participant (Kinsey 1985), and part of the Pinelands National Reserve is in its coastal zone. The CZMP's effectiveness relies heavily on state initiative, especially so in the wake of greatly diminished federal leadership in the 1980s (Archer and Knecht 1987; Galloway 1982; Mitchell 1986; Platt 1985, 1991). This administrative pattern—federal guidance, state administration, and local implementation—is the template for much of our national environmental legislation. In general form at least, it is also the administrative structure for Pinelands planning.

But to what might all this state-level legislative activity of the early and mid 1970s be attributed? A 1973 Rockefeller Brothers Fund Task Force Report, written under the direction of William Reilly (the current Environmental Protection Agency administrator), downplays social factors, but views the "new mood" toward growth as an outgrowth of earlier environmental protests (Reilly 1973; Scott 1975). Other observers find it difficult to pinpoint specific causes for the land use "reform movement" (Popper 1981); instead, they identify general conditions that fostered it. Most important, perhaps, have been rapid population increases in heretofore sparsely settled areas. The new growth in the South and West, in the suburbs, and during the 1970s in nonmetropolitan areas (Beale 1982; Lichter, Fuguitt, and Heaton 1985; Long and DeAre 1988; Popper 1981), conflicts with various vested interests and with other potential uses of land (including open-space preservation).

Several observers cite loss of amenity as a key provocation. To blame are the homogeneous landscapes of fast-food outlets, shopping malls, convenience stores, and gas stations that have replaced the bucolic countryside that once surrounded most towns and cities (Healy and Rosenberg 1979; Popper 1981). In a related vein, threats to agricultural lands provide common justification for increased land use regulation (Healy and Rosenberg 1979; Jackson 1981). Although the United States is in no immediate danger of running short of farmland (Popper 1981; Wolf 1981), persuasive arguments are nonetheless put forth for local farmland preservation. Scattered and piecemeal development—a common occurrence at the metropolitan fringe—consumes vast quantities of agricultural land, much of it prime farmland. Not only is there a general sense of loss when pleasing, productive rural vistas are transformed into tract housing; many see the irretrievable (or nearly irretrievable) commitment of prime farmland to other uses as extremely shortsighted and inefficient.

Popper (1981) sees the proliferation of leisure-home developments in the late 1960s and early 1970s as one factor giving birth to land use reform. Many of these developments were shoddily planned and poorly constructed, and they incurred the wrath of long-time residents faced with fiscal burdens for new schools and other public services. Although construction of seasonal homes has never been much of an issue in the Pine Barrens, concern about large-scale second-home development was a precipitating factor for stricter land use control in the Adirondacks (Graham 1978; Hahn and Dyballa 1981; Liroff and Davis 1981).

Perhaps the most often heard argument for more centralized planning has to do with the inability of local governments to cope with the development pressures being put on them. Indeed, many rural localities have no planning or zoning at all (Rudel 1984). Those that do often are lacking in funds and professional staff, are dominated by development interests, and are readily susceptible to corruption (Popper 1981). Moreover, many developing communities are concerned with maintaining their "character"; in essence, excluding those of lower income (Babcock 1966; Babcock and Bosselman 1973; Danielson 1976; Linowes and Allensworth 1976; Nelson 1977). All these issues are exacerbated in times of economic expansion, diminished in times of recession.

What political forces and interest-group activities have shaped this regulatory phenomenon? Popper (1981) argues that the land use reform movement is liberal rather than socialist. Regulation, therefore, is meant to smooth out market imperfections and injustices, but not to interfere too deeply. In Healy and Rosenberg's (1979) view, large new developments—subdivisions, stadiums, jetports, factories, energy facilities—are not inherently bad because of their size. Indeed, their very scale is a mixed blessing: It creates the potential for harmful impacts, but also the potential for controlling those impacts. This prospect of state intervention to overcome local resistance to unwanted facilities raises an important question: Is the engine that drives the movement essentially one of liberal, "do good" reformism, or are there more insidious forces at work? Heiman sums it up as follows: "Centralized land use regulation attempts to provide an environment conducive to both the expansion of capitalist production and the protection of social and environmental consumption amenities" (1983, 14).

The Quiet Revolution is seen as a consequence of economic conditions associated with a capitalist system of production. Further elucidation of radical political economy perspectives can be found in Birnbaum (1991), Boyer (1981), Edel (1981), Geisler (1980), Heiman (1983, 1988, 1989), Markusen (1981), and Plotkin (1987). Walker and Heiman (1981) claim not to advocate a conspiratorial view of history, but they attribute the land use reform movement largely to the ascendancy of the megadevelopers of housing. They argue that state and regional intervention suits the "new generation" of developers because:

1. Big business is better able to influence decisions at higher levels of government than either the general public or small competitors.
2. Large businesses operate at a geographic scale that makes standardization of regulations (if there must be regulations) more attractive than a scatter of local standards.
3. Intervention can steer development away from obstreperous mu-

nicipalities and those critical environmental areas that cause the greatest public outcry, giving developers some certainty that a project can go forward. (Walker and Heiman, 1981, 72)

Walker and Heiman (1981) see the land use reform movement of the late 1960s and early 1970s as a logical outgrowth of earlier attempts to manage urban growth through such reform-minded, big-business-dominated organizations as the Regional Plan Association of New York (RPA), the Bay Area Council in San Francisco, the Metropolitan Fund, Inc., in Detroit, and the Committee for Economic Development (a national organization). But small developers have not been very supportive of the reform movement. Walker and Heiman contrast the lack of enthusiasm of the National Association of Home Builders, whose principal constituents are small and medium-size builders, with the strong support for the movement's goals expressed by the Urban Land Institute (ULI), which represents larger-scale interests. This was evidenced in the support of large developers for national land use legislation, but the lukewarm support, which later turned to opposition, of the National Association of Home Builders.

After the Revolution

By the mid 1970s, the flames of revolution were flickering (Healy 1983; Popper 1988; Rosenbaum 1976). As noted earlier, the last nail was hammered into the coffin of national land use legislation in 1974. Rosenbaum (1976) points to the rejection of land use legislative proposals in several states in 1974 and finds that comparatively weak powers were granted to governments in states that did pass legislation. He attributes the demise to four factors:

1. Increased fuel costs and the need to discover and use more domestic energy resources.
2. Recessionary trends, which depressed the building industry.
3. Doubts about the constitutionality of vigorous exercise of states' police powers.
4. Ideological opposition from both conservatives and liberals to continuing the trends toward increased centralization of land use decision making. (Rosenbaum 1976, 2–3)

A more long-term view of the Quiet Revolution is provided by Anthony Downs's "issue-attention cycle." Downs (1972, 39–40) postulates that certain "crises" in American life, including that of deteriorating environmental quality, pass through a sequence of five stages:

1. The preproblem stage
2. Alarmed discovery and euphoric enthusiasm
3. Realizing the cost of significant progress
4. Gradual decline of intense public interest
5. The postproblem stage

Public interest, though diminished in intensity, perseveres into the postproblem phase. Perhaps more significantly, institutions, policies, and programs also persist. And spasmodic recurrences of stronger general interest can be expected over time. Simplistic as Downs's typology may be, it has powerful conceptual appeal. Pinelands planning, for example, could be placed in any of Downs's latter three phases.

New federal land use initiatives have not been a hallmark of the postrevolution era. But those that were enacted were immensely significant, especially with respect to federal lands. The 1978 Parks and Recreation Bill, which created the Pinelands National Reserve, also made substantial additions to the Wild and Scenic Rivers System, the National Trails System, and the National Wilderness Preservation System. The 1980 Alaska National Interest Lands Conservation Act classified vast areas of Alaska for preservation, recreation, and resource management—in the process doubling the acreage of the National Park and Wildlife Refuge Systems and tripling the size of the National Wilderness Preservation System. And the mid to late 1970s was the period of brief ascendancy for the greenline park concept: the management of private lands for public purposes in valued regions. Greenline planning is described in Chapter 1.

Though there were few new statewide or regional initiatives during the latter half of the 1970s—the Pinelands legislation was an exception—it would not be wholly accurate to imply that regional and state-level land use activity stagnated after the mid 1970s. Indeed, in many instances, existing legislation was reaffirmed or even strengthened. DeGrove's appraisal in the mid 1980s of seven state programs reveals that most at least held their ground against legislative assaults. In several states—most notably Vermont, Florida, Oregon, and Colorado—broad-based coalitions came forth in support of state land use programs. Some of those coalitions, among them 1000 Friends of Oregon and 1000 Friends of Florida, included both environmentalists and housebuilders. DeGrove concludes that the private sector is becoming increasingly aware that the economy, as well as the environment, may suffer from unwise development. Popper (1981), while not subscribing to a radical political economist's perspective, concludes that, on balance, large developers have benefited from land use regulation. At the same time, development markets have been "stiffened" in a number of ways: Entrepreneurial opportunities for developers have decreased, developers have less planning flexibility, housing costs have risen (though the exclusionary effects of land use regulation tend to be overstated), and project designs have become more aesthetically homogeneous.

For these reasons, as well as individual concerns about property values and rights, local opposition to regional planning was very much on the ascendancy by the mid 1970s. Groups such as the Landowners' Steering Committee and Green Mountain Boys in Vermont, and the Adirondack Local Government Review Board, League for Adirondack Citizens' Rights, and Adirondack Minute Men (D'Elia 1979) were adversaries worthy of regional planners' best conciliatory efforts. And reconcile they did. Both Popper (1981) and DeGrove (1984) describe the reshaping, through bargaining and negotiation, that enabled Quiet Revolution initiatives to adapt to political conditions of the postrevolution period. Popper points to political logrolling and adaptations by personalities on all sides of the issues; Jens Sorensen (1978) characterizes the compromises between top-down and decentralized administration as "collaborative planning." In short, the lesson of the 1970s is that adaptability and willingness to compromise are essential.

The Pinelands program, as we later see, ensures its viability by making concessions to various key interests. In doing so, Pinelands planning takes lessons from its Quiet Revolution predecessors. Although many of those initiatives have fallen short of early ambitions, most of them remain vigorous—and they owe much of their vigor to the aforementioned willingness of proponents and administrators to negotiate and compromise. Still, the results vary considerably. In Hawaii, a comprehensive state plan was adopted in 1978, seventeen years after passage of the state's land use law. But in

1985, requirements for local consistency were virtually eliminated from the state plan (DeGrove 1989).

Florida's Land and Water Management Act of 1972 and Local Government Comprehensive Planning Act of 1975, benchmarks as they were, faltered in their first decade. Local planning under the latter has been viewed as poorly guided, inadequately funded, and ineffectively implemented (DeGrove and Juergensmeyer 1986); and "Areas of Critical State Concern" designated under the former were far fewer than many supporters had initially envisioned (Carter 1974; DeGrove 1984). But, with rapid growth continuing to take its toll in the 1980s, the state acted to overhaul its programs. Florida was in the vanguard of what DeGrove (1989) calls the "second wave" of state actions. In transforming a "bottom-up" system of state planning into a "top-down" one, Florida went further than its second-wave contemporaries (DeGrove and Juergensmeyer 1986). In a series of laws adopted in 1984, 1985, and 1986, the state put into force a comprehensive plan, greatly strengthened local planning requirements and review procedures, more stringently regulated coastal development, and revamped the Development of Regional Impact (DRI) program established in 1972 (DeGrove and Juergensmeyer 1986; Popper 1988; Siemon and Larsen 1985). But at the same time as it made the DRI program more rigorous, the legislature responded to developers' concerns by making it more efficient and "equitable" (DeGrove and Juergensmeyer 1986).

After California's legislature thrice failed to enact coastal zone management legislation, voters in 1972 approved a ballot measure that provided for a state coastal commission, six regional commissions, and adoption of a California Coastal Plan. As they have done in so many other instances, California's voters forced the issue, embracing a rigorous plan that basically left local governments out of the process. Eventually, the regional commissions were phased out and local governments brought back into the process. Even so, they have been reluctant to comply with state planning requirements. Additional legislative changes included a streamlining of administrative procedures, boundary changes, and removal from local jurisdiction of the social welfare function of providing affordable housing (see DeGrove, 1984, 1989; Fischer 1985; Healy et al. 1978; Mogulof 1975; Popper 1981; Sabatier and Mazmanian 1979). Paradoxically, given its early record, California has yet to catch DeGrove's (1989) second wave.

Colorado's Land Use Commission, created in 1970 and statutorily strengthened in 1974, has not, according to DeGrove (1984, 1989), been very dynamic. Largely to placate local concerns, the commission has not used its power to initiate identification, designation, and promulgation of guidelines for "matters of state interest"; thus, a potentially powerful bargaining tool has been allowed to languish. Indeed, the commission suffered from repeated budget cuts in the 1980s, and its role has been limited essentially to one of coordination and persuasion (DeGrove 1984, 1989).

In the early to mid 1970s, Oregon's land use law was viewed as the strongest in the nation. Yet the abilities of its Land Control and Development Commission (LCDC) to regulate activities of statewide significance and establish areas of critical state concern have been greatly compromised (DeGrove 1984, 1989). As Oregon's program evolved, greater emphasis was placed on economic development and local control, and the act's administrative procedures were streamlined (DeGrove 1984; Leonard 1983). Still, at least with regard to farmland protection, Daniels and Nelson (1986) argue that Oregon's programs are more likely to succeed in preserving open spaces than in sustaining economically viable rural landscapes.

Vermont's Act 250 (Environmental Control Act), passed in 1970, established a permitting system, eleven district commissions, and a State Environmental Board, to which appeals of district-level decisions could be taken. But the state land use plan envisioned by the act's framers became a rallying point for Act 250 opponents (DeGrove 1984; Healy and Rosenberg 1979; Heeter 1976; McClaughry 1975; Popper 1981). Not until 1988—well into DeGrove's (1989) second wave—was a plan enacted. But it lacks force. In response to local government concerns, the legislature opted merely to encourage, rather than require, local planning.

North Carolina's 1975 Coastal Area Management Act was scaled back at the start to accommodate local concerns. According to DeGrove: "The focus in North Carolina has been to bring local governments into the process through 'friendly persuasion,' with a minimum use of 'hammers,' which in any case were not that strong" (1989, 26). Interestingly, state goals and policies, reflected in local plans and their implementation, have gradually been strengthened. North Carolina's program now receives high marks among the nation's coastal programs (DeGrove 1989; Owens 1985).

In response to vocal and widespread opposition to regional planning from within the Adirondack Park, significant compromises were forged in the 1970s. In 1976, the Adirondack Park Agency (APA) sought legislative amendments to reduce its own power. The APA agreed to accept local land use controls that only partially met the initial requirements for approval, civil penalties replaced criminal penalties for violation of APA orders, APA jurisdiction over wetlands was narrowed, restrictions on construction of single-family homes were eased, and the development application process was streamlined considerably (see Liroff and Davis 1981; Popper 1981). In addition, the APA worked hard to improve its image, partly by involving Adirondackers more actively in APA activities. Local animosity had diminished by the late 1970s, and the APA's former archenemy, the Local Government Review Board, was becoming something of a "loyal opposition." But, as described in Chapter 8, all this would change in 1989, when Governor Mario Cuomo created his Commission on the Adirondacks in the Twenty-First Century.

In addition to administrative changes, Quiet Revolution programs made economic concessions through the 1970s and 1980s. In an attempt to boost local compliance with state and regional planning objectives, the California, Colorado, Oregon, and Vermont programs provided significant planning funds to localities (DeGrove 1984, 1989; Popper 1981); so did Florida when it overhauled its program in the mid 1980s (DeGrove and Juergensmeyer 1986). Vermont not only offered planning funds but also paid attention to economic development (DeGrove 1984). As part of its land use regulatory program, Vermont emphasized statewide capital investment planning (Heeter 1976), and—more recently—began providing subsidies to help keep farmers farming and established a Housing and Conservation Trust Fund (DeGrove 1989). Increasingly through the 1970s and 1980s, the Adirondack Park Agency stressed the value of tourism and economic development, providing funds for visitor centers and incentives for local economic development. The Commission on the Adirondacks in the Twenty-First Century (1990) called for additional economic development programs, housing subsidies, and health-care and education programs. Rhode Island's 1988 Comprehensive Planning and Land Use Regulation Act provides technical and financial assistance to local governments, while Maine's 1988 land use law provides funds for planning, land acquisition, and provision of affordable housing (DeGrove 1989). Among the comparable actions that have benefited Pinelands communities are the 1984 Tax Stabilization and Reimbursement Act (Chapter 6, "Woodland Township") and infrastructure bond act funding, authorized in 1985 (Chapter 7, "Conformance's Overall Success").

Bioregionalism

An additional development of the post–Quiet Revolution era is the ascendancy of bioregionalism. Its guiding philosophy is one of regional political decentralization that would conform to physiographic (mainly watershed) boundaries and that would be guided by ecosystem principles (Foster 1984; Mason, Solecki, and Lotstein 1987; Parsons 1985; Sale 1985). Not just physiography, but also the traditions and local knowledge of the regions' inhabitants are to be respected. In many ways, bioregionalism is a repackaging of some of the American regionalist visions described earlier. United by intense idealism, its proponents are ideologically rather diverse. They are also small in number, and their agenda faces enormous political and social challenges. Rosalind Williams (1985), in a review of Kirkpatrick Sale's (1985) *Dwellers in the Land: The Bioregional Vision*, makes a poignant observation: "On a practical level, bioregionalism will probably have far less effect than the old-fashioned lobbying efforts of the Sierra Club, which published Mr. Sale's book. At least Kropotkin, a professed revolutionary, understood that the bioregional vision must confront immensely powerful institutions as well as other, maybe far less desirable, visions."

Nonetheless, the notion of the Pine Barrens as bioregion has a certain logic and appeal. But not many Pine Barrens residents—bioregionalists' stated concern for local folk notwithstanding—are likely to share in the bioregionalist vision. Recent confrontations between townsfolk and members of the Greater Adirondack Bioregion Earth First! chapter (Mason 1991) amplify this point. Although it has gained a very fragile foothold in the Adirondacks, bioregionalism scarcely has been mentioned in the Pines.

While many bioregionalists would argue that half a loaf is worse than no loaf, there is no denying that some elements of the bioregionalist vision have surfaced in conventional settings. The Environmental Protection Agency, for example, is beginning to advocate an ecoregional basis for water and land management (Gallant

1989; Hughes 1989; Hughes and Larsen 1988), and is calling for ecosystem-based approaches to risk assessment (U.S. Environmental Protection Agency 1987, 1988, 1990). In its 1972 systemwide plan, the National Park Service (U.S. Department of the Interior 1972) supported comprehensive representation of physiographic and ecological regions. And the Pinelands National Reserve, whether called one or not, is a bioregion.

The Reagan Years and Beyond

One might think that the notion of regional solutions to regional problems would have held some appeal for Reagan-era new federalists. Such was not the case: Regional planning gives legitimacy to yet another level of political administration, clearly something undesirable. Various regional planning agencies, including most of the interstate River Basin Commissions, were disbanded shortly after Ronald Reagan took office. Regional organizations geared toward economic development—among them the Tennessee Valley Authority and the Appalachian Regional Commission—also came under threat.

Reagan's environmental agenda, shaped by the conservative views of James G. Watt and the Heritage Foundation (Kraft and Vig 1984), sought to reduce the scope and effectiveness of federal environmental policies and programs. The means for doing so were (1) regulatory reform relying on cost–benefit analysis to evaluate regulations; (2) decentralization, specifically by shifting of responsibilities, wherever feasible, to state and local governments; (3) reliance, to the greatest extent possible, on the free market in allocating resources; and (4) accelerated extraction of natural resources (Kraft and Vig 1984; Vig and Kraft 1984a, b). Specific strategies included personnel changes, administrative reorganization, budget cutbacks, and more detailed regulatory oversight with greater attention to economic considerations (Vig 1984).

Although the Reagan program was held in check by a public and congressional backlash (Kraft 1984; Mitchell 1984; Vig 1984), it nonetheless succeeded in reducing the scale and effectiveness of environmental regulations. Indeed, reauthorization of the Clean Air Act was stalled for more than a decade. But Reagan's Department of the Interior, potentially a spoiler in the Pinelands, did little to impede the Pinelands plan's general progress. True, the federal government was not the planning partner that some early advocates of the Pinelands program envisioned. Federal money for Pinelands land acquisition was held back, and Reagan's first federal representative to the commission, Ric Davidge, posed pointed and critical questions at times. But that was the worst of it.

Few new environmental programs emerged during the 1980s, and land use initiatives, of course, were scarce (Kenski and Kenski 1984). But there are exceptions—notable among them the 1982 Coastal Barrier Resources Act, which eliminates federal subsidies for development of coastal barrier islands (Gordon 1984), and more recently, the various conservation provisions of the Food Security Act of 1985 (Conservation Foundation 1987) and the 1990 Farm Bill. New federalist policies gave more environmental responsibilities and less money to states and localities. Many of them rose to the challenge, implementing their own stringent regulatory programs. Under New Jersey's Republican governor Thomas Kean, the Pinelands program was sustained, coastal development further restricted, and statewide land use planning begun. DeGrove (1989) describes new land use regulatory programs enacted in Maine, Rhode Island, and Georgia in the late 1980s, as well as expanded programs in other states and additional programs in the works. Popper (1988) argues that we now have more centralized land use regulation than ever. Most of it is not statewide and comprehensive, but specialized and more spatially specific. Popper cites facility siting, farmland preservation (see also Furuseth and Pierce 1982; Hiemstra and Bushwick 1986), wetland and floodplain protection, and sensitive-area protection (such as the Chesapeake Bay) programs (see also Mason and Mattson 1990).

Another response to the changing federal political landscape of the 1980s has been the explosive growth of single-issue, unaffiliated groups that oppose such things as landfills, power lines, transmitter towers, and nuclear waste dumps (Lake 1987; O'Hare 1977; O'Hare, Bacow, and Sanderson 1983; Popper 1985). As we later see, these sentiments abound in the Pine Barrens as elsewhere. There is every reason to believe that these opposition movements will continue to prosper and, in many cases, to provoke preemptive laws and regulations that seek to neutralize them (Plotkin 1987).

As the 1990s unfold, it is becoming apparent that their environmental politics, at least at the federal level, are not all that different from those of the 1980s. Still, the 1990 Earth Day media blitz—along with extensive and continuing coverage of a range of environmental issues—brought forth some new laws and policies. Most of them, however, dealt with such things as solid and hazardous waste management, air and water pollution, and global concerns like ozone depletion and greenhouse warming. Land use regulation is more a consequence of these concerns than the product of direct, comprehensive efforts such as those of the Quiet Revolution.

This review has touched on several themes relevant to Pinelands planning and management: the definition and allocation of public versus private goods, the preservation–conservation (wise use) debate, the historic value of wilderness in the United States, the widespread appeal of small-scale renewable resource activities (e.g., farming, forestry) as part of a harmonious rural landscape, the historic reluctance to embrace the region as an organizing concept except in cursory or single-purpose ways, the persistence through recent years of environmental and land use initiatives of the 1960s and 1970s, the new political conservatism of the 1980s, the ascendancy of single-purpose opposition groups, and the upsurge of environmental interest in the late 1980s and early 1990s. In reconciling urban-based concerns for environmental preservation and the provision of recreational space with rural concerns for local autonomy, conservation, and economic development, the Pinelands program encounters many of the same issues that have been with us for the past century.

The Pinelands effort is rooted in the environmentalism of the 1970s, employs the techniques and strategies of the Quiet Revolution, and embodies a perception of wilderness in which there is minimal human presence. It is also shaped, to a large degree, by local conditions—including the social, economic, and physical settings. The Pinelands, like any other region, are unique—but the broad themes implicit in their management are those that have evolved over the past hundred years or more. In turn, the ongoing debates are influenced, if only to a small degree, by the Pinelands experience itself.

3

One Region or Many?

The greatest challenge for Pinelands planning is one that confronts all regional land use planning: mediating among a bewildering array of physical, political, social, cultural, and economic concerns. If regional planning is to be accepted and understood by the region's residents, then I submit that the area, in all its complexity, must be understood by those doing the planning. This means more than the production of specialized reports on each of the area's key attributes; it means that planners should be conversant with ecology as well as citizens' concerns, with political as well as environmental issues. Their task becomes all the more vexing as they work to transform this knowledge into regional and subregional boundaries at the same time as they try to sort out which "constituents" (residents versus nonresidents, for example) are served in which ways by which planning actions.

What follows is an overview of the Pine Barrens. Principal emphasis is on understanding which attributes are important to whom, and what this implies for Pinelands planning. I begin with a description of the physical region, then consider its human character, and finally turn to the broader questions associated with regional definition.

Physical Character

No great canyons, high mountains, cloud forests, glaciers, or other such breathtaking natural wonders distinguish the Pines. Yet it is the area's physical character that attracts widespread attention from scientists and environmentalists. Foremost on the agendas of planners and interest groups are flora, fauna, hydrogeology, and soils.

Flora

The region's flora, comprising much more than the great expanses of pine trees that linger in so many visitors' minds, have attracted considerable scientific interest through the present century. From the early accounts of Harshberger (1916) and his predecessors (see McCormick and Forman 1979) up to the more recent works of McCormick (1970), McCormick and Jones (1973), Robichaud and Buell (1973), and Boyd (1991), Pine Barrens vegetation has been inventoried and described in some detail. Two major vegetational systems are described: the upland and lowland complexes. The lowland complex is found where groundwater is at or near the surface for at least a part of the year, and the upland complex covers the remainder of the region. Though lowland forests are recognized for their white cedars, other species actually are more abundant. In addition to the cedar swamps, we find maple–gum–magnolia and pitch-pine lowland forests. Many former cedar swamps have been succeeded by hardwood swamps. Despite the general scarcity of light at the forest floor, especially in cedar swamps, shrub and ground layers of the lowland forests are remarkably diverse in species composition (Boyd 1991; McCormick 1970; New Jersey Pinelands Commission 1980).

Lower layers of the upland forests contain far fewer species. Pine–oak forests dominate the central Pines uplands, with pitch pine the dominant tree. Oak–pine forests, with oak dominating, also are widespread, especially around the region's fringes. Much of the Pine Barrens forest (upland as well as drier lowland areas) is fire dependent; many oaks and pines have dormant buds that sprout after fire. Extensive burning tends to favor pine over oak; conversely, the restriction of burning or of conditions conducive to fire tends to favor oak. This is because frequent burning removes thick litter from the forest floor, allowing the tiny pine seeds to take root (Boyd 1991; McCormick 1970; New Jersey Pinelands Commission 1980). Paradoxically, no significant trend toward increasing dominance of oaks is evident, despite a recent history of human influences that has reduced the frequency of fires (New Jersey Pinelands Commission 1980).

One distinct and mysterious vegetative feature, studied by the conservationist Gifford Pinchot around the turn of the century and continuing to draw international scientific attention, is the pygmy forest, or Pine Plains. The Plains actually constitute several distinct areas in the eastern portion of the Pines, in total occupying between 12,200 and 22,510 acres along the Burlington–Ocean county border (McCormick 1970). Dominating the Plains is a closed-cone (serotinous) type of pitch pine; blackjack and scrub oak also are present. With trees typically reaching only two to five feet in height, the visitor to the Plains is treated to a treetop view of large expanses of pine forest. Why do these forests thrive? Researchers have identified a number of causal and contributing factors, including soil fertility, soil moisture, wind, fire, genetic factors, and various combinations thereof. Fire has emerged as the favored explanation, with genetic factors consigned to a significant but secondary role (Good, Good, and Anderson 1979; McCormick 1970; New Jersey Pinelands Commission 1980).

Pine Barrens plant life attracts the interest of amateur and professional botanists alike. Approximately 580 native species and 270 introduced species occur in the Pines, with 71 of the native species classified as rare, endangered, threatened, or "undetermined" (Fairbrothers 1979). What really makes the region botanically distinct is its survival in the midst of Megalopolis as a sort of postglacial arboretum, a refuge for plants that generally thrive elsewhere. According to McCormick (1970), 14 species of northern plants reach their extreme southern limits, or at least Atlantic Coastal Plain limits, in the Pine Barrens. And some 109 kinds of plants reach their northern limits in the Pines. Some of these species occur as disjuncts—distinct outliers from the main species distribution. The climatic and geologic histories of the eastern United States have also placed a number of endemic, relict, and habitat-restricted species in the Pines. Endemic species are those restricted to very small geographical areas; relict species are the remnants, often restricted to quite small areas, of formerly widespread distributions; and habitat-restricted species, while their total population may be widespread, are restricted to specific habitats such as those found only in pine barrens (Fairbrothers 1979). Often overlooked by advocates of Pines preservation is the fact that habitats for many rare and endangered species are created by such human disturbances as clearing, burning, and irrigation (Little 1974; Vivian 1979, 1982 interview).

Geology and Hydrogeology

Many of the Pines' contemporary resource conflicts are defined by geology and hydrogeology. The Pine Barrens occupy a large part of the New Jersey Outer Coastal Plain, which has seen several oceanic advances and retreats over the past 150 million years. Continental deposits from the Lower Cretacious Age (100–136 million years ago) were overlain by deposits of continental and marine origin during the Upper Cretacious Age (65–100 million years ago), and the Tertiary (1.8–65 million years ago) and Quaternary (0.01–1.8 million years ago) Periods. Thus, the Outer Coastal Plain consists of a sequence of unconsolidated quartzose gravel, sand, silt, and clay strata of varying permeability (Rhodehamel 1979).

The region's two major aquifers—the Kirkwood Formation and the Cohansey Sand—were deposited during the Tertiary Period. Composed of sand, pebbles, silt, and clay, the Kirkwood ranges in elevation from 100 feet above sea level to 300 feet below sea level. It is an important source of water in the coastal region. The Kirkwood is overlain by the Cohansey Sand, which occurs in the form of a thick and extensive wedge (New Jersey Pinelands Commission 1980; Rhodehamel 1979). Largely a water-table aquifer, the Cohansey is hydraulically connected to the upper part of the Kirkwood. Collectively, the two aquifers store a vast amount of water; the Cohansey alone holds perhaps as much as 17 trillion gallons.

Groundwater supplies 89 percent of the flow in Pine Barrens streams. Much of the Pine Barrens natural vegetation, as well as cranberry culture, is specifically adapted to the area's extensive wetlands; that is, areas of high water tables. Lowering the water table could prove disruptive to the entire Pine Barrens ecosystem (New Jersey Pinelands Commission 1980). Preservationists, like many residents of the Pines, are alarmed about the prospect of water exploitation. Residents, however, are more likely to be troubled by what they perceive as political exploitation than by threats to ecological integrity.

Groundwater recharge is solely through precipitation, 44 percent of which annually percolates through the sandy soils of the Pines (New Jersey Pinelands Commission 1980). Although recharge of the Cohansey occurs through much of the Pine Barrens, much of the Kirkwood's recharge takes place outside the Pinelands National Reserve, just to its west. Unlike the Pinelands, this area, already largely suburbanized, is not treated as an environmentally sensitive area in New Jersey's state plan (New Jersey State Planning Commission 1988). The apparent incongruity is not lost on Pinelands property owners.

For the most part, the Pine Barrens soils overlaying the Kirkwood and Cohansey aquifers are chemically inert and have low adsorptive capacities; thus they are ineffective in filtering out wastes (New Jersey Pinelands Commission 1980; Rhodehamel 1979; Trela and Douglas 1979). But despite increasing sources of contamination in recent decades, Pine Barrens groundwater remains very pure. Iron levels are high in places, but concentrations of dissolved solids and nitrates are low (Rhodehamel 1979).

As noted, Pine Barrens surface waters are supported mainly by groundwater flow. Eleven major streams, valued for recreational, aesthetic, and ecological purposes, drain into the Delaware River, Delaware Bay, and Atlantic Ocean (Map 5). Generally, surface-water quality is quite high, though there are some significant exceptions. The Comprehensive Management Plan (CMP), in its discussion of surface-water quality, affirms that Pine Barrens streams are quite sensitive to both point and nonpoint sources of pollution. Moreover, the entire regional ecosystem is regarded as highly sensitive to changes in surface-water quality (Hoskins 1984; New Jersey Pinelands Commission 1980).

Soils

Pine Barrens soils are mainly sandy; typical are the gray, sandy, podzolic Lakewood and sandy, droughty Sassafras soils. Yet many variations occur; for example, soils may or may not be layered with ironstone, gley, and clay substrata (Tedrow 1979). Most soils are characterized by a high degree of leaching and only a small accumulation of humus (New Jersey Pinelands Commission 1980; Tedrow

1979). Depth to seasonal high water table and permeability are the main considerations in determining suitability for septic systems. These issues, covered in some detail in the CMP (New Jersey Pinelands Commission 1980), are central to Pinelands planning and management. They form the principal basis for the regional zoning standards prescribed by the CMP and thus are at the root of many of the resultant conflicts.

Fauna

Pine Barrens fauna are very much influenced by the region's unusual combination of environmental conditions, particularly vegetation, fire, moisture, and water chemistry. In all, 299 bird species, 35 species of mammals, 59 reptile and amphibian species, and 91 species of fish were identified as of 1980. The U.S. Department of the Interior listed two species as endangered, and the New Jersey Department of Environmental Protection listed 32 species as threatened or endangered (New Jersey Pinelands Commission 1980). Though considered "rich" in insect species, the Pines are "poor" in bird species (McCormick 1970). While few animal species are unique to the Pines, the area is zoogeographically interesting because within it are the northern limits of the ranges of many southern species.

Among the mammals found in the Pines are beavers, otters, weasels, minks, opossums, raccoons, foxes, squirrels, rabbits, bats, and white-tailed deer. Bobcat and black bear, once common, no longer are present. Of the fifty-nine species of reptiles and amphibians, New Jersey's Division of Fish, Game, and Wildlife listed nine as endangered or threatened (New Jersey Pinelands Commission 1980). The Pine Barrens tree frog (endangered), northern pine snake (threatened), and corn snake (threatened) are widely recognized, even among nonspecialists.

Forman (1979) describes the Pinelands as an ecological mosaic shaped by both natural conditions and centuries of human impact. Indeed, the region's current physical character, even in areas that appear minimally disturbed, might be vastly different had the human presence not been so pervasive.

Human Occupance

The earliest human occupance of the Pine Barrens dates to 10,000 or more years ago (Hartzog 1982; New Jersey Pinelands Commission 1980; Wacker 1979). Prehistoric settlement of the Pines, important to Pinelands planning in terms of archeological understanding and resource protection, is covered in some detail in a volume edited by John Sinton (1982); Buchholz and Good (1983) have compiled a comprehensive annotated bibliography. European settlement of the region has been traced to the early 1700s (New Jersey Pinelands Commission 1980), although Wacker (1979) points out that the portion of the New Jersey Outer Coastal Plain still unsettled as of 1765 resembles in its boundaries Harshberger's (1916) map of the Pinelands. English Quakers and New Englanders settled in the surrounding areas and near the coast, but for the most part avoided the Pines because of their infertile soils (Wacker 1979). Although permanent settlements were few and far between, the Pines' forests were thoroughly exploited in the eighteenth century. As a result, even the inner core of today's Pinelands National Reserve is anything but an "untouched wilderness."

The earliest Pine Barrens settlements grew up around sawmills. Initially, the lumber was used for shipbuilding in coastal locations. Dense lowland stands of Atlantic white cedar were vigorously exploited during this early period (Wacker 1979). Destructive exploitation was encouraged by the fact that large parcels of land were in absentee ownership. Despite state regulation of timber cutting as early as 1707, the region's forests were entirely cut over at least once and in some places twice (Little 1979; New Jersey Pinelands Commission 1986b; Pierson 1979; Wacker 1979).

Since the time of early European settlement, the Pine Barrens have served as a resource hinterland for nearby urban markets. Vast quantities of wood supplied fuel to neighboring cities and stoked steamboat engines. By the mid 1800s, forest depletion—and perhaps competition from imports from other areas—made wholesale commercial sawmilling unprofitable. Many mills were closed, or their systems of ponds were converted for cranberry culture. Others shifted to custom milling of various kinds, and some of these mills persisted well into the present century (New Jersey Pinelands Commission 1986b; Pierson 1979).

Beginning around 1740, the Pine Barrens forests were exploited for production of charcoal needed for ironmaking and other industrial activities. Indeed, vast quantities were consumed by the area's blast furnaces. The charcoal industry prospered well into the 1800s, but gradually declined in succeeding decades. The last colliers in the Pines worked in the Whiting area of Ocean County, and they retired from the business in the 1970s (New Jersey Pinelands Commission 1986b; Wacker 1979).

Probably the best known of the many Pines industries is the iron industry. Limonite, or bog ore, is an abundant renewable resource that occurs in stream-bank deposits throughout the Pine Barrens. Between 1765 and 1865, something in the neighborhood of thirty forges and furnaces operated through the region; some of their ruins persist to the present day. The historic ironmaking village of Batsto, restored by the State of New Jersey, is an important regional tourist attraction.

Over about a three-decade period toward the end of the eighteenth century, the Pines experienced something of an "iron rush." Many iron plantations, often owned by individual entrepreneurs, amassed large acreages in order to maintain secure supplies of ore and fuel, as well as to control the water needed for production (Wacker 1979). In many respects, the iron towns resembled self-contained medieval fiefdoms. But iron production also stimulated settlement on a larger scale. Not only did the iron towns themselves provide employment; sawyers and colliers prospered outside these towns. Tavern towns grew, road networks were developed, and maritime trade prospered during this period (New Jersey Pinelands Commission 1986b). Pine Barrens landscapes were dramatically altered by increased settlement, roads, river landings, water impoundments, and extensive clearing of forests for charcoal (Wacker 1979). But by the mid to late 1800s, the availability of anthracite coal centralized ironmaking and shifted it westward, thus contributing to its demise in the Pines.

By virtue of a vast endowment of wood and sand, the Pine Barrens were well suited to glass production. Between 1800 and 1875, glassmaking thrived. Even after the 1840s, when coal replaced wood as a fuel, glasshouses continued to prosper for several decades. In the mid 1800s there were thirteen glasshouses in the Pines (New Jersey Pinelands Commission 1986b). Like iron, the glass industry contributed to the region's settlement and to the extensive exploitation of its natural resources.

Historically, shipbuilding has been important to southern New Jersey. Most of the activity was in coastal towns, though there were shipyards in a few of the Pine Barrens river communities. Main impacts on the Pines stemmed from demands for wood for shipbuilding, and demands for wood and other resources for trade and use in settlements that grew up around the various seafaring activities (New Jersey Pinelands Commission 1986b).

Many other minor industries were present at various times. Most of them were short lived, such as the paper and textile mills that occupied some of the buildings abandoned after the collapse of the bog-iron industry. There were also wineries and clay factories, as well as a number of other "single-site" industries: a tannery, a turning mill, a chair factory, and a toy factory. The effects of these industries on the region's development were quite limited (New Jersey Pinelands Commission 1986b).

Despite the generally unsuitable soils, agriculture traditionally has been important in the Pines (New Jersey Pinelands Commission 1986b; Wacker 1979). Much of what was initially produced was for subsistence purposes or to provide supplementary income for those employed in the extractive industries. Commercial row crop and truck farming has been and still is rather important in the western part of the Pines, especially in the Hammonton area (see Map 5). Farming practices have played a key role in influencing settlement patterns and choices of architectural styles (New Jersey Pinelands Commission 1986b).

Unfavorable economic conditions and depleted soils conspired to bring about a decline in farming in the late 1700s and early 1800s. With the introduction of marl as a fertilizer, as well as the adoption of other management techniques, farming rebounded during the 1800s. Until late in the nineteenth century, local farms supplied the numerous gristmills associated with Pines settlements. But by the twentieth century, production was limited to those agricultural operations that could survive in a more integrated market economy (New Jersey Pinelands Commission 1986b; Wacker 1979).

Integral to the Pine Barrens as we know them today is berry farming. Indeed, the Pines have given New Jersey its third-place national ranking for cranberry production and second-place ranking for blueberry production. Lowland areas with plentiful water and mucky soils composed of organic materials and alluvium—common in several parts of the Pines—are well suited to cranberry cultivation. Earliest cranberry farming dates to the 1830s; soon after that, farmers learned that flooding the bogs at certain times of the year resulted in better growth. As a result, considerable land clearing and construction of dams, sluices, and reservoirs have accompanied cranberry cultivation (New Jersey Pinelands Commission 1986b). These basic land and water requirements, as well as changing harvesting techniques and labor needs over the years, have significantly influenced landscapes, local economies, and social relations in the Pines. Woodland Township, examined in Chapter 6, illustrates this well.

Commercial blueberry cultivation began early in this century. Experiments conducted by Elizabeth White of Whitesbog (Burlington County) played a key part in the history of blueberry cultivation. White's contributions are recognized in more than this nominal way; the namesake town is now a center for Pinelands education, research, and historic preservation. Both cranberry and blueberry cultivation are important parts of the "new" celebrations of Pine Barrens culture (Chapter 8, "The Pinelands as a Place—or Places").

In short, the Pines are marked by a history of extensive human use—or as Wacker (1979, 20) puts it, "ruinous exploitation of natural resources motivated by thought of immediate gain." Still, the growth of population centers, transportation, and services associated with modern industrialization has bypassed the Pine Barrens almost entirely. Mills and manufacturing sites that did persist were for the most part isolated and unrelated (New Jersey Pinelands Commission 1986b). The advent of the railroads signaled the general decline of the small-scale, local manufacturing prevalent in the Pines. Only one rail line, troubled from its inception, ever operated in the central Pines. As industrialization took place in surrounding areas, the Pine Barrens were left behind—in Lester Klimm's (1953) definition, an "empty area."

Because the Pines held so little prospect for immediate economic development, realtors and promoters were able to amass large tracts of land at low cost by buying from iron, glass, and various other failed or failing concerns (Wacker 1979). Through the mid 1900s, several entrepreneurs attempted, largely unsuccessfully, to develop large residential communities. Indeed, the history of landownership, transactions, and speculation in the Pines is a fascinating, if poorly understood, subject. Though it is too complex and murky to attempt to do proper justice to here (but see Chapter 4, "A Jetport in the Pines?" and Chapter 6, "Woodland Township"), suffice it to say that this history has played no small part in shaping the conflicts and giving rise to the various scandals and scams that have resounded through the region in recent decades (Birnbaum 1989a, b, c; 1991; Goldstein 1981).

Of foremost relevance to current Pinelands management is the fact that much of the region remains sparsely settled and is actually less industrialized than it was in the past. Also important are the legacy of muddled landownership and transactions, the continuing economic significance of berry culture (and to a lesser degree row crops), and the contemporary interest in the region's history and material culture.

Defining the Region

The names *Pinelands, Pine Barrens,* and *Pines* are not so interchangeable as they might seem. Each tends to invoke separate images of place. These images vary not only in terms of geographical boundaries but also in physical and cultural content. Moreover, they differ in clarity and level of detail. And of course people's perceptions of region are informed by political, social, and economic predispositions: The developer's images will differ from those of the environmentalist, which are likely to differ from those of the hunter. The forbidding task for politicians and planners is to try to reconcile the varying perceptions of insiders and outsiders, preservationists and developers, stewards and exploiters, passive and active recreationists. Moreover, the targets move: Who is the insider, who the recreationist, who the developer—and when?

One seemingly unambiguous point of departure for this venture is to delineate physical boundaries for the region. Yet this is not so simple as it might at first appear: Not only must criteria be agreed upon; it is necessary to consider how natural and human processes are altering the physical landscape. Is the landscape contracting? Expanding? Where? At what rates? Is a suburbanized piece of the Pines still to be considered "Pine Barrens"?

The Pine Barrens have been formally delineated on the basis of vegetation, soil types, and hydrogeology. Harshberger (1916) used vegetation patterns; McCormick and Jones (1973) also mapped vegetation features. The Governor's Pinelands Review Committee (1979) and the New Jersey Pinelands Commission (1980) have established regional boundaries with reference to a combination of natural features. Though the various definitions differ, and each has changed over time, there is nonetheless considerable agreement about the spatial extent of the natural region. Thus a natural region has been defined, and in fact constitutes the conceptual basis for Pinelands land use management. The natural and administrative regions, therefore, are one.

But the Pinelands plan is meant to be comprehensive in scope, encompassing regional economy and culture as well as ecology. Can we claim that there is a Pinelands economic region? Pine Barrens economic activities are intimately related to the region's physical features: its pine, oak, and cedar; its bog iron; its sand; its water. These features, in conjunction with a location near the sea and close to major urban markets, have given rise to cyclical patterns of resource-related activity, notably charcoaling, ironmaking, glassmaking, and berry culture. Today's recreation industry also depends on the Pines' physical attributes.

Yet the evidence for regional integration of these various economic activities is at best mixed. In raising the general question of regional integration, the *Pinelands Cultural Resource Management Plan for the Historic Period Sites* (New Jersey Pinelands Commission 1986b) acknowledges that the organization and centralization of industry common in other parts of the United States failed to occur in the Pines. Still, as noted, the iron and glass industries did play a part in fostering a regional socioeconomic structure. The organization of settlements and the development of extensive road networks occurred during the iron and glass periods. Many of the towns are now abandoned or only very sparsely populated, and the sand roads are used only for recreation, but the imprint of formerly thriving local industries is distinct.

In their heydeys, these settlements often supported a variety of commercial and service functions (New Jersey Pinelands Commission 1986b). Yet they were virtually self-contained entities (Fowler 1982; Pierce 1957). Functioning largely in isolation, each iron, glass, or mill site drew on surrounding areas for resources and exported its products to shipping ports or urban centers. Some integration probably did occur, for example, in the way of a shared labor pool (New Jersey Pinelands Commission 1986b). But, generally, the Pine Barrens of the eighteenth and nineteenth centuries constituted a mosaic of independent industrial and agricultural settlements. It was not, by conventional definition (see Hartshorne 1939), a functional region; that is, one unified by transportation networks or trade interaction. Instead, individual settlements and their surroundings may have been the functional regions—just as Hartshorne (1939) alludes to the characterization of agricultural villages as functional regions.

Over the past century (the past twenty years, perhaps, excepted), the Pines have become even less economically integrated and more marginal and isolated. McGarvey (1972) argues that after 1915, negative perceptions of the region and its "Piney" inhabitants led to its avoidance for development. Although his case is overstated, the argument does have merit. By McGarvey's reckoning at least, the differences between insiders and outsiders—as represented by widely differing perceptions of place—are very distinct.

Today's Pinelands are defined for planning purposes as an administrative region. Because the Pinelands plan directs most new development toward the periphery, it is not likely that much, if any, economic integration will be focused around a central regional nodal point or points. It would be more appropriate to speak of economic subregions—for example, recreational subregions where canoe, camping, and other service facilities are present; cranberry regions; blueberry regions; row crop regions; retirement residential subregions; and nonretirement residential subregions. Each of these, to the extent that they can be defined to begin with, is being redefined by Pinelands planning and by changing governmental and public perceptions of the Pines.

More important, perhaps, perceptions of the Pinelands as a whole are shaped by recent events. A legislatively defined area has been recognized as a planning region—not only an ecological planning region, but a "cultural planning" region as well (New Jersey Pinelands Commission 1980). Zelinsky (1973) defines a culture region in these terms: "an intimate symbiotic relationship between man and land . . . one that creates indigenous modes of thought and action, a distinctive visible landscape, and a form of human ecology specific to the locality" (p. 110). A culture region may be defined by common bonds of ethnicity and folkways; a perceptual region by the perceptions of insiders and outsiders to the area. The two concepts are not mutually exclusive; indeed, I would argue that the culture region is at least as much created by our perceptions as it can be defined by "objective" criteria.

Piney is the term most often used to describe natives of the Pine Barrens. But to whom, precisely, is the term being applied? Samuelson (1986) tries to distinguish between Pine Barrens residents (Pineys) and *Pinelanders*. Pinelanders are those residing in the Pinelands protection area; that is, the peripheral area defined by federal and state legislation (see Map 4). Cohen (1985) seeks genealogically and historically to define group membership. Sinton (1981) gives this account of a Piney's self-definition: "A Piney . . . is just a little deeper in the woods than you are" (p. 40). A popular conception of Pineys—still quite widely held, though far less so than in the past—might go something like this: unwashed folk, perhaps incestuous, living in backwoods cabins and subsisting by hunting, gathering, fishing, clamming, woodcutting, and the like (see Sinton and Wills 1978). They engage, in Pinelands Commission parlance, in resource-related activities.

The worst Piney stereotypes probably were inspired by the work of Elizabeth Kite (1913), a researcher at the Vineland Training School for Feeble Minded Boys and Girls. Based on fieldwork she supervised, Kite portrayed Pine Barrens residents as degenerate, lazy, and lustful. "The real Piney," she wrote, "is a degenerate creature who has learned to provide for himself the bare necessities of life without entering into life's stimulating struggle. . . . Like the degenerate relative of the crab . . . kicking food into its mouth and enjoying the functionings of reproduction, the Piney and all the rest of his type have become barnacles upon our civilization" (Kite 1913, 10). In the spirit of Progressive reformism, she argued that we should set about clearing up this "backdoor of our civilization" (p. 40).

Kite's supervisor, Henry Goddard, took matters even further with his notorious book, *The Kallikak Family* (Goddard 1912). Goddard claims that a Revolutionary War soldier, Martin Kallikak (a pseudo name derived from the Greek *kalos* for good and *kakos* for bad), squired two lines. One, consisting of lawyers, doctors, and others of good standing, was descended from his normal marriage; the other, consisting of most of the population of the Pine Barrens, descended from his illegitimate son, whose mother was a feeble-minded barmaid. Goddard's thesis was repudiated even at the time; in more recent times, it was shown to be both grossly exaggerated and misinterpreted (Gould 1981; Smith 1985).

But the damage was done. Goddard's and Kite's findings were

widely publicized, prompting further "investigations" and a tour of the region by Governor James F. Fielder. Goldstein (1981) reports the following gubernatorial quotation from the *New York Sun* of June 29, 1913: "I have been shocked at the conditions I found. Evidently these people are a serious menace to the State of New Jersey. . . . They are inbred and lawless and lead scandalous lives 'til they have become a race of imbeciles, criminals and defectives. . . . The state must segregate them, that is certain. I think it may be necessary to sterilize some of them" (p. 44).

A regional identity was indeed established. Needless to say, these images of Pineys do not match the realities of the present, just as they inaptly described Pineys of the past. Yet the myth persists in subdued forms; in some people's minds, in radically altered form. In some quarters, Pineys are romanticized—seen, perhaps, as the American Indians of Megalopolis. The current generation are the proud bearers of a rich but threatened folk culture; one that must be documented and protected by those whose business it is to understand and appreciate folklore (Berger and Sinton 1985; Hufford 1986; Moonsammy, Cohen, and Williams 1987; *New Jersey Folklife* 1987; Samuelson 1986).

The mysterious Pineys have been mythologized, among other places, in *Reader's Digest* (Mallowe 1985), as well as in a newsletter distributed to AT&T credit union members (AT&T Employees Credit Union 1989). The latter depicts the Pineys as virtually unchanged for generations, "keeping to themselves, living off the products of their forests and swamps." Pineys are seen as self-sufficient, having little need to trade with the outside world. Ironically, this same article urges readers to take their AT&T VISA cards with them when visiting this isolated region so far removed from the mainstream.

In trying more earnestly to figure out who the Pineys are, we must return to the question of where they live. Samuelson (1986) spatially defines Pineys by linking them with the core "preservation area" delineated by the Pinelands Commission (Map 4). Stansfield (1983, 202) believes that the myth of "an isolated, homogeneous culture, crystallized in a time past by isolation" may bear some relationship with reality in the Mullica River watershed in the central Pine Barrens. The largely Anglo-Scottish-Irish population, mostly Methodist and second- or third-generation New Jerseyans, was quite homogeneous in the nineteenth century. Sinton and Masino (1979), in a study of Washington Township (central Pine Barrens) in the 1800s, note that cultural homogeneity was extremely high in the nineteenth century—in fact, they seem to generalize these findings to all of "Piney society." Significantly, they note the literacy rate was 70 percent in 1850 and 90 percent in 1900 (Sinton and Masino 1979, 181). Although most Pineys hunted and produced food and timber for themselves, they produced a surplus that tied them into the regional market economy. Many also had jobs, such as cranberry harvesting, charcoaling, roadwork, or timber cutting. Sinton and Masino (1979) view Piney society as a historically stable and unified one, tied into the mainstream, yet isolated by choice from the nearby urban society. As we later see, the concept of choice is very relevant to today's Pine Barrens residents—Pineys or not.

If the population of the central Pine Barrens was culturally homogeneous, that of the southern Pines was not (Map 2). Elizabeth Marsh (1979) describes the southern Pine Barrens as an "ethnic archipelago." It lacks the Pineys found farther north and more closely resembles "small-town America." Its uplands—islands in a sea of extensive swampy areas—have seen concentrated settlement only within the past hundred years. With the demise of local industries, the penetration of the railroad, and the availability of commercial fertilizer in the mid 1800s, the area became ripe for settlement. Groups of German, Italian, "Yankee," Polish, Jewish, black, Puerto Rican, Russian, Ukrainian, and even Mongolian and Japanese immigrants settled in the region, engaging in such activities as truck farming, poultry farming, and railroad work.

Thus, while the southern Pines are much too ethnically diverse to be labeled a single culture region, the central Pines are identified, at least by some historians, as the seat of Piney culture (Sinton and Masino 1979; Stansfield 1983). But in the contemporary context, there is little to distinguish the central Pines from rural "cultures" elsewhere in the United States (Berger and Sinton 1985; Rubinstein 1983). Indeed, Zelinsky (1973) points out that, in general, differences among American culture regions appear to be slight and shallow when compared with those in older countries. Yet many make the assumption that the Pines—to some, the entire Pinelands National Reserve—constitute a culture region; this assumption is embedded in Pinelands planning. Research addressing this question is scarce, though Marsh's (1982) identification of one material feature of the landscape, the "South Jersey house," lends some support to the notion of regional culture. The South Jersey house, with its

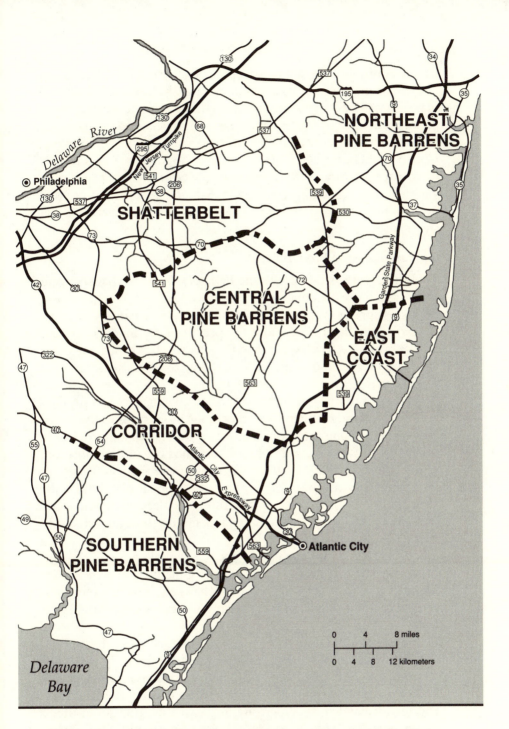

Source: Jonathan Berger and John W. Sinton, *Water, Earth, and Fire: Land Use and Environmental Planning in the New Jersey Pine Barrens* (Baltimore: Johns Hopkins University Press, 1985), 165. Boundaries reproduced with permission.

MAP 2. PINE BARRENS SUBREGIONS

front door in the middle and ridgepole parallel to the road, has been influenced by Yankee English, Quaker English, and later Pennsylvania culture. Marsh maintains that even though this house design can be found outside southern New Jersey, it has persisted longer in the Pines than elsewhere because of the region's isolation. Moonsammy, Cohen, and Hufford (1987) describe the "South Jersey wagon" that took crops to market in the nineteenth and early twentieth centuries. But in a more contemporary context, Samuelson (1987) found that no regional thread unified the various festivals and celebrations that she studied throughout the Pines.

Musicians and Storytellers

Until recently, students of Pine Barrens folk culture have concentrated much of their analytic energy on music and folktales. These popular expressions may give some clues as to what, if anything, is particularly distinctive about the people of the Pines. They may also inform us as to how the Pine Barrens are currently being packaged and presented to outsiders—and how residents are shaping or reconstructing their own regional images.

To the extent that music can be considered indigenous to any contemporary place, there appears to be none indigenous to the Pines. Nor is there a long tradition of adapting folk music imported from other places. But folk traditions are sustained by cultural diffusion; music, for example, does not just spring from the soil. Whatever its various sources, music enjoys a rather special place and fairly long tradition in the Pines. In the 1800s, fiddler Sammy Giberson was one of the Pines' better-known folk figures (see Halpert 1947). In the 1920s, Sam Hunt, a local craftsman, hunting and fishing guide, and banjo player, gained some renown, often playing to out-of-town visitors at nearby shore resorts (Gillespie and Ayres 1979; Mendell and Yedinsky 1981). The Pinehawkers, of which Hunt was one, played not only at local gathering places but also for Atlantic City and New York City radio stations and at the 1941 National Folk Festival in Washington, D.C. (Gillespie and Ayres 1979).

Meanwhile, local musicians congregated for Saturday night jam sessions at Joe Albert's cabin in Ocean County. This informal group, known as the Pineconers, was joined by Sam Hunt after the Pinehawkers disbanded. Its repertoire included "traditional, old-timey, string band and contemporary pop-country selections" (Gillespie and Ayres 1979). The Pineconers now form the core of the Pinelands

Cultural Society (Ayres 1981); it meets regularly in the building that houses the Waretown Flea Market, and its "Sounds of the New Jersey Pines" attracts large crowds. The society is thriving.

Suzi Jones (1976) views the regionalization of folklore as a "rhetorical strategy." Folklore is seen not only as a form of entertainment but also as a means of making an argument and a tool of persuasion. Thus, as tales are told, songs sung, and so on, they are modified to persuade their audience. At the regional level, details of the local environment may replace details of distant people and places. Jones sees this localization as a rhetorical strategy because it is used by the performer to elicit desired effects and responses from the audience.

Ayres (1979) sees the activities of the Pinelands Cultural Society (PCS) as a rhetorical strategy for regionalization. He states that "the cultural stance of the Pinelands Cultural Society is, thus, one which argues for the validity of past values in the face of a threatening future" (p. 229). The avowed purpose of the PCS, he argues, is to preserve and present to the public the spirit of the old gatherings at Joe Albert's cabin; thus, the PCS is arguing in favor of old Pinelands values versus those represented by newcomers of the past ten or fifteen years.

This argument is true, at least in part. It is not so clear, however, that the old-timer–newcomer dichotomy is as powerful as Ayres would suggest. Indeed, not all Pineconers are themselves Pine Barrens natives (Gillespie and Ayres 1979). Many nonnatives have adopted a "Pinier than thou" ethic (Sinton, 1982 interview); in asking "Where are the Pineys?" Sheppard (1989) wrestles with this business of self-ascription as a basis for group identity. In Waretown, "newcomers" and "outsiders" may be creating a demand for a certain kind of music and atmosphere more than performers are trying to persuade their audiences. Gillespie (1979) concludes that the Pineconers' repertoire is a response (1) to the taste and message of individual members of the group, especially Gladys Eayre; and (2) to the tastes of different audiences. While Gladys Eayre describes the group as "just a bunch of country shitkickers," she maintains a record shelf at home that includes Gilbert and Sullivan, Debussy, and Handel (Gillespie 1979, 235). Gillespie, quoting from Douglas Green's *Country Roots*, adds: "Over the years the Pineconers have attracted a large audience of Ocean County residents by following a formula that can be described as "sentimental, nostalgic, 'old-time' music," guaranteed to remind the agrarian listener of a happier, simpler, more carefree time" (p. 235). Thus, while the Pineconers may have a message to convey, the message is probably more informed by the changes taking place in the mass society than by some naive longing on their part for an idealized past. Without doubt, they hate to see the old days end, but they are adapting creatively to changing times, rather than simply pining for the past.

The songs sung by the Pineconers are not, for the most part, localized in their content (Gillespie 1979). Nor do the Pineconers necessarily represent the Pine Barrens as a whole; it would be more accurate to see them as representing a small part of the Pines. Although they are not passing on a long tradition of Pine Barrens music, there are some recent traditions that they may help to keep alive. While the atmosphere and emotions they evoke do have some local distinctiveness, and probably should be regarded as a part of present-day Pine Barrens culture, they are not very strongly linked with the past. Although some music may be linked with seasonal rhythms of Piney lives and livelihoods of the past (Hufford 1986), this is only minimally reflected in the music and activities of the Pinelands Cultural Society. What may be more important than this is the simple fact that there was music in the Pines, and there still is. Granted, most of the songs can be heard elsewhere. But it is the choices of songs—the repertoires—that help set the Pines (or parts of the Pines) apart from their surroundings. Those repertoires give regional and subregional distinctiveness to the Pines. True, that distinctiveness may be rather contrived in the contemporary context, but that is how regional definitions are made, sustained, and reconstructed. For many visitors, the Saturday-night Waretown experience *is* the Pines.

Not just Pine Barrens music, but folktales too have received considerable attention. As with music, though, scholarly research is rather scarce. The outstanding basic reference on folktales and legends is the exhaustive compilation found in Herbert Halpert's (1947) doctoral dissertation. Various other accounts—mostly popular ones—also describe Pine Barrens folklore (see Beck 1936, 1937, 1947, 1956; Buchholz and Good 1983; Cohen 1982; Feinstein 1963; Hufford 1986; Irwin 1978; Lawrence 1953; McCloy and Miller 1976; McMahon 1964, 1973, 1980; McPhee 1967, 1974; Mayer 1859; Moonsammy, Cohen, and Williams 1987; *New Jersey Folklife* 1987; Sinton 1979, 1982; Weygandt 1940). Though folktales were being told as recently as the 1940s (Halpert 1947), very few, if any, were passed along to the present generation.

Halpert (1947) attempts to trace some of the relations between Pine Barrens folktales and other American tales, as well as European, especially British and Celtic, traditions. The evidence regarding regionalization of folktales in the Pines is much more abundant than that for the regionalization of music. This may be partly—but probably not entirely—a function of Halpert's careful and extensive documentation of folktales. Most stories were told by itinerant storytellers, for whom storytelling was an avocation rather than a profession. They would travel the main routes across the Pines, bringing news as well as stories, but not staying at any one place more than a night at a time. Devils, spirits, wizards, strong men, fools, and clever fellows were the subjects of their tales. Their guiding strategy was simple: Entertain the audience. This meant recalling details accurately, using the right intonation, using the right gestures, delivering the tale at the right speed, and so forth. Localization was important—elements of familiarity added to the entertainment value. It seems that most of the stories would be made local to a fairly small subarea of the Pines, such as an industry town and its surroundings. Indeed, some tales would vary from place to place within the Pines. A reading of Halpert (1947) conveys the impression that audiences knew their own small areas well, but probably did not identify with the Pine Barrens as a larger entity. As with music, though, the present-day recognition—and it seems to be an increasing recognition, judging by the number of recent books on the subject—that folktales were told in the Pines tends to enhance the notion of the Pine Barrens as culture region.

Contemporary Regional Consciousness

How firmly entrenched in the contemporary mind, then, is the perception of a Pine Barrens or Pinelands region? Unfortunately, most evidence regarding regional recognition is anecdotal. But the few studies that have been done would seem to indicate that, at best, the regional image is blurry. As noted, Samuelson's (1987) study of festivals revealed that there was no common Pine Barrens theme. Stansfield (1983), however, argues that South Jersey, which encompasses a greater area and has a much larger population than the Pines, appears to be a vernacular perceptual region with con-

siderable regional self-consciousness. This conclusion is based on
(1) the pro-secession votes cast in a 1980 referendum by residents of
all southern counties except Ocean, (2) an examination of regional
identifiers in telephone-directory listings, and (3) a survey of college students directed at eliciting their regional perceptions. Before
she conducted her study of festivals, Samuelson (1986) argued that
Pine Barrens residents identify both with South Jersey and the Pine
Barrens.

Results of an Eagleton Institute (1981) poll also lend some support to the notion of a separate South Jersey consciousness. This
north-south dichotomy resembles divisions found in several states.
When a more developed, prosperous portion of a state possesses
greater wealth and political power than some other part of the state,
animosity often becomes a powerful basis for regional identification
in the "outcast" region (Elazar 1984; Waterfield 1986). Not only is
this the case in New Jersey, but also in such states as New York, California, and Illinois. Yet none of these cases are so clear-cut as they
may at first appear. In South Jersey's case, the Pine Barrens are rather
isolated, even within the South Jersey context. Some parts of South
Jersey—at least to a greater extent than the rest of the region—tend
to be aligned with the greater New York and Philadelphia regions.

Much of the period between Goddard's and Kite's stigmatiza-
tions of the Pines early in the century and the first fledgling attempts at regional planning in the 1960s was marked by widespread
ignorance of the Pine Barrens. But regional recognition has been
boosted over the past twenty-five years or so by various popular,
academic, and planning definitions of the Pines. John McPhee's
popular book *The Pine Barrens* (McPhee 1967) and his article in
National Geographic (McPhee 1974); various recent planning definitions (Governor's Pinelands Review Committee 1979; New Jersey
Pinelands Commission 1980); 1982 recognition of the Pinelands as
a UNESCO biosphere reserve (Batisse 1982, 1985; U.S. Man and the
Biosphere Program 1989); and studies of the area's peoples and cultures (Berger 1980; Berger and Sinton 1985; Hufford 1986; Sinton
1979, 1980, 1982) have undoubtedly fostered greater recognition
of the Pines as a region. New education programs and increased
media interest surely have bolstered general recognition of the Pines
in northern New Jersey, southeastern Pennsylvania, and to a lesser
extent outside the immediate megalopolitan vicinity. Moreover,
concern about and opposition to Pinelands planning may have en-

hanced regional consciousness in the Pines and the rest of southern New Jersey. Still, there is no clear evidence that either insiders or outsiders identify specifically with the regional boundaries defined by state and federal legislation.

Increased recognition of the Pinelands as a distinct region would seemingly help planning and preservation efforts. Yet the various images of the Pine Barrens created by publicity, education programs, and even music do not, for the most part, represent Pine Barrens history very faithfully. Indeed, the past tends to be selectively romanticized, spatially as well as culturally. Nevertheless, much of the recent attention may do service by helping persuade outsiders that culture, as well as ecology, is important. But this yearning for cultural protection, while not rejected by all residents of the Pines, is only rarely informed by their contemporary concerns.

The Comprehensive Management Plan (CMP) treats the Pinelands as a single political region, directing the bulk of future development away from the core and toward the fringes (especially the Atlantic City region). In New York State's Catskill Park, in contrast with its northern Adirondack Park, comprehensive regional planning never took hold. Dyballa (1979) attributes this failure of New York State's Temporary State Commission to Study the Catskills to the fact that residents do not necessarily feel united as a region; that the Catskills do not hold together well socially or politically.

One way to treat the planning area is as a series of subregions. While given some mention in the Pinelands plan (New Jersey Pinelands Commission 1980), a subregional planning approach has not been practiced. Jonathan Berger and John Sinton, harsh critics of the way in which the plan has been implemented, strongly advocate a subregional approach (Berger 1980, 1982; Berger and Sinton 1985; Sinton 1980, 1981). They argue that traditional indigenous activities—such as agriculture, hunting, fishing, and gathering—can be encouraged by promoting the appropriate land use patterns in the appropriate places. Shown in Map 2 are water-table regions, delineated on the basis of surface drainage patterns and seasonal depth to high water table. Berger and Sinton further divide these units, in each Pinelands county, into a series of politically defined subregions. Those subregions consist of clusters of towns, and each tends to be dominated by one or more major land use patterns. Berger and Sinton call for a "bottom-up" approach to regional planning, with the policy subregions serving as loci for important decision making.

Whatever its merits, this is not the approach adopted by the Pinelands Commission—except when elements of it happen to coincide with the broad regional approach embraced by the commission. While Berger and Sinton's specific proposals leave much to be desired, their guiding logic remains persuasive: If the "culture" of the Pine Barrens is to be defined and planned for spatially, then it is far more appropriate to do so at the subregional than the regional level.

4

Evolution of Planning and Management

Before Regional Planning

Given the intense political activity of the past decade, one might easily conclude that lawmakers and planners had all but forgotten about the Pines during preceding decades. Such was not the case. Indeed, as early as 1707, restrictions were imposed on woodcutting in the Pines. In the late 1800s, when the industrialist Joseph Wharton sought to develop a system of reservoirs, canals, and conduits to carry Pine Barrens water to nearby Philadelphia, the New Jersey Legislature thwarted his designs, at the final hour, by passing a law prohibiting conveyance of waters out of state. Thus, in 1884, was the first strong public stand taken on behalf of a resource as coveted then as it is now.

In 1915, Wharton's heirs offered to sell their land to the State of New Jersey for $1 million. A referendum was put on the ballot, and voters rejected the purchase 123,995 to 103,456 (Berger and Sinton 1985, 67). Finally, in 1950, New Jersey purchased the 100,000-acre tract. It became the Wharton State Forest, New Jersey's largest. Several smaller state forests had been established much earlier in the century. Other public landholdings include several large federal military facilities, the 28,000-acre Edwin B. Forsythe National Wildlife Refuge, and state and county parks, wildlife management areas, natural areas, and historic sites. Among the larger public preserves, besides Wharton, are the following, listed by number of acres (New Jersey Pinelands Commission, 1987a):

	Date established	Acreage
Lebanon State Forest	1908	29,413
Peaslee Wildlife Management Area	1954	14,276
Lester G. McNamara Wildlife Management Area	1933	12,438
Colliers Mills Wildlife Management Area	1941	12,211
Belleplain State Forest	1928	11,270
Bass River State Forest	1905	9,100

In conjunction with the New Jersey Department of Environmental Protection's Green Acres office, the Pinelands Commission carries out its own acquisition program. In 1980, the CMP recommended that 100,000 acres be purchased; between 1981 and 1990, 61,000 acres had been acquired (New Jersey Pinelands Commission 1991). Although Congress appropriated $14.5 million in 1988 for Pinelands acquisition (to be matched by state funds), only $1 million had been appropriated by 1991. The appropriated funds are to be used to acquire small parcels whose uses have been greatly restricted by the CMP. In total, approximately one-fourth of the Pinelands National Reserve is now in public ownership (Map 3).

Compared with New York State's Adirondacks, early public interest in the Pine Barrens was sporadic and limited. The Adirondacks achieved distinction in the nineteenth century as a vacation mecca for the elite and in the twentieth century became much more accessible to the middle class. The Pine Barrens, despite the reputations of Lakewood, Medford Lakes, and Cassville as health meccas and summer resorts (see Moonsammy, Cohen, and Hufford 1987), and despite fairly wide recreation use in recent years, never achieved the same level of recognition. But, as noted in Chapter 3, the Pines have drawn scientific interest at least since the turn of the century. And widespread negative publicity associated with the Kite–Goddard reports brought a notoriety to the region that has persisted through

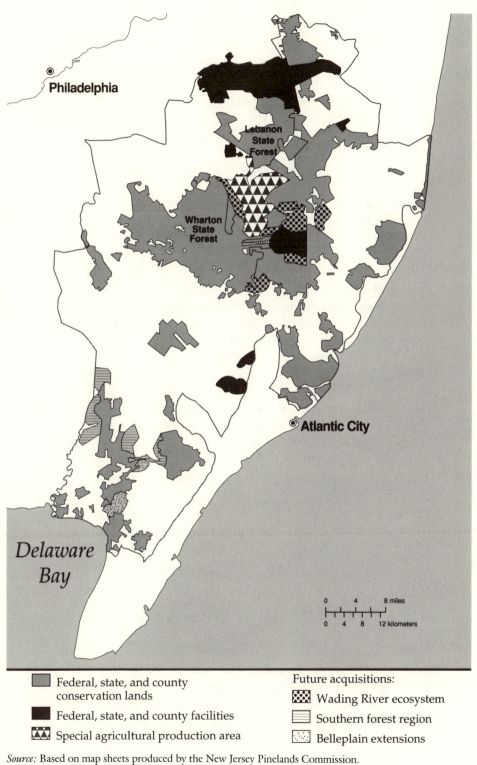

Philadelphia

Lebanon
State
Forest

Wharton
State
Forest

Atlantic City

*Delaware
Bay*

| 0 | 4 | 8 miles |

| 0 | 4 | 8 | 12 kilometers |

Federal, state, and county
conservation lands

Federal, state, and county facilities

Special agricultural production area

Future acquisitions:

Wading River ecosystem

Southern forest region

Belleplain extensions

Source: Based on map sheets produced by the New Jersey Pinelands Commission.
MAP 3. PINE BARRENS LANDS IN PUBLIC OWNERSHIP

much of the present century. Still, overall outside interest—probably even basic awareness of the existence of the Pines—remained very limited until the early 1960s.

A Jetport in the Pines?

Latent interest in the special qualities of the Pine Barrens was transformed into active concern around 1960, when a huge intercontinental jetport was proposed for Burlington County. In fact, several of those who got their start opposing the jetport remained active in subsequent Pinelands planning efforts (Table 1). From a broader regional and national perspective, it appears that the Pine Barrens site would not have been chosen for the jetport anyway. Even in the early 1960s, before the advent of environmental impact and various other legal and procedural requirements, the social, political, and economic obstacles that stood in the way of choosing a specific site were formidable. The jetport scheme for the greater New York region never came to fruition.

Nevertheless, the Pine Barrens and the Great Swamp area of northern New Jersey had both been potential sites. Strong support for the Pine Barrens site came from the Burlington County Board of Chosen Freeholders. In 1960, the Boards of Chosen Freeholders of Ocean and Burlington counties established the Pinelands Regional Planning Board. The boards commissioned Herbert H. Smith Associates to undertake a comprehensive planning study for the bicounty region. First, a series of technical studies was completed; then the actual plan for the region (Herbert H. Smith Associates 1963, 1964). Individual members of the Pinelands Regional Planning Board, as well as the reports Smith generated for them, were strongly biased toward maximizing regional economic development.

Thirty years ago, Walter Rostow (1960) developed a five-stage typology of national economic development: traditional society, preconditions for takeoff, takeoff, drive to maturity, and age of high mass consumption. In a rather similar manner, the 1964 report argued that the Pinelands had to reach a "takeoff point," after which substantial economic development could occur. The takeoff was in this case to be spurred by development of an intercontinental jetport, which would serve the New York and Philadelphia metro-

TABLE 1. PINELANDS PLANNING TIMELINE

1960–1964	Pinelands Regional Planning Board.
1967	Pinelands named as prime jetport site.
	Department of Interior declares that parts of Pinelands are of "national significance" (McCormick 1970).
1968	National Park Service releases "four alternatives" study (U.S. Department of the Interior, n.d.).
1968–1972	Pine Barrens Advisory Committee.
1972–1977	Pinelands Environmental Council.
1975	Pinelands Environmental Council releases "Plan for the Pinelands."
1976	Bureau of Outdoor Recreation report offers three protection options for Pinelands (U.S. Department of the Interior 1976).
	Governor Brendan Byrne convenes Pinelands conference in Princeton.
1976–1978	New Jersey Department of Environmental Protection upgrades central Pine Barrens water standards.
1977	New Jersey Executive Order 56 creates Pinelands Review Committee.
1977–1979	Pinelands Review Committee.
1978	National Parks and Recreation Act creates Pinelands National Reserve.
1979	Executive Order 71 creates Pinelands Commission and imposes eighteen-month building moratorium.
	New Jersey Pinelands Protection Act passed.
	Pinelands Commission established.
1981	Comprehensive Management Plan for Pinelands adopted.

politan areas. Several options were laid out, and a "jetport–new city" plan was recommended. Had the jetport scheme ever come to fruition, land speculators probably would have made fortunes. But along with the potential for private gain, much of it ill gotten, the scheme promised a garden city, perhaps as visionary as the ideas of Ebenezer Howard. From "raw earth" would rise a "renaissance city." It was an elaborate prospect, reflecting the technological and quasi-utopian aspirations of a dawning supersonic jet age. Undoubtedly, some of its principal proponents believed, in all sincerity, that their plans could bring only good to the region: jobs, graceful living, and the preservation of open space. Although open space was seen as an almost unassailable virtue, only a small number of "nature nuts," bird watchers, and scientists were seriously concerned with the Pine Barrens' ecological assets.

After wealthy and politically astute northern New Jersey suburban interests successfully laid to rest the proposal for a jetport in the Great Swamp (see Cavanaugh 1978), and as other potential sites in the New York metropolitan area met with strong opposition, local attention focused by default on a Pine Barrens site. According to Goldstein (1981, 70): "The Pinelands, which was considered by the FAA to be an unrealistic and altogether unworkable choice in 1961, became the choice site in 1967."

Significant opposition to a Pine Barrens site emerged in the early 1960s, when the idea first surfaced. Goldstein (1981) sees two major jetport opponents: conservationists and the military. The Pine Barrens Conservationists, a loosely organized group formed in 1957 to advise the state on botanical development of the Wharton Tract, had a membership consisting mainly of old-stock, wealthy, conservative Republican Yankees. These conservationists took pleasure in studying, photographing, and botanizing in the Pine Barrens. Elmer Rowley, who later became chair of the New Jersey Audubon Society, was very active in this group. While these genteel conservationists did their best to lobby against the jetport proposal, they were not as numerous or vocal as the "new" environmentalists of the 1970s, with whom many of them would later join forces.

The army, air force, and navy—major landowners in the Pines— had their own plans for those lands and did not want to transfer acreage to New Jersey for use as a jetport site. But even though they shared a concern about the jetport threat, military and conservation interests did not forge an alliance. And on other issues they were antagonists. Indeed, reports Goldstein (1981, 73), the Citizens Committee to Save State Land—a conservation group— actively and successfully opposed a National Guard plan for a tank training ground in the Pine Barrens.

Goldstein (1981) sees the jetport issue as finally being put to rest during the 1969 gubernatorial campaign. The jetport was a LULU (Locally unwanted land use) or NIMBY (Not in my backyard) issue (Lake 1987; O'Hare 1977; Popper 1985) of monumental proportion. Precious few New Jerseyans would have wanted it in or anywhere near their backyards. Indeed, by the time of the 1969 gubernatorial campaign, it had become a prominent state-level political issue (*New York Times* 1969a, b; Sullivan 1969). Goldstein (1981, 75–77) tells how Republican candidate William T. Cahill shifted his stance from one of support for McGuire Air Force Base as a jetport site to opposition to a jetport anywhere in New Jersey. This occurred shortly after a well-attended (largely by senior citizens) anti-jetport meeting of FOCUS (Federation of Conservationists United Societies, Inc.). Cahill's opponent, Robert Meyner, had chosen to leave the question open (*New York Times* 1969a). Cahill won the election, and the issue was apparently laid to rest.

Through this entire jetport episode, then, local entrepreneurial elites sought wider regional control and personal profit; conservationists, based mainly in the surrounding metropolitan region, sought to stymie those efforts. Conservationists prevailed, though not necessarily because their own opposition tactics succeeded. Larger economic and political forces were also at work. But the conservationist legacy was established—in the form of an enduring Pine Barrens protectionist movement.

The Pinelands Environmental Council

Formal federal recognition of the importance of Pine Barrens preservation came in the late 1960s. A 1967 study, commissioned by the U.S. Department of the Interior and conducted by Jack McCormick of the Philadelphia Academy of Natural Sciences (see McCormick 1970), found that parts of the Pine Barrens were of "national significance." This finding moved the Department of the Interior to direct the National Park Service to study alternative means for Pine Barrens preservation (Ocean County Nature and Conservation Society, n.d.). The Park Service study commenced in September 1968.

Word of the Park Service activity spread rapidly, and cries of "The Feds Are Coming" were heard locally. A tempestuous meeting aimed at keeping them out was held in the Burlington County village of New Gretna. The outcome of this and other local meetings was the formation of a Pine Barrens Advisory Committee, appointed by the Burlington and Ocean County Boards of Chosen Freeholders (Goldstein 1981; Governor's Pinelands Review Committee 1979; Ocean County Nature and Conservation Society, n.d.; Pinelands Advisory Committee n.d.; U.S. Department of the Interior 1976).

This is not at all unlike the local response to Adirondack land use planning in the early 1970s, when the Local Government Review Board was created, and again in 1990, when in response to the report of the Commission on the Adirondacks in the Twenty-First Century (1990), various proposals for greater local participation in regional affairs emerged (Mason 1991).

In 1969, the National Park Service released a report (U.S. Department of the Interior, n.d.) that put forth four alternative plans for the Pine Barrens. Because national park or monument designation would have precluded such existing land uses as agriculture and hunting, neither was recommended. Instead, these alternatives were proposed:

1. The Pine Barrens as a national scientific reserve. As recommended by McCormick, a 175,000-acre central Pine Barrens area would be designated. Landowners would enter into voluntary agreements with the federal government or, alternatively, there might be acquisition along with regulatory programs.
2. The Pine Barrens as a national scientific reserve. This is similar to the preceding alternative, but a larger area would be regulated and more acreage would be acquired.
3. The Pine Barrens as a state forest preserve or national recreation area. A 267,000-acre area would be managed through acquisition and conservation easements. Major existing land uses would not be disturbed.
4. The Pine Barrens as a state pinelands region. A 373,000-acre region would be managed through acquisition and zoning. A regional council would represent eighteen towns, four counties, and state, federal, and other interests.

Each scenario would have kept substantial proportions of land in private ownership and would have attempted to maintain existing patterns of land use. Each, therefore, could be considered an application of the greenline planning concept (see Chapter 1, "Larger Planning Contexts").

Meanwhile, the Pine Barrens Advisory Committee had taken on a life of its own, separate from the federal initiative. In a July 1970 report, it recommended that a land use review commission be established and that acquisition proposals from the Park Service study be endorsed. The result, in 1972, was creation of the Pinelands

Environmental Council (PEC), an organization comparable in structure and powers to the widely criticized Tahoe Regional Planning
Agency (Constantini and Hanf 1973; Strong 1984).

The PEC's jurisdiction was limited to the central Pine Barrens (see
Map 2 for an approximation), an area considerably smaller than that
which would be regulated by subsequent executive and legislative
actions. Though authorized by state legislation and funded through
the Department of Environmental Protection, the council was to
be an independent body. Its membership was composed largely of
county and municipal officials from Burlington and Ocean counties,
along with individuals specifically representing conservation interests, fish and game concerns, agriculture, and the Department of
Environmental Protection. The PEC's formal powers were advisory
only: It could provide assistance and encouragement to localities,
conduct studies and hearings, make recommendations to the state,
and produce reports. But the procedural requirements attached to
the PEC's advisory role did give it a means of exerting leverage.
Specifically, the council was authorized to review projects; the time
required to do this (as specified by law) could result in project delay
and perhaps modification or even abandonment of projects. The initial review period was thirty days; if the PEC found that the project
might not be in conformance with its comprehensive plan for the
Pinelands or that it might have an unreasonable adverse effect on
Pinelands resources, it was empowered to enjoin the project for an
additional sixty days (Pinelands Environmental Council 1975).

During that sixty-day period, the council's findings would be
communicated to public agencies having review or approval powers
over the project in question and would also be widely disseminated
to the public. In addition, the PEC's statutory authority explicitly
allowed the enjoining of any agency or person violating any provisions of the authorizing legislation. Legislative and administrative analogues can be found in the National Environmental Policy
Act (NEPA) and some of its state-level progeny. NEPA cannot stop
projects or legislation, but its provisions requiring environmental
impact statements for federal agency actions provide an avenue for
public review and procedural legal challenges on a wide range of
actions. As a result of NEPA, many projects and proposals have been
modified or even canceled; some proponents, perhaps, were dis-
suaded even from putting proposals forward (see Anderson 1973;
Andrews 1985; Liroff 1985). Arguably, NEPA has improved envi-

ronmental decision making, but at the same time it has resulted in considerable, perhaps often unnecessary, expense and delay.

Opponents charged that the PEC "had no teeth" (see New Jersey Senate 1979). NEPA likewise has no teeth, yet it has been effective— at least in many circumstances—in forcing agencies and project proponents to take account of environmental impacts. Federal agencies can, for example, refuse to issue water-discharge permits or wetlands-alteration permits based on certain environmental information. In other words, the federal government uses either purse strings or legal consent requirements as levers to ensure compliance with certain environmental objectives. This general policy approach is embodied in various forms in many federal and state laws— to name a few, the Clean Air and Water acts, Food Security Act, National Flood Insurance Act, Coastal Zone Management Act, and Coastal Barrier Resources Act (Davis and Lester 1989; Mason and Mattson 1990). When applied forcefully and consistently—which, for various political and economic reasons, often it is not—this approach can be quite effective.

Suppose we make a somewhat dubious assumption: If all parties had worked in earnest, most of the PEC's goals could have been met. Then the poignant questions become these: Did the PEC's *Plan for the Pinelands* provide for an adequate balance among land uses in the Pines, and were the project review standards and procedures sufficient to protect the resources of the Pines? To some, the answer was a resounding No! David H. Bardin, then commissioner of the New Jersey Department of Environmental Protection, labeled the PEC's 1975 *Plan for the Pinelands* a "developer's dream," since it proposed half-acre zoning—essentially a suburban density—in developable areas of the Pines (Goldstein 1981, 106).

Two distinct elements of conflict present themselves here: conflict of interest (preservation vs. economic gain), and conflict of attitudes and values (a commitment to local control vs. assertion of the collective interest in the resource). It is difficult, if not impossible, to sort out fully the components of the conflicts that were brewing in the Pinelands during the 1970s. But from a strategic perspective, the PEC can be characterized as a successful coping strategy (see Wood 1976). Local economic and political interests were responding to the threat of strengthened federal and state regulatory presence in the Pines. For a time, the coping strategy worked.

Indeed, a theme that pervades the recent history of Pinelands management is that the threat (implied or otherwise) of extrare-gional intervention prompts a concerted local response. That re-sponse may take the form of some sort of locally based initiative (like the PEC), or at least a thorough defense of local motives and abilities—based on the record—to meet the broad environmental goals that created all the fuss in the first place. At any rate, the PEC was philosophically committed to local control. Even the conserva-tionists on the council were for the most part old-line and politically conservative. Morton Cooper, a highly respected Ocean County conservationist and staunch defender of home rule, exemplified this well. In its *Plan for the Pinelands*, the PEC explicitly declared its respect for "the traditional rights of ownership and use of land." Perhaps its philosophy is best summed up in this rather curious excerpt:

> The Council believes that all landowners in the Pinelands bear a responsibility to protect the region's resources. No owner of a parcel of land should have the privilege of utilizing his land so in-tensely that if all similar parcels were so utilized, the region would suffer degradation. Otherwise, a time may come when no further development may be permitted to occur, unfairly punishing those who did not develop their land early. The proposals which follow are based upon this principle. (Pinelands Environmental Council 1975, 8)

Echoes of Garret Hardin's (1968) "tragedy of the commons" can be heard here, though in Hardin's scenario the land is in common, rather than private, ownership. Hardin's story is one of animals sharing a limited amount of pastureland. The common resource begins to deteriorate as soon as one shepherd—acting out of self-interest and in the belief that his act will go unnoticed—makes the decision to add one animal beyond his fair share. The individual benefits, but there is a small negative consequence for the resource as a whole. In the absence of rules and sanctions, other shepherds soon follow suit, and this leads to severe degradation or destruction of the pasture. Marvelous a metaphor as this is, there are some obvious difficulties in calculating a resource's carrying capacity. In the Pine Barrens planning region of the early to mid 1970s, the PEC had the task of making the necessary value judgments, as well as promulgat-ing the requisite standards ("mutual coercion," in Hardin's words), to ensure that the carrying capacity of the Pine Barrens would not be exceeded.

Resources can be defined and valued in a virtually infinite number of ways. The PEC's plan for the central Pine Barrens would have set aside certain "critical" areas where development was to be either discouraged or prohibited. "Developable" lands were defined as those where depth to the water table is greater than five feet. "Marginal" lands were broadly defined as those that fall in between the critical and developable categories. The PEC's scheme would have encouraged one-acre zoning in many developable areas. Had developable areas actually been built out to that density, groundwater still would have been protected to the "baseline" satisfaction of the PEC, but not to the satisfaction of other interests, as evidenced by the more stringent standards later adopted by the New Jersey Department of Environmental Protection. The PEC plan presented little in the way of scientific justification for its determinations. But the PEC had expressed a sincere interest in conservation, motivated though it was by the threat of further state or federal intervention in the Pines. The council then attempted, up to the limits of local political acceptability, to translate that concern into action.

In essence, the PEC was a search for common ground between local political acceptability and state- and federal-level interest in ecological protection and preservation of open space. But state- and federal-level thinking shifted in the 1960s and 1970s, responding to growing public desires—sometimes imperatives—for stronger, preservation-oriented measures for valued areas like the Pines. At this ethereal level, at least, the notion of private property rights was no longer held so sacred; indeed, the idea that land is a resource, rather than a commodity, was gaining currency (see Goldstein 1981). Unfortunately, though, this resource versus commodity debate—widely accepted as it is as a framework for discussion and analysis—tends grossly to simplify the complex, and sometimes inherently contradictory, ways in which Americans value land (see Wolf 1981).

The "new environmentalism's" view of the common resource differed from the PEC's view. For one thing, the resource encompassed a larger geographical area (see Governor's Pinelands Review Committee 1979). Also, carrying capacity was defined differently; deterioration was *already* well under way, with much more threatening to occur. "Carrying capacity," as based on the PEC's principle, was replaced by an ecosystem perspective—a preservation philosophy that seeks to sustain conditions suitable for protection of rare and endangered species, maintain the pristine quality of Pine Barrens groundwater, and preserve the sense of remoteness and wilderness qualities of the Pines. The preservationist community, while far from unitary in its views, often had fairly little regard for the human presence in the Pines. Perhaps preservationists felt that local interests were more than adequately represented (or overrepresented) through the existing political structure.

Why did the more preservationist, extralocal view not prevail in the late 1960s and early 1970s? Given the environmental fervor of the period, the time should have been right. One factor often regarded as a precondition for strong state-level land use legislation is a serious and visible threat to the land resource—as was the case, for example, in Hawaii in the early 1960s and Vermont and the Adirondacks in the early 1970s. In the Pines, the jetport proposal was just such a threat—and, indeed, associated controversy did greatly heighten public concern. But the threat was laid to rest. More insidious threats—for example, second-home development, rapid suburban encroachment, or aquifer depletion or deterioration—seemingly would have prompted stronger state responses. Although all these things were in fact happening in the Pines—development, for example, was proliferating in parts of Ocean County in the 1960s—threats to the area's integrity apparently were neither sufficiently visible nor alarming to evoke more than a rather muted state-level response.

Nor was there much interest on the part of the Rockefeller family or other nationally influential conservationists. The Pines were, and still are, perceived much differently from the Adirondacks, the Vermont countryside, the Columbia River Gorge, Lake Tahoe, or the California coast. The contours are much more subtle, without dramatic peaks or valleys, large lakes, or rugged stretches of coastline. The Pines are valuable open space, an important recreational resource, they store vast quantities of pure water, and they are highly valued by scientists worldwide. But this was not enough, in the early 1970s, to bring forth powerful land use legislation. One key missing ingredient was a strong state-level political commitment to Pine Barrens preservation; indeed, the Republican administration of the time was not a friend of strong, centralized regulation. This was to change with the 1973 election.

Brendan Byrne's Critical Role

In 1973, New Jersey voters overwhelmingly elected Brendan T. Byrne as governor. Byrne proved to be a very strong supporter of Pinelands preservation. Indeed, it was he who often prodded his staff on Pinelands issues, at times acting in ways that seemed to defy political prudence (Linky, 1985 interview). Byrne hopes that he will long be remembered and credited for his Pinelands efforts (Meyner et al. 1983; Byrne and Linky, 1985 interviews).

During Byrne's first term as governor, the PEC was to lose what support it enjoyed from the governor's office. In 1974, the state dropped its share of funding for the PEC. In 1975, Byrne's commissioner of environmental protection labeled the PEC's *Plan for the Pinelands* a "developer's dream." After the state funding cutoff, Burlington and Ocean counties underwrote the council on their own—until a 1976 superior court ruling found that the counties' support was illegal without state aid. Late in 1977, an appeals court panel overturned the earlier ruling, allowing the counties to resume support of the PEC.

The PEC's history was even more tumultuous than thus far indicated. Its first chairman, J. Garfield De Marco, was charged with conflict of interest because of his large landholdings (see Chapter 6, "Woodland Township"); he finally resigned in 1977. Joseph Portash, the first executive director, was convicted of accepting money from a developer in return for favors. Though the conviction was overturned several years later, Portash would be linked with other scandals late in his subsequent tenure as Manchester Township administrator (see Chapter 6, "Manchester Township"). At any rate, the PEC did reorganize and try to set a rather different course for itself in 1978. But the reincarnation was short lived. The PEC was rapidly eclipsed by other events of the mid and late 1970s.

In 1976, Governor Byrne convened a conference in Princeton, where he made public his commitment to develop a more effective preservation plan for the Pinelands. In 1977, he issued Executive Order 56, creating the Pinelands Review Committee (PRC). In addition to citizens appointed by the governor, committee membership included the secretary of agriculture and commissioners of the Departments of Environmental Protection and Community Affairs (or designated representatives). The PRC was charged with reviewing state activities affecting the Pinelands and proposing plans, guidelines, or standards for achieving the goal of making state actions consistent with the stated aims of protecting Pinelands resources and encouraging "compatible" development. Late in 1978, the PRC set forth its recommendations in the form of a draft report. Key among them was the proposed establishment of a Pinelands Planning and Management Commission, whose members would be appointed by the governor. This recommendation came as no surprise—given Governor Byrne's interest in a regional (or, more accurately, state-wide) approach to Pinelands planning and the PRC's membership and mission.

The PRC was also charged with identifying boundaries for the Pinelands. This was done in rigorous detail, with the committee relying in its deliberations on the substantial body of technical information already in existence. The latest addition to that body of information was a study by Rutgers University's Center for Coastal and Environmental Studies (Merrill et al. 1978), conducted under contract to the Mid-Atlantic Regional Office of the National Park Service. The boundaries derived by the PRC are similar to those of the final Pinelands map of 1980 (Map 4). Within these boundaries were designated an inner, more ecologically sensitive "preservation area" surrounded by a larger "protection area." The 1.1 million-acre total area—virtually the basis for the plan later adopted—compares with only 320,000 acres under the planning jurisdiction of the Pinelands Environmental Council. Key factors in drawing the expanded boundaries were hydrogeology and vegetation. Included in the enlarged area is a substantial coastal zone segment. Although it differs markedly in physical appearance from the interior Pine Barrens, it is hydrologically and historically linked with them.

During the same period (1976–1978), the New Jersey Department of Environmental Protection (DEP) had been working toward upgraded water-quality standards for the central Pine Barrens area. This process began in 1976 with a policy statement by Brendan Byrne and was later cast concretely in the language of Executive Order 56. The DEP held a series of hearings on its proposals for nondegradation of surface and groundwater. As a response to those hearings, as well as legislative sentiment of the time, four task forces were formed. Their recommendations resulted in modifications to the DEP proposals (Governor's Pinelands Review Committee 1979). Interim guidelines were developed in mid 1977 and remained in effect until final guidelines were adopted in 1978. The storm of criticism aroused by the standards is reflected in the record of a hearing held in January 1978 before the Senate Committee on Energy and Environment (New Jersey Senate 1978). Patterns of support and opposition were typical: support mainly from environmental organizations and opposition mainly from small housebuilders, tradespeople, and their representative organizations.

This was a time when several local threats to the integrity of the Pinelands emerged. The PRC (Governor's Pinelands Review Committee 1979) expressed concern about growing impacts associated with retirement-home projects and growing recreational demands. A more discrete development was the approval of casino gambling in Atlantic City; this was expected to generate growth that would spread into nearby Pinelands communities. During the late 1970s, development of Outer Continental Shelf oil and gas seemed imminent—and associated pipelines through the Pinelands would have posed environmental risks (Governor's Pinelands Review Committee 1979). These factors, although not sufficient to account for the strength of the Pinelands plan that ultimately emerged, were important in generating the concern that made it possible.

The Federal Role

The 1976–1978 period also witnessed movement at the federal level. In 1976, the Bureau of Outdoor Recreation released a study report that set forth options for federal participation in Pinelands preservation. Three options were presented (U.S. Department of the Interior 1976):

1. Joint federal–state land acquisition and management
2. Federal and state land acquisition and state management
3. State land acquisition and management (with federal designation of a national ecological reserve and special consideration of requests for matching funds from the Land and Water Conservation Fund).

The report urged a concerted state–federal effort in choosing among the alternatives for managing an area of approximately 920,000 acres.

First stirrings of congressional activity came in 1977, when Representative James J. Florio, a Democrat from Camden County (elected New Jersey governor in 1989), introduced a bill for the establishment of a Pine Barrens National Ecological Reserve (U.S. Congress, House, 1977a). Florio's interest in a Pine Barrens protection scheme was kindled by a phone call to his office from Charles E. Little. Little, then with the Congressional Research Service, mentioned his 1975 paper on greenline park planning (U.S. Congress, Senate, 1975). In brief, greenline planning involves public management of private lands; the concept is more fully considered in Chapter 1. Florio was keenly interested in the idea, and work soon got under way on drafting a bill (Little, 1985 interview). Little, along with George Davis of the Adirondack Park Agency, Jack Hauptman of the Northeast Regional Office of the Bureau of Outdoor Recreation, Donald Humphrey of the National Park Service, and Pope Barrow of the House Legislative Counsel's Office, came together as a task force (Little 1983).

True to the greenline approach, the bill called for a federal–state–local partnership for the Pines. Up to 50,000 acres of ecologically critical land would be acquired by the secretary of the interior and managed by a broad-based commission. A separate state commission would develop detailed boundaries and plan for and manage land use within the region. Also to be established was a citizens' advisory committee, with thirteen members appointed by the governor. The secretary of the interior would establish guidelines, and if the secretary disapproved the plan developed by the commission, the secretary would be able to withhold federal planning assistance (up to 75 percent of the total costs), reassert federal control over federal lands within the reserve, acquire lands, and enter into direct agreements with local governments. This potentially powerful federal role in some ways resembles that embodied in the "Cape Cod formula." Towns are not directly required to comply with federal zoning standards; instead, the secretary of the interior, under the 1959 Cape Cod National Seashore Act, is empowered to condemn private property selectively in towns whose zoning ordinances do not comply with federal standards for the Cape Cod National Seashore (Thomas 1985). A similar scheme is in place at Fire Island National Seashore.

The burgeoning interest in greenline parks persuaded New Jersey Senators Clifford Case and Harrison Williams to develop a generic greenline bill (U.S. Congress, Senate, 1977); in the process, they brought together some of the "best thinking in the field" (Little 1983, 4). The Pinelands were to be the first unit in a nationwide system of reserves. But because the Carter administration withheld support—with the apparent intention of strongly endorsing the greenline concept during Carter's second term of office (Little 1983, 1985 interview)—greenlining's moment in the sun indeed turned out to be a brief one. Yet even though Congress never did consider greenline legislation, the idea of a Pinelands National Reserve lived on. And in the late 1980s, revived interest in the greenline concept, or at least a scaled-down version known as *greenways* (Little 1990; Presidents Commission on Americans Outdoors 1987), brought renewed attention to the Pinelands model (Chapter 1, "Larger Planning Contexts").

In addition to the Florio bill, New Jersey Representatives Edwin Forsythe and William Hughes introduced a Pinelands Preservation Act (U.S. Congress, House, 1977b). This bill directed the secretary of the interior to undertake a comprehensive study of the 970,000-acre Pinelands region and develop a proposal and management plan for a National Wildlife Refuge not to exceed 50,000 acres. The remaining acreage would be eligible for inclusion in "ecological management units." The units would receive federal funds but would be managed through cooperative agreements among local governments and within the state government. If local governments failed to act, the state would be encouraged to establish a commission to manage the units in question, the inducement again being federal monetary assistance, since Congress cannot actually require the state to establish a planning commission. The federal funding carrot—an essential element in so many of our environmental laws (Mason and Mattson 1990)—once again found favor.

The Forsythe–Hughes proposal relied much more on local initiative than did the Florio bill; in this regard, it might be compared with New York State's Tug Hill program (Dyballa, Raymond, and Hahn 1981; Marsh 1981). That program, much less intrusive even than the Forsythe–Hughes proposal, was generally accepted by local residents because it did little to threaten their interests, and because a great deal of effort went into consultation and gentle persuasion. Under the Forsythe–Hughes approach, local governments would be treated gently—but they would act, the thinking went, because the state would intervene if they failed to do so.

Supporters of the Florio proposal argued that a regionwide approach was needed (U.S. Congress, House, 1977a; U.S. Congress, Senate, 1979); Forsythe and Hughes countered that the legislation necessary to establish a Pinelands planning commission might not get through the state legislature. If that were the case, their logic went, at least the localities would have tried to plan—it would not have been "all or nothing." This scenario is difficult to evaluate. Perhaps, on the expectation that the state legislature would not really come down on them, reluctant localities would have refused to act. Or they might have feared that there was enough statewide sentiment favoring regional planning that they had better act in order to preserve as much local control as possible. Key elements of the Forsythe–Hughes proposal, in short, were that it gave local governments the chance to prove themselves before being overruled by a regional agency, and it called for a subregional approach to planning.

The 1970s, then, brought to light various plausible scenarios for Pinelands management, ranging from stringent federal controls to strengthened local planning. The area to be protected ranged in size from 175,000 to more than 1 million acres. Most proposals were accompanied by threats, directed toward localities, of state or federal financial and other negative incentives. Greatest political progress was made by the Florio and Forsythe–Hughes bills.

But neither bill was reported out of committee; instead, the proposal for a Pinelands National Reserve became part of the lengthy and complex National Parks and Recreation Act of 1978 (Public Law 95-625). Senators Clifford Case and Harrison Williams, who had earlier proposed the generic greenline bill, worked out a committee amendment to the omnibus parks bill. The amendment enjoyed broad support from the New Jersey congressional delegation, state officials, and environmental interests (see Van Abs 1986 for a more detailed description of the law's evolution).

Section 502 of the National Parks and Recreation Act established the 1.1-million-acre Pinelands National Reserve. Congress also directed that the secretary of the interior ask the governor of New Jersey to establish a planning entity to develop a comprehensive management plan for the reserve. The fifteen-member entity was constituted as follows: one member appointed by the secretary of the interior, seven members appointed by the governor, and one member appointed by each of the governing bodies of the seven counties with lands in the reserve. The county appointees were meant specifically to represent local viewpoints, while interests such as agriculture and conservation were to be represented somewhere—but not necessarily through "assigned" interest-group appointees—within the entity's overall membership. If one assumes, perhaps rather unrealistically, that state and federal appointees represent the larger public interest, while county appointees represent local viewpoints, then interests based outside the region have a slight political edge. In practice, of course, the balance of interests depends very much on gubernatorial inclinations, as well as various local (county- and municipal-level) interests and political considerations.

Financial assistance for plan development and land acquisition (up to 75 percent of costs) would be the secretary of the interior's responsibility. The comprehensive plan was to include a resource assessment, detailed boundary map, policy statements, and a provision for maximum local government and public input. On November 10, 1978, the National Parks and Recreation Act became law.

New Jersey's Role

In March 1979, Governor Byrne issued Executive Order 71. This order established the Pinelands Commission as it currently exists: a fifteen-member body consisting of seven gubernatorial appointees, one member each from the governing bodies of the seven Pinelands counties, and one member appointed by the secretary of the interior. The commission was empowered to prepare a comprehensive management plan for the nearly 1-million-acre area that was the focus of the Pinelands Review Committee Report (Governor's Pinelands Review Committee 1979). In essence, the planning provisions of Byrne's order concurred with the federal legislation.

But Byrne took an additional and bold step: He imposed an eighteen-month Pinelands building moratorium. State agencies and departments were barred from taking final action on permits and grant applications, except in cases of "compelling public need" or "extraordinary hardship." In essence, this was a ban on nearly all construction in the Pines. One of the moratorium's effects—indeed, an intended effect—was to put pressure on the legislature to pass a Pinelands planning bill. Not surprisingly, the New Jersey Builders Association challenged the executive order in court. The Attorney General's Office advised the Governor's Office—in fact, before the executive order was even signed—that the case probably would be lost. But by the time the case reached the New Jersey Supreme Court, the moratorium had already been eclipsed by state legislation, and the case was declared moot.

On February 13, 1979, Senate President Joseph Merlino and Senator Charles Yates introduced S. 3091, the Pinelands Protection Act, in the New Jersey Legislature. Gathering legislative momentum, fueled by both the federal directive and Byrne's moratorium, expedited the bill's progress. Somewhat unclear is just which individuals pushed hardest to get the bill through. A number of persons would like to claim a major share of the credit for the legislative effort, including Senator Frank Dodd, Senator Merlino and Governor Byrne (Byrne, Catania, and Dodd, 1985 interviews). At any rate, all played integral parts in shaping and directing the process.

Frank Dodd, chair of the Senate Energy and Environment Committee, conducted a series of hearings on the bill (New Jersey Senate 1979). Predictably, environmental organizations and a few key individuals, mostly from northern New Jersey, testified in favor of S. 3091. Farmers, tradespeople, local officials, and small businesspeople for the most part testified against it—arguing that it went too far, was a land grab, violated the intent of the federal legislation, and, in a related vein, that the governor's actions were dictatorial. No one, however, contended that there was no need for development restrictions in the Pines. Indeed, those most vehemently opposed to the legislation were sure to stress the need for some controls. Perhaps this was simply opportunism. The writing was on the wall, and some willingness to compromise was essential. But, as is further addressed in the case studies of Pinelands townships in Chapter 6, opportunism was not the sole motivating factor.

Although many of the region's residents share in the desire to prevent "overdevelopment," this very value-laden notion is the stuff of rancorous disagreements at public hearings. Preservationists often are opposed to any intrusion into what they portray as wilderness, but they will reluctantly accept some. Their opponents are willing to accept more intrusion and generally feel that planning decisions should be made at the local level, with only advice and guidance from above. The exchanges that occur in public forums are dramatic, if not very informative. Still, underlying differences in values and interests frequently do manage to reach the surface. Many Pinelands residents feel that the Pines are theirs, and to bolster their claims, they may cite lines of ancestry reaching back to colonial times. At the same time, they say they are willing, especially if monetary compensation is forthcoming, to share the wealth. "Outsiders" feel that these lands belong to everyone, but "everyone" may in fact be a relative few who wish to use the area's scenic and scientific resources with only minimal interference from other potential users.

These broad issues and arguments notwithstanding, the immediate role of the hearings was to produce a workable bill. Yet, in another sense, they were a ritual; they gave many individuals a chance to express views and let off steam. Arnstein (1969), Burke (1968), and Wengert (1976) describe this as "therapy." Still, and perhaps more important, the hearings did act as working sessions of sorts, providing committee members with constructive guidance for fleshing out and amending the legislation.

The Merlino–Yates bill prevailed over a bill introduced by Senator John Russo (S. 3138), which would have required an economic impact assessment as well as a secure funding source (bond issue or other form of financing) to reimburse towns for lost tax revenues. Despite much redrafting, the Merlino–Yates bill emerged as a surprisingly strong piece of legislation. Several individuals intimately involved in the process later commented that they fully expected the planning-area boundaries to be substantially pared down (Catania and Linky, 1985 interviews). In fact, nothing of the kind happened.

In June 1979, Brendan Byrne signed the Pinelands Protection Act into law, declaring that "it's the bill that 100 years from now I'll be most remembered for" (Panzer 1980, 12). While affirming the development moratorium, the act allowed exemptions for expansions to individual homes as well as for improvements for agricultural or horticultural purposes. The act validated in law the fifteen-member Pinelands Commission and charged it with producing a comprehensive plan by August 8, 1980. The following planning goals—the basic principles that guided Pinelands management through its first decade—are set forth in the legislation.

For the outer protection area:

1. Preserve and maintain the essential character of the existing Pinelands environment, including the plant and animal species indigenous thereto and the habitat therefor;
2. Protect and maintain the quality of surface and ground waters;
3. Promote the continuation and expansion of agricultural and horticultural uses;

4. Discourage piecemeal and scattered development; and
5. Encourage appropriate patterns of compatible residential, commercial and industrial development, in or adjacent to areas already utilized for such purposes, in order to accommodate regional growth influences in an orderly way while protecting the Pinelands environment from the individual and cumulative adverse impacts thereof.

For the inner preservation area:

1. Preserve an extensive and contiguous area of land in its natural state, thereby insuring the continuation of a Pinelands environment which contains the unique and significant ecological and other resources representative of the Pinelands area;
2. Promote compatible agricultural, horticultural, and recreational uses, including hunting, fishing, and trapping, within the framework of maintaining a Pinelands environment;
3. Prohibit any construction or development which is incompatible with the preservation of this unique area;
4. Provide a sufficient amount of undeveloped land to accommodate specific wilderness management practices, such as selective burning, which are necessary to maintain the special ecology of the preservation area; and
5. Protect and preserve the quantity and quality of existing surface and ground waters.

The Comprehensive Management Plan

The commission then set about the hurried task of drafting a comprehensive plan for the Pinelands. As noted, the commission had already been established and working over the several months that had elapsed since Brendan Byrne issued Executive Order 71. Because the commission had drawn up interim development standards and dealt with development applications, certain issues had crystallized. But the head start did little to lessen the commission's daunting workload. Moreover, the commission had no permanent staff (it had to rely on state agency personnel, mostly from the Department of Environmental Protection) and was plagued by absenteeism, especially on the part of county appointees. Nonetheless, the commissioners got to know each other quite well, creating an atmosphere that minimized acrimonious debate and allowed the group to get on with its work (Russell, n.d.).

The commission had to work under extraordinary time and budget constraints—a source of consternation to many local residents, who felt (and continue to feel) excluded from the planning process. Once funding was secure, the commission moved rapidly in awarding consulting contracts for work on the plan. In all, about twenty consultants produced a large collection of reports that constitute the background documentation and basis for much of the Pinelands Comprehensive Management Plan (CMP) (New Jersey Pinelands Commission 1980). Prominent among the consultants was the Chicago-based firm of Ross, Hardies, O'Keefe, Babcock, and Parsons. This large law firm has been in the vanguard of the "Quiet Revolution in Land Use Control" (Chapter 2, "The Quiet Revolution"), promoting the revolution and writing associated laws and regulations (Walker and Heiman 1981). Smaller local consulting firms, as well as nonprofit institutions such as Rutgers University's Center for Coastal and Environmental Studies, also were brought on board. The full set of consultants' reports is described and referenced in the CMP.

General Plan Provisions

The CMP provides a careful and rather exhaustive description of the Pinelands physical environment, inventories prehistoric and historic sites, and describes settlement patterns and the distribution of ethnic groups within the region. Also included are results of a Pinelands scenic study and lists of actual and candidate rivers under the federal and state wild and scenic rivers programs. Brief mention is made of various "perceptions of the future," ranging from maximum allowable development (given certain basic standards) to a strong assertion of the national interest in the region.

Regional land use patterns and infrastructure (sewer and water systems, landfills, transportation facilities, recreational facilities, governmental installations, and mining operations) are described, population trends and land use transactions are detailed, and population projections to the year 2000 are presented. These are more than neutral baseline data; they serve as the basis for estimating housing demand and developing growth scenarios for the Pines. In short, these data and the consultants' reports from which they were derived are the foundation for the prescriptive part of the CMP.

Thus it comes as no surprise that the CMP's projections, and the assumptions they embody, have proved contentious during the plan's implementation.

Critical Pinelands areas are delineated in the CMP. Criteria are included for identifying critical ecological, perceptual, cultural, economic, and natural-hazard areas. But the greatest emphasis, by far, is on critical ecological areas; this is justified by the reference given to them in the federal and state legislation. Because the specification of critical ecological areas was such a contentious issue, the detailed procedure for doing so is spelled out in the CMP (New Jersey Pinelands Commission 1980; Russell, n.d.). The approach might be described as clinical. A series of criteria that could be applied to any or all critical areas was rank-ordered by commission staff, scientists, consultants, and participants at public meetings. Critical areas were then assessed on the basis of point totals derived by summing the generic importance ratings for each of the factors applicable to each critical area. The areas themselves were not specifically ranked or evaluated by participants. Broad principles, not the uniqueness of places, guided this process.

The commission adopted a set of resource goals and a somewhat more specific set of policies. The goals generally resemble those found in the state legislation, though in addition to protection and preservation, they include enhancement of ecological, cultural, agricultural, and recreational values. "Enhancement" is a particularly elusive term, meant to satisfy a variety of concerns (Russell, n.d.), but doing so in a deliberately vague way. General and ambiguous as they are, though, the goals and policies do set the tone for the CMP and its implementation. The long discussions over choices of words and phrases are still referred to by Pinelands commissioners, often when one of them wishes to allay public concerns about a philosophical point that was debated extensively during the plan's formative stages.

Land Use, Water Quality, and Quality of Life

Central to Pinelands planning and management is the land-capability map that separates the region into zones (Map 4). Preservation and protection area boundaries had already been established by the state legislation. In the preservation zone, "low intensity" or "appropriate" uses—such as berry agriculture, forestry, selected recreational uses, and limited resource extraction—are permitted.

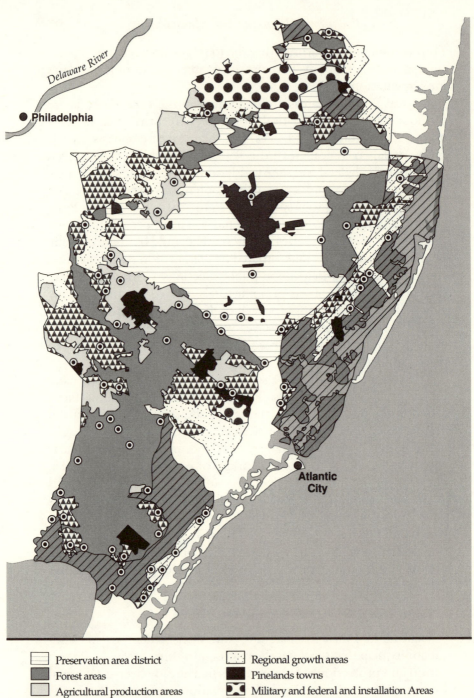

Delaware River

● Philadelphia

Atlantic City

Legend	
☐ Preservation area district	⣿ Regional growth areas
▨ Forest areas	■ Pinelands towns
☐ Agricultural production areas	⬚ Military and federal and installation Areas
■ Special agricultural production areas	◉ Pinelands villages
▲▲▲ Rural development areas	⧄ Within Pinelands National Reserve but outside state-designated Pinelands Area

Source: From a brochure produced by the New Jersey Pinelands Commission.

MAP 4. PINELANDS COMMISSION LAND CAPABILITY MAP

Residential development outside designated towns, villages, or agricultural areas is restricted to those who can demonstrate a "cultural, social or economic link to the essential character of the Pinelands" (New Jersey Pinelands Commission 1980, 393). To qualify for this "Piney exemption," an applicant must be a member of a two-generation extended family of at least twenty years' residence in the Pinelands, or his or her primary source of household income must be "employment or participation in a Pinelands resource-related activity" (New Jersey Pinelands Commission 1980, 394). This is defined as "including, but not limited to, forest products, berry agriculture and sand, gravel or minerals" (New Jersey Pinelands Commission 1980, 350). Considerable latitude has been granted in the interpretation of these definitions.

Both the protection and preservation areas are subdivided into several planning areas (Map 4). This was done by developing and overlaying sets of criteria in the form of "factor maps." This process yielded a first-cut set of maps, which was revised after comments were received from local planners, Pinelands residents, and interest-group members (see Russell, n.d.). These are the management areas:

1. Agricultural production areas. Found in both the preservation and protection areas, these zones consist of major areas devoted to agricultural uses, as well as adjacent lands so suited. Allowed uses are those related to agriculture, though municipalities have limited options for permitting other uses.
2. Special agricultural production areas. Designated by municipalities in the preservation area, these are meant to protect areas devoted to berry production and native horticultural uses, as well as adjacent watershed lands.
3. Military and federal installation areas. These are major existing federal landholdings.
4. Forest areas. These are largely undeveloped areas that represent the "essential character" of the Pinelands. Low-density residential development is permitted (average densities for each township are specified in the CMP), as well as certain other uses that would not greatly alter the character of these areas.
5. Rural development areas. These are meant to serve as buffers between more and less developed areas, as well as reserves for future development. Municipalities are afforded wide discretion in determining land uses in rural development areas, though there is an overall density cap of 200 dwelling units per square mile.

Within rural development areas, municipalities have the option of designating "municipal reserves." Reserves are meant to absorb future growth beyond the capacity of existing regional growth areas (see below). Before an area's status can change from reserve to regional growth, a series of environmental conditions must be met. Regional growth area standards then apply to the reserve area.

6. Regional growth areas. These are in or adjacent to already developed areas, are experiencing growth pressures, and have been deemed capable of accommodating growth. The commission allocates dwelling units and maximum densities for each town's regional growth districts. Regional growth areas are meant to absorb growth demands generated by Atlantic City casino development, coastal growth pressures, and suburban expansion from the Philadelphia metropolitan area.

7. Pinelands towns and villages. These are existing settlements. Limited development is allowed in and around the center of the settlements, with a 3.2-acre maximum lot size for houses using conventional septic systems and a 1-acre minimum for those using alternative and innovative on-site treatment systems.

Although the 212,000 coastal acres of the Pinelands National Reserve are subdivided into the zones described here (Map 4), they are not under the jurisdiction of the Pinelands Commission. Instead, New Jersey's Division of Coastal Resources (DCR) has direct planning responsibility for these lands. To the extent that its statutory authority permits, the DCR is to implement the CMP, and the Pinelands Commission and affected municipalities are to act as reviewing agencies for CAFRA (Coastal Area Facilities Review Act) permit applications handled by DCR. But CAFRA regulations are less stringent than Pinelands regulations, and this discrepancy would quickly lead to conflicts and concerns about overdevelopment in the coastal zone (Collins and Russell 1988).

A distinctive feature of Pinelands planning is its transfer of development rights (TDR) scheme. Development credits are allocated to lands in the preservation area, agricultural production areas, and special agricultural production areas. In the preservation area, except in wetland and agricultural areas, property owners are entitled to 1 credit per 39 acres (or fractions thereof). In wetland areas, they receive .2 credits per 39 acres. In agricultural and special agricultural production areas, the formulas are 2 credits per 39 acres of upland, berry bogs, or fields; and .2 credits per 39 acres of wetlands not in agricultural use. Credits may be purchased for use in the regional growth areas. Developers who do so are entitled to 4 bonus units per credit; they are used in accordance with regulations of the receiving municipality.

When the TDR question was raised during the drafting of the CMP, two viewpoints emerged (Russell, n.d.). One held that the program was necessary compensation for loss of property value; that is, the imbalances created by the Pinelands regulations had to be remedied. The other held that the TDR program was a bonus: The CMP did not constitute a "taking" and thus was on firm legal ground (see Randle 1982); therefore the TDR plan was at best unneeded, at worst unjustified. Indeed, Russell (n.d.) reports that the consultants (Rogers and Golden) were at first not favorably disposed to the idea. Ultimately, the pro-TDR view prevailed, perhaps in large part because of unflagging advocacy by Pinelands Commissioner B. Budd Chavooshian (Russell, n.d.; Chavooshian, 1983 interview). Today, the TDR scheme, although firmly in place, remains a source of considerable controversy.

The CMP includes program recommendations for vegetation and wildlife, water quality, wetlands, fire management, forestry, air quality, agriculture, waste management, resource extraction, recreation, housing, and capital improvements, as well as more detailed recommendations on the financial aspects of plan implementation and public participation in the process. Some of these elements, such as vegetation and agriculture, are absolutely critical to the plan's stated and implied objectives. But perhaps no aspect of the CMP is more integral than its water-quality standards.

Amid much controversy (see Russell, n.d.), the commission opted to extend existing water-quality standards for the central Pine Barrens (Chapter 4, "Brendan Byrne's Critical Role") to the entire Pinelands National Reserve. The two-parts-per-million-nitrate standard, applied through a dilution model that determines anticipated levels of nitrates at property lot lines, serves as the basis for establishing lot-size requirements. The minimum lot size for on-site disposal systems for *any* management area is 3.2 acres, but this can be altered in cases where an alternative disposal system is used.

Questions may be raised about the assumptions embedded in the water-quality standards and the scientific rigor of the models on

which the standards are based. Yet there is a clear resource protection rationale for water-quality standards of some sort. The same
cannot necessarily be said for the CMP's provisions requiring use
of native vegetation in landscaping. Other requirements, including
those that seek to restrict and eliminate outdoor signs and those
that make undergrounding of utilities mandatory, are much further
removed from resource protection; their bases are purely aesthetic.
The impulse for an ecologically harmonious cultural landscape was
taken even further in the report of the Governor's Pinelands Review
Committee (1979); it contemplated incentives for low-technology
lifestyles. In this ecotopian Pinelands, one would have found energy-
efficient homes, "sonic clothes washing," and industrial activities
limited to such pursuits as weaving, potting, and woodworking.
Some individuals actually envisioned guidelines at this level of detail
(Patterson, 1984 interview), but the CMP, however ecotopian the
thinking of some of its proponents, stopped far short of this.

Plan Administration

A key element of the CMP, considered further in Chapter 7, is
the local-conformance requirement. Initially, counties and municipalities were given one year to bring their master plans and zoning
ordinances into conformance with relevant provisions of the CMP.
The deadline was later extended for towns that failed to meet it
but were judged to be making a good-faith effort to comply. Major
elements of a certifiable plan/ordinance are a natural resources inventory, a capital improvements plan, adoption of the CMP's design and
development density standards, provision for notifying the Pinelands Commission of development review actions, provisions to
accommodate Pinelands development credits (where appropriate),
and adoption of the CMP's management programs and minimum
standards. Local plans must address each of the CMP's program elements, but considerable latitude is allowed in doing so. Specific
minimum requirements must, however, be met: prohibition of development in or within 300 feet of wetlands, exemption of agricultural operations in agricultural and special agricultural production
areas from local nuisance ordinances, and adoption of wastewater
and septic-disposal standards, detailed sign provisions, fire management and housing standards, and conditions for resource-extraction
operations.

The Pinelands Commission itself is responsible for all development review decisions in uncertified municipalities. Its decisions are rendered through application of the CMP's standards and provisions. Certified towns make their own development review decisions, but the Pinelands Commission must be formally notified at key points in the review process. The commission reserves the right to "call up" and review local approvals (preliminary or final) that raise "substantial issues" with the CMP. This procedure is designed to encourage towns to conform with the CMP, reduce the Pinelands Commission's potential workload, and make the commission's presence less directly felt at the community level. But its presence, if less directly felt, is little diminished; indeed, the commission retains full and ultimate authority over much decision making in the region.

These, then, are the CMP's essential elements. The commission worked with great dispatch, completing a draft plan on June 6, 1980. Approximately two months remained until scheduled adoption of the CMP. Though the protests along the way may have seemed intense (see New Jersey Senate 1980), they pale in comparison with the firestorm of criticism unleashed by release of the draft CMP.

Plan Adoption

In June 1980, the New Jersey Assembly sent a strong message to the governor. It approved, 64–5, a bill calling for a five-month delay in approval of the Pinelands plan, and giving the legislature power to veto the plan. An earlier version of this bill went much further, clearing the way for immediate development of up to 17,000 houses (Weissman 1980). Though there was widespread sentiment that the Pinelands plan was perhaps too much, too fast, the Assembly's vote was not an unequivocal message to ease up on the restrictions. As noted, the provision that would have done so was rejected.

The governor, still committed to a preservation plan of his own shaping, conferred with legislators to work out a compromise. The result was the elimination of the legislative veto provision from the bill, adherence to the August 8 adoption date for the inner (and much less controversial) preservation area part of the CMP, and a delayed adoption date (November 14) for the outer, more controversial protection area. The compromise was unanimously approved by both houses of the legislature (Panzer 1980).

Thus a strong preservation plan was put into place for the core section of the Pinelands, and an opportunity was presented for considerable modification of the protection area plan. During this period, the commission conducted workshops and hearings. Amid the mountains of papers produced, circulated, commented on, and revised, two important documents stand out. One is the "alternative plan," submitted by the Coalition for the Sensible Preservation of the Pinelands (1980a, b, c, d; see Chapter 5 for more on the coalition's activities); the other, an environmental impact statement prepared by the Heritage Conservation and Recreation Service of the U.S. Department of the Interior (1980). The latter examines various Pinelands planning alternatives and, not surprisingly, supports the proposed plan.

The coalition, an organization dominated by development interests, produced a multivolume critique of the Pinelands plan (Coalition for the Sensible Preservation of the Pinelands 1980a, b, c, d). Its efforts culminated in an "alternative plan" that called on the Pinelands Commission to adopt performance standards for the protection area and develop a targeted housing allocation program for Pinelands towns. The scheme called for three maps: an ecological constraints map, a development opportunities map, and a composite of the two. The Pinelands Commission's plan was one of prescribed zoning densities, with some latitude for localities to allocate these densities. The coalition's scheme, by contrast, relied heavily on environmental performance standards. But even if those standards were stringent, the "alternative plan," if enacted, would probably have yielded less regional control over the landscape than does the CMP. The coalition's claims notwithstanding, much more time probably would have been needed to develop and implement its plan—and the plan would have allowed more scope for bargaining at the local level. The constraints–opportunities mapping, as proposed by the coalition, might have imposed stringent constraints on development in sensitive areas, but rather intense development probably would have been permitted in areas in between. The coalition's plan probably would have yielded fewer and smaller expanses of minimally disturbed landscapes (minimally disturbed, that is, in recent years). Allowing even for well-designed buffers, the sort of "mottled" landscape that might have resulted does not mesh well with environmentalist thinking calling for large-scale ecosystem protection, extensive undisturbed (or minimally disturbed) areas, and natural corridors for migration of plants and animals.

Long and heated debate during the fall of 1980 did result in some changes to the CMP; changes, that is, that were largely favorable to individual landowners and developers, especially in the protection area. Nonetheless, the protection area plan is a powerful land use plan; indeed, some key actors, looking back on this period, express surprise that the protection area plan survived at all. They expected to lose this part of the region in the final negotiations (Catania and Dodd, 1985 interviews). The compromises that secured the protection area's survival basically allow for more housing than initially would have been permitted. Grandfather provisions for development approvals were made more generous (individuals owning an acre or more before the imposition of Byrne's moratorium would be allowed to build a single-family home without Pinelands Commission approval), a higher *overall* density of development was permitted within the forest area (1 unit per 15.8 acres, as opposed to 1 per 39 acres), and growth-area municipalities were allowed, if they could demonstrate sufficient need, to increase total acreages where development would be permitted.

This, to the chagrin of some environmental organizations, is the compromise that was forged. It was approved by the Pinelands Commission, Governor Byrne, and finally Secretary of the Interior Cecil Andrus. Andrus's approval came only four days before Ronald Reagan took office. But a final hoop through which the plan had to jump was Congress. For a period of ninety days after Andrus's approval of the CMP, Congress could have opted to review the plan, and if it so chose, force changes by withdrawing federal funding. South Jersey Representatives William Hughes and Edwin Forsythe, ardent opponents of the plan as adopted, seemed interested in some sort of congressional action. Yet they were never very clear as to just what (*New York Times* 1981). In fact, in a preview of smooth legal sailing to come, these potential legislative threats to the CMP did not materialize. Federal funding came more slowly than originally anticipated, but it was never cut off. By the spring of 1981, plan implementation was well under way.

5

Actors and Interests

Interest-group politics, legal maneuvering, bureaucratic infight-ing, personality conflicts, and personal and institutional alliances all have played their parts in Pinelands planning. But beneath the rhetorical veneer of conflict and compromise lies a wide range of images and ideas regarding the Pinelands region and its future. In public debate, they tend to crystallize into a few well-represented and politically powerful viewpoints. The resultant Pinelands man-agement program represents an equilibrium of sorts among various political interests: a regional-level version of the pluralist model of equilibrium democracy (MacPherson 1977). In a fashion similar to an economic marketplace, competing interests interact continually through bargaining and negotiation. In Lowi's words: "The role of government is one of ensuring access particularly to the most effectively organized, and of ratifying the agreements and adjust-ments worked out among the competing leaders and their claims" (Lowi 1969, 71). In short, the interest groups become the whole of the relevant public. Those groups most influential in Pinelands planning and management represent three interests: environmen-tal preservation, housebuilding, and agriculture. Table 2 lists the

TABLE 2. MAJOR NONGOVERNMENTAL INTEREST GROUPS

Name	Geographic Area of Concern	Year Founded	Organizational Aims	Membership	Budget	Paid Staff	Pinelands Activities
Environmental							
Environmental Defense Fund	National	1967	Environmental and public health protection through education, legislative reform, legal and administrative action	52,641	$3,165,609	35	Since late 1970s; testimony, monitoring, legal action, research, political organizing
Friends of the Pine Barrens (defunct)	Mainly near Pines	1982	"Preservation, protection, and enhancement of Pinelands ecosystem"	N.A.	N.A.	0	Since 1982; testimony, monitoring, research
Natural Resources Defense Council	National	1970	Environmental protection through litigation, legal services, education, watchdog functions	43,000	$6,654,000	95	Since late 1970s; testimony, monitoring, research
New Jersey Audubon Society	New Jersey	1897	Preservation and protection of habitat through education, research, maintenance of sanctuaries	7,700	$675,000	16	Since late 1960s; testimony, monitoring, education, legal support
New Jersey Conservation Foundation (founded	New Jersey	1964	Land protection through purchase, holding for public purchase, lobbying, research,	4,000	$272,892	13	Since mid 1960s (unofficially) and 1976 (officially); testimony, monitoring, legal action, edu-

Organization	Location	Year	Purpose	Membership	Budget	Staff	Activities
as Great Swamp Committee)			political organizing, legal action				cation, public events, Town of Whitesbog preservation
Pine Barrens Coalition	Mainly near Pines	1977	Long-term protection of Pinelands and their resources	75–100	None	0	Since 1977; testimony, monitoring, legal action, umbrella for members
Sierra Club	National	1892	Protection and conservation of natural resources through research and education	350,000	$17,160,000	185	Since late 1970s; support to local chapters for testimony, lobbying, legal action, research
Sierra Club, New Jersey	New Jersey	1972	See Sierra Club	10,332	$45,000	.5	Since mid 1970s; see Sierra Club
Sierra Club, West Jersey	Southern New Jersey	1975	See Sierra Club	N.A.	N.A.	0	Since 1975; see Sierra Club

Development

Organization	Location	Year	Purpose	Membership	Budget	Staff	Activities
Builders League of South Jersey	Southern New Jersey	1940	See New Jersey Builders Association	425	$500,000	3	Since late 1970s; see New Jersey Builders Association
Coalition for the Sensible Preservation of the Pinelands (disbanded)	New Jersey	1979	To promote "economic retention, enhancement, and health of South Jersey"	N.A.	$300,000 (approx. total spent on Pines)	0	Since 1979; see New Jersey Builders Association
New Jersey Builders Association	New Jersey	1949	Support building and related professions through lobbying, education, research	2,500	$924,000	21	Since late 1970s; testimony, monitoring, legal action, research

TABLE 2. MAJOR NONGOVERNMENTAL INTEREST GROUPS (*Continued*)

Name	Geographic Area of Concern	Year Founded	Organizational Aims	Membership	Budget	Paid Staff	Pinelands Activities
Agriculture							
New Jersey Farm Bureau	New Jersey	1919	Represent interests of New Jersey farmers	5,010	N.A.	14	Since mid to late 1970s; testimony, monitoring, lobbying

NOTE: Data are for 1983–1985, an important time for interest-group activity in the Pinelands. After a period of relative quiescence, the Pinelands Preservation Alliance was created in 1989. An umbrella environmental organization, its major activities are monitoring, provision of testimony, education, and research. Its projected operating budget for FY 1991–1992 was about $160,000.

salient characteristics of the most active interest groups in the 1983–1985 period, an important time in setting the course for Pinelands planning.

Key individuals also have played very important parts in initiating and guiding Pinelands planning and management. Some of these people are active interest-group members (e.g., Carol Barrett of the Sierra Club, Nan Walnut of the Pine Barrens Coalition); others are politicians (e.g., Governor Byrne, Senators Case and Williams). Without their respective frameworks of institutional and political support, these individuals probably would have been far less effective in their efforts; conversely, without these individuals, interest groups and governing bodies would not have been able to muster such a vigorous Pinelands protection campaign.

Environmental Advocates

By mere virtue of the fact that a strong regional land use plan is in place, we can conclude that environmental interests are well represented in Pinelands decision making. But the task of defining an environmental interest is far from simple. Pepper's (1984) analysis explores environmentalism's conceptual complexity by considering its historical, philosophical, and ideological contexts. O'Riordan (1981) sees environmental ideologies as fundamental and persistent, related to systematic and logical structures of thinking. He views environmentalism across a continuum, ranging from "ecocentrism" to "technocentrism." Lowe and Worboys (1980) view "popular ecology" as politically naive; its ecological determinism ignores, or sometimes even masks, underlying social divisions and conflicts. Other observers take a less dim view. Bouchier (1987) and Boyte (1980; Boyte, Booth, and Max 1986; Boyte and Riessman 1986), for example, look to grass-roots activism as a form of empowerment and a force for progressive social (including environmental) change. Deep ecologists, such as Devall and Sessions (1985) and Tobias (1985), advocate "biocentric equality," whereby human needs are not intrinsically of greater value than those of any other species.

All these ideological bents can be found in various U.S. contexts; many are manifest in the Pine Barrens. Noticeably absent, though, are any forceful expressions of deep ecology or bioregionalism—with their biocentric, radical social and political implications. Instead, an overtly apolitical form of ecocentrism—akin to Lowe and Worboys' popular ecology—has dominated Pinelands environmental thinking. Pinelands environmental politics, superficially at least, are those of developers versus preservationists rather than those of social standing, race, or wealth. Social and economic divisions are of course relevant to Pinelands planning, but these issues usually enter the public debate only when disgruntled residents, whose credibilities more often than not are tarnished by some combination of unconstrained anger, political naïveté, and inexperience in bureaucratic settings, accuse planners and politicians of environmental elitism.

For present purposes, I define environmental interests as those whose main mission is either or both of the following: open-space protection and ecosystem preservation (i.e., ecocentric). Generally, the latter perspective is less accommodating of a human presence in the Pines than is the former. Specifically excluded from my definition are organizations, such as hunting clubs and campground and canoe rental associations, for whom environmental protection is important, but not the *main* organizational focus or reason for existence. At any rate, most such groups have played only very limited roles in Pinelands planning.

Government Advocacy

Environmental interests, although they have not achieved all their goals, have clearly prevailed in Pinelands decision making. But it is important to distinguish between environmental interests and environmental interest groups. Indeed, political impulses favoring Pinelands preservation were not directly fomented by environmental organizations. Instead, governmental advocacy emanated from several key sources, among them New Jersey Governor Brendan Byrne, the U.S. Department of the Interior, Congressman James Florio, and Senators Clifford Case and Harrison Williams. Much, though clearly not all, of this interest reflects political astuteness: Wise, or at least fortunate, politicians raise the right issues at the right time. Moreover, the Pinelands project was one that offered more than just immediate political gain. Because a protected natural area becomes an enduring and visible part of the landscape, those involved in saving it may hope to secure for themselves a place in the history books and the collective consciousness.

But something more was at work in the Pines. Governor Byrne

pursued the Pinelands cause with a dedication that exceeded most definitions of short- or long-term political opportunism. As noted, he prodded his staff on Pinelands issues (Linky, 1985 interview). Although Governor Byrne is the foremost political figure associated with Pinelands preservation, other politicians also played crucial roles. Central to the Pinelands program were the efforts of then Congressman James Florio, who had a very strong environmental record, especially regarding the regulation of toxic and hazardous materials and the public's right to know about associated risks. Florio's highly visible concern, as well as that of other New Jersey politicians, in part reflects the severity of environmental problems engendered by New Jersey's economic base and high population density. Whatever their origins, the concerns and initiative of individual politicians have perhaps been equal to or even greater in importance than the actions of environmental interest groups in the Pines. Individual politicians were, of course, able to tap successfully into strong preservationist interest in the urban and suburban regions that surround the Pines. But, absent this political leadership, it seems highly unlikely that environmental interest groups could have come together to force adoption of a planning program as spatially expansive and rigorous as the one now in place.

By the mid 1970s, state and federal interest in Pinelands planning had taken on something of a life of its own. One example was the federal initiative in promoting greenline park planning. In short, greenline planning calls for innovative management of private lands for public purposes (for a fuller description, see Chapter 1). The greenline banner has been carried by the former Heritage Conservation and Recreation Service (Department of the Interior) and subsequently by the National Park Service, especially its Mid-Atlantic Regional Office and Denver Service Center.

Despite a cool-to-disinterested attitude at high levels in Washington (Eugster, 1985 interview), the greenline initiative was supported by lower-, middle-, and even some high-level Park Service staff. In effect, they were gently subverting the ideology of a conservative Department of the Interior. We might compare this with the more overt campaign of subversion being waged in the late 1980s and early 1990s by Forest Service employees disgruntled with agency policies regarding timber sales and forest management (Kern 1990). At any rate, Foresta (1984) observes that environmentalist values of the 1960s and 1970s became widespread among

Park Service rank-and-file employees. That orientation has persisted to the present, exemplifying what Downs (1967) characterizes as an ideological lag common in large bureaucracies. Indeed, the environmentalist ideology so pervades the rank and file that decades might pass before a markedly different set of beliefs penetrates widely and deeply.

But such a massive shift may not be in the cards; by the mid 1980s, signs of an ideological softening were evident. Controversial Secretary of the Interior James Watt was forced to resign in 1983, and National Park Service Director William Penn Mott (appointed in 1985) seemed more favorably inclined toward greenline park planning than his predecessor (Eugster, 1985 interview). Moreover, the 1987 report of the President's Commission on Americans Outdoors proposed that a system of "greenways" link the nation's metropolitan areas. None of this necessarily signals a major federal commitment to innovative land management—indeed, significant new legislation has not emerged—but the report does lay some groundwork for future policies more receptive to greenline-type initiatives.

Citizen Organizations and Public Institutions

Congressional and Park Service actions notwithstanding, national interest in the Pine Barrens has been neither overwhelming nor widespread. Indeed, it has been limited mostly to a small scientific community keenly interested in the region's biota. Nevertheless, major national environmental interest groups did actively support the amendment to the 1978 National Parks and Recreation Act that established the Pinelands National Reserve.

Although the participation of national organizations diminished after passage of the federal legislation, some continue to monitor the Comprehensive Management Plan's (CMP's) implementation and provide support for locally based activities. But the bulk of the environmental activism has been "locally" based, emanating from the heavily populated megalopolitan centers of suburban northern New Jersey, the Philadelphia area, and New York City. Here we find the greatest knowledge of, interest in, and experience with the region. Because New Jersey is a small, densely populated state, the Pines are very accessible to its residents. So, too, is the seat of political power in Trenton. In terms of sheer physical accessibility, Trenton is no more than a couple of hours away from New Jersey's farthest hinterlands and is much closer to the bulk of the state's population. New Jersey's spatial and demographic character thus facilitates political organization.

Within most small and medium-size voluntary organizations, it is one or a few individuals who are deeply dedicated to the tasks at hand and who take on much of the work. Behind these individuals are the financial resources, access to expertise and advice, and organizational standing provided by the general membership, most of whom are passive supporters of the group's activities. In the Pine Barrens, the Sierra Club's early involvement came largely through the local leadership of Carol Barrett. Other Sierra Clubbers were active, but none so much as she. Barrett grew up near Camden, New Jersey, and visited the Pine Barrens frequently. Her involvement and leadership in Pines issues grew from her work with a local watershed association. She worked full-time, unpaid, for the passage of Pinelands legislation and the development of a comprehensive plan. It was Barrett who first chaired the Pine Barrens Coalition, an umbrella group of environmental organizations. Through its Princeton and West Jersey groups, as well as its New York office, the Sierra Club continued to maintain its distinct presence and pursue its own Pine Barrens concerns, but eventually it was overshadowed by the Pine Barrens Coalition.

Barrett has always been outspoken, at times acting in ways that have embarrassed her environmental allies. For example, the Sierra Club was the only environmental group to oppose adoption of the CMP by the governor and secretary of the interior. Club members felt that too many compromises had been made. Barrett, of course, led the club in its opposition.

Eventually, there was a realignment within the Pine Barrens Coalition. Barrett reverted to acting on her own behalf and that of the Sierra Club (and eventually "burning out"), and Mae Barringer and Nan Walnut, both Pine Barrens residents (but relative newcomers), took the reins at the coalition. The coalition kept member organizations informed about Pinelands issues, communicated with the Pinelands Commission, gave testimony where appropriate, and sometimes joined in other environmental organizations' lawsuits. The coalition neither supported nor opposed individual political candidates and appointees, and it maintained good working relationships with the Pinelands Commission. As of late 1991, the coalition continued to exist in name only, its role having been eclipsed by changing Pinelands environmental politics.

Other organizations have had longer interests in the Pine Barrens. The New Jersey Audubon Society and New Jersey Conservation Foundation both serve as bridges between old-line, politically conservative pre-1960 conservation, and the "new" environmentalism of the 1960s and 1970s. These organizations have been active in Pines issues at least since the jetport controversy of the 1960s. Their early interests grew from the personal concerns of what Goldstein (1981) calls "old-line conservationists": wealthy, conservative, well-connected, influential Republicans.

The New Jersey Conservation Foundation, known in its first incarnation as the Great Swamp Committee, illustrates this. Formed in opposition to a proposed jetport in northern New Jersey's Great Swamp, the committee counted among its members and backers many wealthy and influential individuals (see Cavanaugh 1978). Indeed, the Great Swamp sits in the midst of what John Fraser Hart (1975) calls the "gentleman farmers' belt," an exurban area adjacent to the northeastern megalopolis. Its inhabitants possess the inclination, clout, and money to preserve and protect pleasing, productive rural landscapes.

After the jetport proposal was defeated (see Chapter 4, "A Jetport in the Pines?" for details of a subsequent proposal for a jetport in the Pines to serve the Philadelphia–New York area), the Great Swamp Committee became the North Jersey Conservation Foundation. As its interests in land use and environmental conservation continued to broaden, it became the New Jersey Conservation Foundation (NJCF). NJCF is still true to its mission of conservation, with much of its work directed toward preservation of valued agricultural and rural landscapes. Its trustees are mostly bankers, attorneys, and corporate officers; the organization receives many large corporate gifts. NJCF's thirtieth-anniversary gala, a black-tie affair, recently brought together Brendan Byrne, Governor Florio, AT&T vice-chairman Randall Tobias, and actor Christopher Reeves. Franklin Parker, a New York attorney, friend of the Rockefeller family, and chairman of the Pinelands Commission from its inception in 1981 until 1988, is a former president and current trustee of the foundation.

Of all the environmental organizations, NJCF has maintained the most consistent presence in the Pines. For several years, the foundation maintained an office in the historic Pine Barrens town of Whitesbog, in a building leased for a nominal fee from the State of New Jersey. Michelle Byers, now based at NJCF's northern New Jersey office, lived in Whitesbog, closely monitoring Pinelands activities and keeping in close contact with the Pinelands Commission (Byers, 1985 interview). During the earliest years of Pinelands plan implementation, the Association of New Jersey Environmental Commissions, an organization involved in environmental planning activities statewide, also had several staff members in residence at Whitesbog.

One might be tempted to conclude that NJCF and the powerful interests affiliated with it have succeeded in setting aside the Pinelands as a preserve largely for their own benefit. But the record of events does not bear this out. NJCF's role in Pinelands protection and land acquisition, especially in working with Burlington County (Shinn, 1982 interview), has indeed been important, but not of the same caliber as its efforts in the Great Swamp campaign. NJCF is best characterized as an integral contributor to, and supporter of, the larger effort to protect the Pines.

The other group with a long record of Pine Barrens activism is the New Jersey Audubon Society (NJAS). Incorporated in 1901, the society remained entirely voluntary (i.e., with no paid staff) through the early 1950s. Its board of directors was, and is, politically conservative (Jackson, 1985 interview), but its members represent a somewhat lower caste than NJCF's wealthy and influential trustees. Although the society's traditional base of support and organizational interest had been in northern New Jersey, it became very active in opposing the Pine Barrens jetport. NJAS has remained active on Pinelands issues, and much of its interest can be attributed to the keen concern of Elmer Rowley, a former NJAS president whose crusading style has been likened to John Muir's (Jackson, 1985 interview). Like those of other organizations, society activities reached their zenith when Pinelands planning legislation and the CMP were being drafted and acted on.

While environmentalists usually close ranks on crucial Pinelands issues, they have diverged markedly on strategies and specific concerns. This represents not so much an old-line–new-environmentalist split as it reflects differing tactics, approaches, personalities, and clamoring for position and recognition among key individuals. More generally, much of the early energy that went into securing a Pinelands plan was gradually replaced by a sense of complacency once the plan had been put in place. Not unexpectedly, key environmental leaders (Jackson and Walnut, 1985 interviews) view that complacency with considerable apprehension.

In short, the leading Pinelands environmental groups are (or have been) the Pine Barrens Coalition, New Jersey Conservation Foundation (which maintained an office in the Pines), Sierra Club (especially the Princeton and West Jersey groups), Environmental Defense Fund (New York office), Natural Resources Defense Council (New York office), and—only very recently—Pinelands Preservation Alliance. The Pine Barrens Coalition assumed something of a separate identity, built on but also distinct from the interests of its individual members. The Environmental Defense Fund, Natural Resources Defense Council, and Sierra Club's New York office have been involved mostly from a distance. Their energies have been directed principally toward providing testimony, participating in lawsuits, and, on occasion, spearheading initiatives or providing limited staff support for activities initiated by other organizations (Bloom, Hoskins, and Speer, 1985 interviews). These activities represent the more professional, managerial modus operandi that had by the 1980s all but permeated mainstream American environmentalism (see Borelli 1988; Ingram and Mann 1989; Thompson 1985). It differs dramatically from the environmentalism of ten to twenty years earlier—an environmentalism that is still alive and well, but largely relegated to the obstructionist fringe of the mainstream environmental movement. Carol Barrett's personal, emotional, and—at least during its time—rather effective brand of environmentalism typified that more confrontational style.

I now turn to a subchapter of the Pinelands interest-group story that was very much informed by environmental currents and countercurrents of the 1980s. In the fall of 1982, Governor Thomas Kean replaced the two most outspoken "preservationists" on the Pinelands Commission, Gary Patterson and Floyd West, with more "moderate" appointees. Seeking to create an organization more in tune with their concerns, the dispossessed former commissioners (especially Patterson) helped assemble an ad hoc group that later acquired the name Friends of the Pine Barrens. Its meetings were organized under the official auspices of the Sierra Club, Environmental Defense Fund (EDF), and New Jersey Environmental Lobby. Although a broad range of environmental organizations were involved, the bulk of the organizational effort originated in the offices of the EDF. Though this was a departure from EDF's mainly legal activities of earlier years, it was in keeping with EDF's diversification of its national activities.

Two EDF staff people were assigned to the project: Caron Parker, a researcher, and Adam Stern, a skilled community organizer. Stern, along with James Lanard of the New Jersey Environmental Lobby, sought to organize a massive, well-funded effort to monitor implementation of the CMP. It was to be a watchdog organization, politically more active than the Pine Barrens Coalition. On meeting notices, Carol Barrett's name appeared as Sierra Club representative. But her role was limited; Stern and Lanard used their organizing skills to control and direct the organization's meetings. They were the professional environmentalists—committed to the general cause, if not familiar in great detail with the region and its particular management issues. They sought the support of such activists as Barrett and long-time preservationists like Walnut and Barringer. Walnut attended meetings and supported the group's efforts, but was puzzled about the organization and a bit angered that members of the Pine Barrens Coalition had jumped onto the Friends' bandwagon (Walnut 1985, interview).

The Friends of the Pine Barrens was short lived; its January 1984 meeting was sparsely attended, and the discussion focused exclusively on rare and endangered Pine Barrens plants. In sharp contrast with the situation only a couple of years earlier, environmental interest-group activity was on the wane. In part, this can be attributed to divisiveness, bitterness, and burnout. Barringer (1984, interview) saw herself "just coasting" by this point, while Barrett was being isolated by other environmentalists (Jackson and Walnut, 1985 interviews). Most probably, it was not so much individuals' lethargy as it was a general complacency that plagued Pinelands environmentalism. Good organizational management dictated that scarce resources be diverted to other causes, where the payoffs would be greater.

Environmental interest-group activity did not come grinding to a halt. By the mid 1980s, the Pinelands Commission was fully engaged in a mandatory three-year review of the CMP, a process that itself consumed about six years. The review created many new opportunities for interest-group participation. Major participants, with the exception of forestry interests, were the key interest groups that had been active all along. Best represented were environmental organizations, in part because of the sheer number of environmental groups in comparison with other interest groups and in part because Pinelands Commission staff tended to be more receptive to the ideas and suggestions of the plan's natural supporters. Political expediency dictated that they also listen carefully to the development community and other interests not wholly supportive of regional planning. Commission responsiveness to these various interests was further shaped by the working relationships established at the staff level. Those relationships ranged from close personal friendships to deep animosity.

In a rare departure for the likes of an Adirondack Park Agency, California Coastal Commission, or other powerful regional land use agency, the Pinelands Commission's initial solicitations produced genuine participation, limited though it was to the aforementioned interest groups. First, meetings between interest-group representatives and the Plan Review Subcommittee were not straitjacketed by the time pressures typical of many Pinelands subcommittee meetings. Also, the groups had ample notice of meeting dates, giving them sufficient time to develop their positions and prepare written comments. Many of the initial meetings were held in the evening during the fall of 1983—a time and season conducive to good meeting attendance. Dialogue and wide-ranging discussions were the norm. But as the plan review process wore on, it became much more routinized and, to many participants, seemingly endless. Early comments had to be distilled and classified by commission staff, sorted into categories of importance by the Plan Review Subcommittee, distributed in draft report form, commented on at public hearings, reclassified, evaluated in greater depth where appropriate, organized into another draft report (New Jersey Pinelands Commission 1985e), commented on at public hearings, reworked into a final report for submission to the full commission, drafted—where appropriate—into potential CMP amendments, submitted for further public review, adopted formally by the commission, and approved by the governor and secretary of the interior. Like a raging bureaucratic brush fire, the plan review process seemed to consume everything around it. For a time, the inferno seemed to guarantee a virtually infinite bureaucratic rationale for the commission (see Simon 1976). But while the commission had its work cut out, interest groups and individuals were being drained of energy and resources. They simply could not afford to participate in or even track the review process in the meticulous way that they had dealt with issues before it. Public participation was in no way officially discouraged by the Pinelands Commission, but its costs had become so high as to preclude all but the most dedicated, patient, and well financed.

Increasingly complacent environmental groups were nevertheless given a jolt by the plan review process. The major organizations endured the process, providing input at the designated "entry points." Some (Moore and Walnut, 1985 interviews) viewed the plan review as a potential threat because it offered an opportunity for agriculture and development interests to weaken the CMP. Clearly, environmental interests would have been negligent had they not expressed their concerns and reaffirmed their support for the CMP. And this indeed is what they did, but without the vigor and institutional support of earlier days. They did pool their scarce resources, first by producing a joint task force report to the Pinelands Commission (Environmental Defense Fund et al. 1984) and later by developing joint strategies for testifying at public hearings. Spearheaded by the Environmental Defense Fund, the task force also included the Sierra Club West Jersey group, New Jersey Conservation Foundation, New Jersey Audubon Society, Natural Resources Defense Council, Friends of Warren Grove, and what remained of Friends of the Pine Barrens. Thus an ad hoc coalition had emerged apart from the Pine Barrens Coalition, which by this time found itself "drifting" (Walnut, 1985 interview).

During this period, Pinelands Commission staff began scheduling meetings with environmental organizations. Jackson (1985 interview) attributes this to the changing relationship between commission staff and commissioners. In the early years of plan implementation, the staff in effect developed policy, and the commission gave consent (Batory, 1982 interview; Jackson, 1985 interview). But by the mid 1980s, the commission was no longer so eager to give that consent; new commissioners appointed by Governor Kean and several counties were less preservation oriented than their predecessors and more prone to raise critical questions about staff actions. A mostly young, idealistic, and ecocentric staff responded by seeking greater public support, in part by trying to reach out to environmental groups. But they could not rid their environmentalist supporters of the complacency that had set in, and attendance at the meetings took an early and sharp decline.

In 1985, the Sierra Club West Jersey group responded to the

lethargic state of affairs by boldly calling for creation of a 67,000-acre "wilderness area." Central to the proposal was a ban on motorized vehicles in the Four Rivers (Nescochauge, Batsto, Wading, and Oswego) and West Plains natural areas; it also called for additional protection adjacent to the 40-mile Batona hiking trail. The vehicular-access issue had already been on the Sierra Club's agenda for some time, as well as on the agendas of the Pinelands Commission, New Jersey Department of Environmental Protection, Outdoor Action Cooperative, and other recreation groups.

Dismayed with the glacial pace at which the issue was being resolved, the Sierra Club began its own study in 1983, which led to its 1985 wilderness proposal (Carney 1985b; Sierra Club 1985). The club argued that its proposal restricted motorized access in less than 8 percent of the Pinelands, while allowing it in over 92 percent of the region. Not surprisingly, sportsmen's groups objected strongly to the proposal. Composed mainly of hunters, these groups had been ambivalent about Pinelands planning. Many of their members support strong protection measures but at the same time are deeply concerned about excessive government interference in local affairs. Typically, responsible sportsmen abhor irresponsible use by recreationists, but they do not wish to preclude totally vehicular use over large areas. The Sierra Club, citing the efforts of Aldo Leopold and Bob Marshall, sees wilderness areas as places able to accommodate only the lowest intensity of recreational use. Nowhere, perhaps, are these conflicts about recreational use in greater evidence than the Adirondack Park. The 1990 report of the Commission on the Adirondacks in the Twenty-First Century (1990) proposed a 400,000-acre wilderness area in the northwestern part of the park. Local opposition was intense. But an Adirondack regional chapter of Earth First! proposed to go much further in excluding people from the park. In the Pines, as noted, such draconian biocentric perspectives have yet to emerge.

Although the Pinelands Commission responded to the wilderness challenge by initiating yet another study, nothing much came of it beyond some additions to New Jersey's Wild and Scenic River system. In 1991, however, the Sierra Club made apparent its interest in reviving the wilderness proposal. If recent Adirondack experience is any guide, wilderness proponents may be in for a protracted battle.

In 1989, environmental leaders came together to form a new coalition, the Pinelands Preservation Alliance. The alliance, much better financed than the Pine Barrens Coalition, is able to support a full-time executive director. Headquartered in historic Whitesbog, the alliance counts among its key members the New Jersey Audubon Society, Association of New Jersey Environmental Commissions, Sierra Club, League of Women Voters of New Jersey, New Jersey Conservation Foundation, and Environmental Defense Fund. Brendan Byrne serves as honorary chair, and the organization's staff work with seven program committees. Major elements of the alliance's mission include monitoring the Pinelands Commission; coordinating environmentalist participation in the 1992 Pinelands plan review; acting on major current issues (among them aquifer protection, forestry management, and development approval decisions); and promoting research, education, stepped-up enforcement of regulations, and changes in a variety of specific land use programs.

David Moore, executive director of the New Jersey Conservation Foundation, was the leading force in creating the alliance. In addition to Moore and Byrne, trustees include Beryl Robichaud Collins (Center for Coastal and Environmental Studies, Rutgers University), Buntzie Ellis Churchill (president, World Affairs Council of Philadelphia), Franklin Parker (Trust for Public Lands; former Pinelands Commission chair), and Nan Hunter-Walnut (Pine Barrens Coalition). Inspired by such predecessor groups as 1000 Friends of Oregon and the Adirondack Council, the alliance hopes to mobilize a network of citizen eyes and ears that would make it a powerful environmental watchdog.

With its influential trustees and base of foundation support, the alliance does in some ways mimic the Adirondack Council, a preservation-oriented group whose principals are mainly wealthy downstate landowners. Yet the alliance differs in significant ways. It does not enjoy (at least not yet) the comfortable relationship with the Pinelands Commission that the Adirondack Council has traditionally had with the Adirondack Park Agency. Alliance staff and trustees are, however, trying to establish working relationships with Pinelands commissioners. Though their presence is welcomed, their mission is still viewed with some weariness by the commission (Price, 1991 interview).

The alliance is trying to reach out to, or at least recognize, constituencies that share interests with, but often are alienated from, the environmental community. Those constituencies include long-time residents, hunters, all-terrain vehicle users, and farmers. Moreover, a part-time alliance staff member is seeking to establish relationships with Pinelands towns. This is something the Pinelands Commission has largely failed to do; in most cases, towns come to the commission, rather than the commission going to the towns. It will be interesting to see whether the alliance can, over the long term, establish trust in Pines localities. Its greatest potential for doing so may be in allying itself with citizens opposed to such environmental, aesthetic, and public health threats as power lines, transmitter towers, road extensions, airport expansions, and landfills.

I have concentrated mainly on major environmental interest groups that have had a continuing presence in the Pines. Others, large as well as small, have come and gone. The National Parks and Recreation Association and Wilderness Society, for example, were active in early efforts to secure passage of Pinelands legislation and adoption of the CMP. Many other organizations, for whom Pinelands issues may be important, but not central, have articulated their interests through membership in the Pine Barrens Coalition or Pinelands Preservation Alliance. For them, involvement tends to be passive and low key.

Then there are ephemeral organizations that coalesce around specific local issues—LULUs, or locally unwanted land uses (Popper 1985)—noted earlier. These include landfills, transmitter towers, airport runway expansions, or mining operations. Collectively, this phenomenon is known as the NIMBY (Not in my backyard) syndrome (O'Hare 1977). Historically, the Pines have been a dumping site for industry, the military, and midnight dumpers. The region has its share of Superfund abandoned hazardous waste sites, and in the mid 1980s, revelations about decades of waste mismanagement at military bases hit the headlines (Birnbaum 1991; Carney 1985a).

LULUs abound in the Pine Barrens. Examples of local opposition groups include the Friends of Warren Grove, conceived in opposition to exploratory drilling for natural gas storage; STOP (Serious Taxpayers Opposed to Pollution), a landfill-related group; Pinelands People Against the Dump, opposed to the temporary storage of radium-contaminated soil in a wildlife management area located in the Pinelands preservation area; the Atlantic County No-GWEN Committee, opposed to air force plans to site 300-foot-tall communications towers in the county; and the Stop the Roc-a-Jet Incinerator Project group. Some of these organizations long outlive the issue that gave birth to them (Friends of Warren Grove has confronted several issues); others disappear as soon as the crisis is resolved. Either way, participants usually become more aware of larger environmental and social issues as a result of their personal experience. Often, individual environmental consciousnesses are permanently raised. Witness, for example, former opponents of Pinelands planning for whom a proposed landfill near their home is a revelation. Their testimony at public hearings sometimes resembles that heard in a television Bible hour. This newfound support for regional planning can be valuable in both actual and symbolic terms to the Pinelands Commission, and it adds support to the environmental community's efforts. Indeed, the commission's role in overseeing the closure of remaining Pinelands landfills in 1990 made it a saviour in the eyes of many residents. Conversely, when the commission is on the "wrong" side of an issue, it can find itself confronting formidable adversaries who can do serious damage to its public image—as, for example, was the case when it granted an operating extension for a landfill in Cape May County.

Finally, consistent support for Pinelands protection efforts has come from Rutgers University, mostly through the Center for Coastal and Environmental Studies (CCES). This has consisted principally of planning and management studies and the sharing of staff and facilities. In 1988, Rutgers opened the Pinelands Biosphere Reserve Research Station at the Pinelands Commission headquarters in New Lisbon. As noted, Beryl Robichaud Collins of the CCES sits on the board of trustees of the Pinelands Preservation Alliance. The center's support and activities are generally guided by the assumption that ecosystem protection is the overriding goal. The work is scientifically credible; the ideology is usually ecocentric. As a source of reputable institutional support, CCES is helpful in advancing Pinelands Commission aims and activities, just as "institutional volunteers" assisted the California Coastal Commissions in the 1970s (Healy et al. 1978). Unlike California, though, the Pinelands-related research is well supported by grant funding.

Overall, Pinelands environmentalism has two components: the bedrock support of the several large organizations and the variable, but often critical, support of local groups. The major groups are always there, but they are far from consistent in the strength of their support. Conversely, many individual members of smaller regional organizations are perpetual environmental boosters, even as the various organizations break apart, reform, shift alliances, and otherwise metamorphose. The strongest environmental leaders have been women, among them Carol Barrett (Sierra Club, Pine Barrens Coalition), Nan Walnut (Pine Barrens Coalition), and Mae Barringer (Pine Barrens Coalition). All live either in or near the Pines and are dedicated to the preservationist cause. Their successes owe at least as much to conviction and perseverance as well-honed political skills. Remarkably, two of the three held full-time jobs during their years of peak Pinelands activity.

By contrast, agriculture and development communities have been represented not by outstanding leaders but by competent professionals who are predominantly white, male, and well paid. Given the overwhelming male domination of these industries, the fact that they are represented by men is no great surprise. To be sure, there have been male environmental leaders as well (e.g., Elmer Rowley of the NJAS, Gary Patterson as Pinelands commissioner and Friend of the Pine Barrens, and Adam Stern of the EDF), but none has been so consistently politically active as the women leaders.

While women fill the ranks and lead many local environmental struggles, it is primarily men who are the national and state-level leaders. In the Pines, the women who initially led the efforts maintained crucial links with, but worked largely outside, the "traditional" environmental advocacy infrastructure. Once the Pinelands protection cause became thoroughly institutionalized, the roles of individual activists, including these women, diminished greatly. But women are again in the vanguard of local Pinelands resistance movements; indeed, they are the leaders and prime supporters of most of the antilandfill and other NIMBY campaigns. In contrast, minorities have been noticeably absent from virtually all Pinelands environmental endeavors.

Development Interests

The development community, composed mainly of small housebuilders along with a few larger firms, has expressed continuing interest in Pinelands regional planning issues at least since the early 1960s. Organized activity, however, was not much in evidence until the late 1970s (Fisher, 1985 interview). It was after Brendan Byrne's 1979 building moratorium that the Coalition for the

Sensible Preservation of the Pinelands came into being. This organization brought together the New Jersey Builders Association, the state's nine local builders' associations, the National Association of Home Builders, and realtors, contractors, engineers, architects, planners, and other allied trade, business, and industrial organizations. The coalition acted as a sort of countervailing force to the Pine Barrens Coalition.

Though the Coalition for the Sensible Preservation of the Pinelands has been inactive since the mid 1980s, its key member organizations have by no means put Pinelands issues behind them. Most of the coalition's Pinelands activities were initiated by the New Jersey Builders Association and Builders League of South Jersey, and both organizations remain active on Pines issues. But those operations are much diminished in scope; the Pinelands no longer constitute the issue they did during the early years of Pinelands planning.

In its heyday, the coalition was well funded through member organizations; former New Jersey Builders Association official David Fisher (1985 interview) estimates that $250,000 was spent fighting the Pinelands plan. The coalition engaged in extensive lobbying at the state level, and, as noted in Chapter 4, commissioned consultants' reports on water quality, wetlands protection, septic design and impact, and stormwater management (Coalition for the Sensible Preservation of the Pinelands 1980a, b, c, d). Moreover, a great deal of effort went into developing and articulating an "alternative plan" for the Pinelands (Coalition for the Sensible Preservation of the Pinelands 1980d); it was based on overlay mapping of environmental constraints (see Chapter 4, "Plan Adoption"). The coalition's plan would have applied to the protection area; the core preservation area had already been "written off" (Fisher, 1985 interview). Though the coalition's thinking did not prevail, Fisher (1985 interview) claims that some concessions were gained when Governor Byrne worked out a compromise with the legislature. Support for the Pinelands program, as it had developed to that time, was flagging in the Assembly. In considerable part, this might be attributed to the concern and efforts of small homebuilders. Not only were those concerns evident in the testimony offered before legislative committees, they were also echoed in the responses of some Assembly members (New Jersey Senate 1979).

Though its membership includes builders of all types and sizes, the New Jersey Builders Association (NJBA) represents *mainly* small residential builders and allied professions. Fisher (1985 interview) estimated in 1985 that 80 percent of its 2,300 members build fewer than twenty-five houses a year. Many, perhaps most, of those builders have no direct interest in the Pinelands; nonetheless, there is consensus that excessive intrusions into local affairs must be opposed. And indeed, during Pinelands-related hearings, the pleas of small, community-based builders prompted some of greatest concern and compassion on the part of state legislators. If the megadevelopers— in the Pinelands context, builders of senior citizen communities in Ocean County and residential and commercial projects in Atlantic County—were active, it was not in a very public way. Smaller builders, in contrast, took advantage of their plight (real or exaggerated) by calling public attention to it. As Walker and Heiman (1981) have pointed out in the national context, small developers, unlike their larger brethren, have been uniformly and conspicuously unenthusiastic about liberal land use reforms.

After adoption of the CMP, the Coalition for the Sensible Preservation of the Pinelands came under greater dominance by its two major member organizations: the NJBA and the Builders League of South Jersey (BLSJ). Eventually, the coalition fell into inactivity. But the NJBA and BLSJ remain active. For the most part, they monitor plan implementation, attend meetings, testify where appropriate, and meet regularly with the Pinelands Commission's executive director and staff. After the coalition's breakup, Sean Reilly went to work for the BLSJ. Reilly, interestingly enough, was a former insider. Before he "defected" to the builders, he was the Department of Environmental Protection's Pinelands expert. His move may have been prompted by his not being appointed executive director of the Pinelands Commission, a job that went to seasoned administrator Terrence Moore.

The housebuilding community participated fully in the Pinelands Commission's plan review process. But in contrast to even the best-financed environmental advocates, the builders possess the financial wherewithal to represent themselves fully and professionally. By the mid 1980s, though, they had narrowed the scope of their activities mainly to monitoring Pinelands Commission activities and pursuing only matters where they might expect a reasonable return on their investment of organizational resources. They did participate in the first Pinelands plan review and worked to secure Hamilton Township's (a major growth town) conformance with the CMP. Increasingly, the NJBA and BLSJ have found it worthwhile to work within the confines of the regional planning structure—but by no means have they become true friends of regional planning. It has been argued elsewhere (Heiman 1988; Plotkin 1987) that small builders, unlike many megadevelopers, are most comfortable dealing with local planning boards, where their interests tend to be well represented. If there is to be regional planning, better that it be locally inspired than imposed by outsiders. But in the Pines, the CMP has virtually precluded the former in all but a pro forma sense.

Agricultural Interests

The agricultural community completes the triad of major, active Pinelands interests. At the federal level, the relationship between agricultural interests and the government has been marked by diversity and contradiction (Waterfield 1986; Wilson 1978). The farm bloc (more specifically, commodity organizations) has succeeded beyond all reasonable expectations in sustaining a system of subsidies that disproportionately benefits megafarmers; other elements of the farm community have sought better working conditions for farm labor and, ostensibly at least, greater equity for the small farmer. But despite their successes in preserving subsidies, farm interests have lost a great deal of political ground in recent decades (Fite 1981).

Rural and farm interests continued to dominate many state legislatures long after most states' populations had become predominantly metropolitan. But a 1964 Supreme Court decision requiring states to reapportion on a one-person, one-vote basis (rather than on the basis of territory) went a long way toward breaking this pattern (Fite 1981; Rohrer and Douglas 1969; Waterfield 1986). Yet, a quarter of a century after the Court decision, rural interests in many states continued to yield political power beyond their demographic due.

In New Jersey, according to Burch (1975), farmers have long held political power out of proportion to their small share of the state's population (even in the 1930s, farmers constituted only 4 percent of New Jersey's population). One reason for this is that before court-mandated reapportionment, one state senator was elected from each county, regardless of population. The presence of the rural-dominated Republican caucus system was strongly felt. Also, there was and continues to be a rather loose alliance between the state's agricultural interests and major business interests. And, perhaps to a greater degree in New Jersey than in more rural states, agriculture benefits from our urbanized society's widely held view of farming as a good way of life.

Burch (1975) points to the enormous postwar erosion of influence of New Jersey farm groups. Still, their influence lingers. They have a strong voice, for example, in the organization of the state's Department of Agriculture and the selection process for the secretary of agriculture. Perhaps some of that lingering influence helps explain the priority given by the Pinelands plan to "preserving and enhancing" agriculture. Clearly, this special attention to agriculture is also nourished by the widely held sentiment that farming is a compatible and vital part of the rural landscape. Even though fertilizers, herbicides, and pesticides contribute enormously to the pollution of surface and groundwaters in the Pinelands, romantic agrarian notions persist, making farming more acceptable, even to the environmental community, than many other land uses. Concern for the economic plight of the small farmer plays into this, as well as a fear—perhaps exaggerated—of the political influence farmers possess. Only a few lone members of the environmental community are willing to proclaim vigorously that agriculture, on balance, may be more harmful than beneficial to the cause of ecological protection.

As a result, the CMP has bestowed on agriculture an exalted status. Most farmers affected by the plan, however, do not view their position as privileged. Most prominent among their concerns has been the perceived devaluation of farmland resulting from CMP restrictions. Such a devaluation in turn reduces the value of the land as collateral for loans. Although a Pinelands Commission study concluded that the plan has had little effect on farm credit (New Jersey Pinelands Commission 1983b), a state-appointed Agricultural Study Commission concluded that the CMP has disrupted farm credit markets in the short run and may have serious long-term effects as well (Pinelands Agricultural Study Commission 1985). The agricultural community also has been highly skeptical of the transfer of development rights program. The study commission report argues that the program has not met expectations; farmers feel that the credits are undervalued. Farmers also object to what they see as onerous state restrictions on farm-related construction. Other farmers' concerns, addressed in the study commission report (Pinelands Agricultural Study Commission 1985), include incompatibility between the CMP and a separate statewide Agriculture

Retention and Development Program, and rising municipal taxes resulting from Pinelands land use restrictions. Interestingly, the report concedes that the latter issue is not a major concern of farmers. That it was taken up at all is really more a reflection of farmers' political convictions than a statement about economic matters that affect them directly.

Several individual farmers have been adamant in their opposition to certain aspects of Pinelands planning. But the only nongovernmental agricultural interest group involved in Pinelands affairs is the New Jersey Farm Bureau. The bureau is the largest of only a few farm interest groups in the state, and the only one that engages officially in lobbying activities (Burch 1975). The Farm Bureau has monitored implementation of the Pinelands plan, has given testimony where appropriate, and has participated in meetings and other activities.

But how well does the Farm Bureau represent agricultural interests? Given the diversity of farm concerns in New Jersey—a highly urbanized state with a vibrant agricultural economy—this is indeed an elusive question. Bureau President Arthur West, testifying at a 1979 hearing on state Pinelands legislation (New Jersey Senate 1979), claimed that the organization represents 4,300 farm family members and is the "voice of agriculture in New Jersey." West contended that the secretary of agriculture, who supported the legislation, simply represented the governor. West argued that even though the secretary is nominated by the State Board of Agriculture, which itself is elected by farm groups, the governor has final say over the appointment.

Bedeviling the Pinelands Commission is the question just how faithfully the concerns of a few vocal farmers represent the feelings of the larger farm population. The commission had, in the mid 1980s, planned and secured funding for a survey of farmers, but the project never came to fruition because of financial and other practical difficulties. Whatever the true breadth and depth of negative feelings about the CMP, the discontent so far articulated by the farm community has been powerful enough to provoke considerable official concern. Most notably, the governor assembled the Agricultural Study Commission to listen to farmers' concerns and make recommendations. Though the commission's findings reflect a broad range of concerns, some of them are rather weakly supported by evidence.

Perhaps by giving little more than lip service to farmers' concerns, the report was designed to placate the farm community at minimal political cost. But this does not appear entirely to be the case. Some of the report's recommendations were, in fact, implemented, though not solely at the bidding of farmers. A state Pinelands Development Credit bank was established, and a bond issue to fund infrastructure development in regional growth areas (which should in turn encourage use of PDCs) was put on the 1985 ballot and approved by the voters. Also, as part of the plan review process, CMP amendments allowing cluster development in agricultural areas were considered. In the end, they were not adopted.

Pinelands planners have not responded to farmers' concerns by reducing the Pinelands plan's geographic scope or regulatory severity. Early on, however, they did create the PDC program, largely to placate farmers. Publicly, at least, it seems so far to have done just the opposite. Still, as PDC sales increase (they finally began to do so in the late 1980s and early 1990s), support may grow. The Pinelands Commission's Agriculture Subcommittee continues to try to open communication channels with farmers; the Agricultural Study Commission also sought to address farm concerns. Farmers, meanwhile, continue publicly to urge the Pinelands Commission, New Jersey Board of Agriculture, and Governor Florio to be far more responsive to their concerns.

In sum, then, a handful of environmental, agricultural, and development interest groups have most influenced Pinelands planning and management (see Table 2). Environmental interests have been active at least since 1960, and a rather ecocentrist perspective became institutionalized with the creation of the Pinelands Commission in 1979. That philosophy persisted through the commission's early years. Even though the Pinelands Commission is a bureaucratic entity, not an advocacy group, many of its actions have been guided by a preservationist outlook. The ecocentric perspective gained institutional support from Rutgers University's Center for Coastal and Environmental Studies and, in a more tempered form, from the U.S. Department of the Interior.

But environmental advocacy alone was not sufficient to transform the idea of a Pinelands National Reserve into reality. In fact, the authorizing legislation was a product largely of political opportunism mixed with personal dedication to the preservation cause, mainly on the part of former New Jersey Governor Byrne, Representative Florio, and Senators Case and Williams. Other figures, such as former New Jersey Senate President Joseph J. Merlino and Senate Committee Chair Frank Dodd, also were central. This political interest prospered in a climate of statewide public opinion that was at least indifferent toward, if not mildly supportive of, regional environmental planning (see Andrews 1980 and Healy and Rosenberg 1979) on the strength of general, latent support for environmental and land use initiatives).

Organized interests *responded* to the idea of a Pinelands National Reserve and had a role in shaping and directing the process. Indeed, key environmentalists—most notably Carol Barrett (Sierra Club, Pine Barrens Coalition), Nan Walnut (Pine Barrens Coalition), and Mae Barringer (Pine Barrens Coalition)—have been active throughout the Pinelands planning and management effort that began in the 1970s. And they have been very important to its success. Other individuals made vital contributions as well, but these three women were the most active during the critical early years. Yet, while organizations rely on the deep commitment of individuals, individuals need the support and backing of their respective organizations.

Agriculture and development interests, and to a much lesser extent forestry and mining interests, have been well represented in Pinelands decision making. By and large, professional organizations and paid lobbyists, rather than voluntary organizations or government agencies, represent these interests. Some environmental groups also are represented by paid professionals, but most such individuals work for much less money than their counterparts in the building and resource-related industries. The modus operandi, personalities, and special interests of the paid lobbyists are all of some importance, but not nearly so important as the interests and personal characteristics of the environmental leaders. The environmentalists' dedication to the cause helps explain why the preservationist viewpoint became firmly established in the structural framework for Pinelands planning and management. The decline after the mid 1980s in the intensity of their efforts offers a partial explanation for the shift in the Pinelands program toward the more technocentric (O'Riordan 1981). All three major interests, though, have retooled and for the most part adapted remarkably well to changing political circumstances.

6

Three Communities

This chapter introduces the community as a distinct unit of analysis. Saunders et al. (1978) argue that local political decisions are still important in many rural areas, especially to persons employed locally in agriculture and related service industries. In other words, surrender to the institutions of mass society (Vidich and Bensman 1968) is far short of total. Indeed, Pinelands planning and management constitute a discrete and very important junction between local social and political forces and those of the larger society. Not only do local individuals and institutions guide regional management after the laws have been passed, but some of them actually helped define the process from the outset.

New Jersey enjoys a strong tradition of local control over local affairs, but contrary to popular notion, it is not a "home rule" state (Houston 1984). The powers delegated to local governments are not absolute (they aren't even in the home-rule states); the legislature can preempt any of them, at any time. But the perception is otherwise; local officials, especially, seem to believe that planning and zoning, law and public safety, and finance and private property powers are theirs and theirs alone. Little does it matter that a great

135

deal of local control has in fact been surrendered to the federal and
state institutions that control so many health, safety, welfare, transportation, and other programs. When Vidich and Bensman (1968)
tried to make this point, townsfolk in the community they studied
staged a parade and burned them in effigy. Indeed, the myth of local
control is so central to local political culture that only in exceptional
circumstances are state legislatures willing visibly to tamper with
whatever balance of power is in place. Pinelands planning is one
such exceptional circumstance.

Although real control is vested principally at the state level, the
"working level" for Pinelands planning and management is municipal government. Many of the interests—including farmers, small
residential builders, and owners of sand and gravel companies—
that have felt most threatened by the Pinelands program are active
in local affairs. They conduct much of their business within a small
geographic area and have firm links with local leaders; indeed, they
often hold local political offices. While support for the Pinelands
program has for the most part come from state, metropolitan, and
national constituencies, the origins of most of the opposition can
be traced to the local level. Although local interests have not been
powerful enough to stop or seriously hinder the Pinelands program,
they have influenced the course of the plan's implementation. They
had to be accommodated. The skill and success the Pinelands program has shown in doing so goes far toward explaining the degree
to which regional planning has prospered in the Pines.

Some of those accommodations are described in Chapters 4, 5,
and 7. The case studies presented in this chapter, while not representing the full range of local responses to regional planning, examine
three communities where key issues have been raised (see Map 5 and
Table 3). Two of the three municipalities—Woodland and Hamilton townships—have been pivotal to the conformance process. The
agreements forged with these towns became precedents and models
for surrounding communities.

Woodland Township is one of only two townships located entirely in the Pinelands preservation area. With its small population
(2,063 in 1990), large area (95.4 square miles), and minimal industrial and commercial development, Woodland lives up to the image
of the small Pine Barrens town. Because the Pinelands planning
scheme creates an inner preservation and outer protection area, it
is a model for the core–buffer management approach favored by

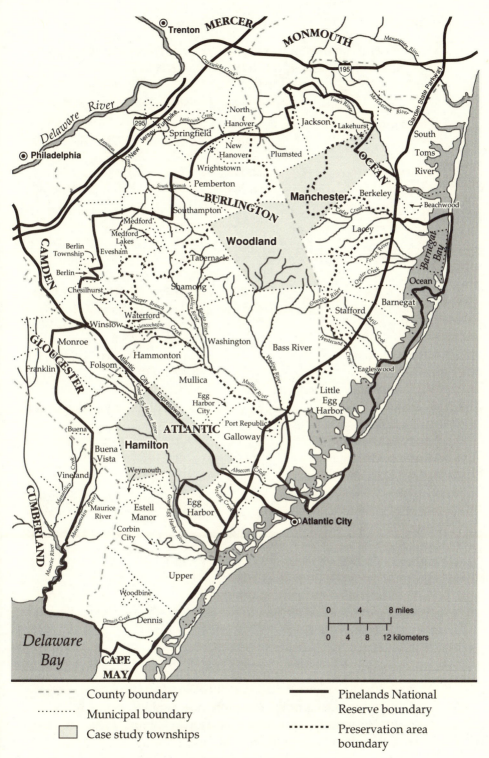

Source: Based on map sheets produced by the New Jersey Pinelands Commission.

MAP 5. PINE BARRENS TOWNSHIPS

TABLE 3. DEMOGRAPHIC CHARACTERISTICS OF CASE-STUDY TOWNSHIPS

	Woodland	*Hamilton*	*Manchester*	*New Jersey*
Population				
1990	2,063	16,012	35,976	7,730,188
1980	2,285	9,499	27,987	7,364,823
1970	2,032	6,445	7,550	7,171,112
1960	1,904	6,017	3,779	6,066,782
Age (1990)				
Under 5 years	99	1,252	1,116	532,637
	(4.8%)	(7.8%)	(3.1%)	(6.9%)
5–20 years	341	3,551	3,896	1,592,904
	(16.5%)	(22.2%)	(10.8%)	(20.6%)
21–44 years	1,031	7,342	5,688	3,010,415
	(50.0%)	(45.9%)	(15.8%)	(38.9%)
45–64 years	404	2,565	4,470	1,562,207
	(19.6%)	(16.0%)	(12.4%)	(20.2%)
Over 65 years	188	1,302	20,806	1,032,025
	(9.1%)	(8.1%)	(57.8%)	(13.4%)
Income (1980)				
Median household income	$16,810	17,764	12,038	19,800
Percentage of persons for whom poverty status is determined	11.8	8.9	5.5	9.5
Race (1990)				
White	1,815	12,966	34,460	6,130,465
	(88.0%)	(81.0%)	(95.8%)	(79.3%)
Black	202	2,365	1,176	1,036,825
	(9.8%)	(14.8%)	(3.3%)	(13.4%)
Other	46	681	340	562,898
	(2.2%)	(4.2%)	(1.0%)	(7.3%)

Sources: U.S. Department of Commerce (1982) and Summary Tape File 1A data.

the U.N. Educational, Scientific, and Cultural Organization for its worldwide system of biosphere reserves (Batisse 1982, 1985; U.S. Man and the Biosphere Program 1989). Woodland Township, therefore, offers an outstanding venue for studying local planning issues encountered in the core area of a developed country's reserve. Not only is Woodland representative of, and important to, the towns that surround it; it also became the regional stage on which several conflicts between major Pinelands actors were played out.

Intense growth is rapidly obliterating Hamilton Township's cherished rural character. Between 1970 and 1990, its population increased from 6,445 to 16,012, a jump of almost 150 percent. In part, this is explained by growth pressures associated with Atlantic City casino gambling. In addition, Hamilton is one of the Pinelands plan's growth nodes; in other words, growth is directed there. As a result, conflicts have emerged between large corporate developers and "controlled growth" sentiment in the township. Much Pinelands Commission time and energy went into securing Hamilton's conformance with the Pinelands plan. Hamilton's conformance was especially important not only because of the financial interests at stake but also because surrounding towns, slated to similarly absorb growth, were carefully watching Hamilton (see Schiff 1986).

Manchester Township also experienced tremendous growth in the 1970s, but for different reasons. Manchester's increase of 270 percent between its 1970 population of 7,550 and its 1980 population of 27,987 is explained largely by the development and growth of retirement communities. Even though the Pinelands plan sharply curtailed the township's growth potential, local leaders were cooperative in implementing the plan's goals. But Manchester is an anomaly in Ocean County; other towns have not conformed so quickly or easily.

Conflicts between regional objectives and local prerogatives take different forms in different parts of the Pinelands. The three community case studies that follow seek to illustrate some of the key variations within the region and their implications for defining conflicts as well as shaping accommodations between local concerns and the broader interest in environmental planning and management. The conclusions drawn from the cases, while not sufficient to cover all possible kinds of conflict and accommodation within the regional setting, should nonetheless help convey a sense of the Pinelands' political texture.

Woodland Township

Publicly at least, the Pinelands Commission is likely to maintain that all towns are equally important. But Woodland Township is in fact more important than many others. It is a regional "keystone."

Chatsworth, the traditional economic, governmental, and social center of the township, is considered by many to be the "capital of the Pines" (New Jersey Pinelands Commission 1983a). This small burg has gotten more attention than a quiet woodland village might expect, mainly because of its recognition in John McPhee's popular book, *The Pine Barrens*, and his subsequent article in *National Geographic* (McPhee 1967, 1974). Chatsworth evokes images of continuity through generations of Pine Barrens life. It is a small, isolated village that on first impression seems little more than a tiny, but cozy, clearing deep in the pine woods. Yet it has never really been isolated from the outside world.

The first European settlement of Woodland Township has been traced to the early 1700s (Woodland Township 1976). Settlers engaged in a variety of activities including farming, charcoal burning, carpentry, and bog-iron production. Local forges, here as elsewhere in the colonies, supplied iron for cannonballs and shells used by the Revolutionary Army. In the 1800s, several sawmills were built, and by the late 1800s, cranberry production had begun. By 1866, when Woodland Township was officially organized by carving pieces from the townships that surround it, there were several small settlements, such as Lebanon, Pine, Shamong Station, Woodmansie Station, and Harrison Station. These places exist today only as names on maps and in the minds of some of Woodland's older residents.

Chatsworth has survived the vagaries of changing regional economies. But Chatsworth was not always known as Chatsworth. Before 1900, it was known both as Chesilhurst and as Shamong. Chatsworth came to be known by its present name in a rather peculiar way. In the late 1890s, Prince Mario Ruspoli de Toggio-Suiza, an attaché to the Italian Embassy in Washington, married a wealthy American debutante whose family held large acreages in the Pines. Prince Mario built her a grand villa on the shores of what was then known as Lake Shamong, in what is now Woodland Township. Guests who came to take the salubrious pine air included the Morgans, Vanderbilts, Drexels, Astors, Goulds, and Vice-President Levi P. Morton. Eventually, a large and lavish country club was built. The Tudor mansion was said to be a reproduction of the estate of the Duke of Devonshire in Chatsworth, England. Coincidentally, the Chatsworth estate in England is located in what is now the Peak District National Park—like the Pinelands, a park surrounded by a large metropolitan population. As a retreat for the eastern elite, Chatsworth was one of only a few places in the Pines that could be compared with the great camps and resorts of the Adirondacks. Although the country club was destroyed by fire in 1910, Shamong's town fathers had renamed their town Chatsworth in 1901. The name remains, and so do the memories of a bygone era (Buzby, 1984 interview; Brower, 1985 interview).

Until 1949, Chatsworth was a stop on the Central Railroad of New Jersey; there was daily service to both New York and Philadelphia. Today, Chatsworth is situated at the intersection of two well-maintained county roads, and a well-traveled state highway passes through the northern part of Woodland Township. By no means is the town truly isolated, nor has it been for at least the past century. But it is rather out of the way; away from the roar of traffic on State Highway 72, it is quiet and woodsy, with scattered homesites, cranberry bogs, and blueberry fields. A second concentration of settlement, aside from Chatsworth, is Lebanon Lakes, a development of about sixty houses located on the western edge of Woodland Township. Also located within the township is the New Lisbon State School (for mentally retarded men). It is an enclave of about 1,250 residents, more than half of Woodland's official 1990 population of 2,063. The school is also a regional employment center.

General awareness of Chatsworth and the rest of Woodland Township has increased in recent years, despite their location half an hour away from even convenience shopping. Indeed, to many people's thinking, Woodland represents the Pine Barrens. Its "discovery" was hastened by McPhee's (1967, 1974) writings, general interest arising from Pinelands planning efforts, and the growing realization that the county highway offers a quick route to the Jersey Shore on busy summer days. Many summer wayfarers stop at Buzby's general store, a venerable local institution and Chatsworth landmark since 1865. Owners Tom and Charlotte Hedge have tried to retain something of Buzby's traditional character, at the same time making it attractive to out-of-town visitors (Hedge, 1984 interview). Another attempt to package and present Chatsworth to the world outside can be seen in efforts to restore the crumbling Shamong Hotel. Though considered an example of vernacular architecture, it was for at least a part of its history a retreat for the rich. Led by local attorney and environmental activist Mary Ann Thompson, a group of citizens is raising funds and marshalling volunteer labor and other contributions to renovate the structure. The ultimate aim is to turn it into a self-supporting commercial folk-art/community center.

As noted, Woodland Township is of special interest to the Pinelands Commission because it is one of only two municipalities situated entirely within the preservation area, and it is a regional political power base. Because of its powerful, entrenched political interests, Woodland's conformance with the Pinelands plan did not come easily. Indeed, local officials were concerned that their preservation area designation was overly restrictive and would seriously reduce the township's tax base. A great deal of discussion and negotiation between the Conformance Subcommittee and Woodland officials took place before certification was ensured.

In the early 1970s, Woodland became a stage for reenacting some classic conservationist–preservationist battles. The 1976 bicentennial booklet for the township (Woodland Township 1976) articulates community sentiment as follows: "What does the future hold for Chatsworth? Many residents readily say, 'Let's keep it like it is!' But the answer lies with the future."

This enigmatic declaration sums up the dilemma experienced by many a small town (see King and Harris 1989). On the one hand, there is the abiding desire to preserve all that is good about Chatsworth; local planners, builders, and the rest of the citizenry would not want to pave over the township, even if it were possible and would make them richer. Yet there is more than a hint of resignation in their thinking. Berger and Sinton describe this dilemma: "Many, if not most, Pinelands residents still resent the formal planning . . . many residents want to retain the old landscape while at the same time being able to sell their land for the highest possible price to a developer. The mixture of conservative rural values, suspicion of outside authority, and love of the land with its attendant nostalgia creates a difficult climate in which planning must proceed" (1985, 142).

One reason that the preservation–development dichotomy oversimplifies Woodland's situation is that it excludes an important political layer. J. Garfield DeMarco, one of the largest cranberry growers in the Pinelands, has a big economic stake in Woodland Township. Although he resides in nearby Hammonton, the family cranberry operations are based in Woodland. Family patriarch Anthony DeMarco was an immigrant success story: He came to the Pines and built a thriving cranberry empire. Anthony was active in local civic and political affairs, as have been his sons, Garfield and Mark.

To some, the name DeMarco evokes thoughts of scandal and intrigue. Any talk of political power in the township inevitably makes reference to Garfield DeMarco. Garfield was at one time a Democrat and was active in the Kennedy presidential campaign. He was also a Rhodes Scholar. And he was Burlington County Republican party chairman for many years. Despite rapid suburban residential and commercial growth in the western part of the county (mostly outside the Pines area and associated with the Philadelphia region), Burlington County retains something of New Jersey's "agrarian tradition" of considerable political power vested in rural locales (McCormick 1975; Moakley and Pomper 1975; Carpenter, 1984 interview). Republicans enjoy strict control of the County Board of Chosen Freeholders, and DeMarco, at least when he was party boss, was alleged to "call the shots" (McIntyre 1980; Shrom 1982). The picture of DeMarco gleaned from interviews and newspaper accounts is one of a power broker with a controlling behind-the-scenes interest in Burlington County and Woodland Township politics.

DeMarco is a good example of the ubiquitous "rural land baron." In this case, the connections between local, regional, and state politics are particularly important. Robert Shinn, a former Burlington County freeholder and later state assemblyman, served as the Pinelands Commission's first vice-chairman. Although it would be difficult to attribute any direct benefits to Woodland Township to Shinn's position, the connection is nonetheless a significant one.

Before the Pinelands Comprehensive Management Plan (CMP) came into being, Woodland relied on its large share of vacant land to keep property taxes relatively low for homeowners. In effect, the taxes paid by owners of vacant lands subsidized homeowners. But Woodland's residents did not reap extraordinary benefits; the levels of service they received in return for their low taxes were appropriately minimal. Before the CMP's enactment, Mayor John Bowker and other town fathers argued that the plan's land use restrictions would render much of Woodland's vacant land worthless and that, as a result, the taxes on those lands would have to be lowered.

Indeed, a year after the CMP took effect, there were numerous tax appeals, mostly from large landowners. In order to make up for the resulting shortfall, Woodland cut back on local services and raised its local-purpose tax rate by almost 400 percent in one year. In 1982, a reassessment markedly lowered the assessed value of vacant lands in the township. The heavy burden that fell on homeowners created an uproar and turned the tide of local opinion—as evidenced by news reports and local recollections—overwhelmingly against the Pinelands plan. A number of local environmentalists—Glassboro State College professor Gary Patterson (1984 interview) was prominent among them—argued that the entire tax episode was engineered; the intent was to turn public opinion against Pinelands planning. Although there are no clear answers, some evidence partly upholds his contention, some disputes it (see Birnbaum 1989b). It would seem that many local officials accepted as inevitable the success of tax appeals, claiming that they could not justify pre-CMP assessments when "nothing could now be done with the land." Yet they also claimed that much of the land in question was unsuitable for development anyway (even under pre-Pinelands planning) and that the pace of development was glacial and likely to stay that way.

One might ask, therefore, whether the development potential of the vacant lands was being overestimated before there was a CMP. Clearly, large landowners have reaped tax benefits as a result of successful tax appeals. While town officials pin all woes on the CMP, over a thousand tax-defaulted properties remain on the town's tax rolls. No taxes are collected on them, the town does not foreclose on them, and dozens of them are owned by township attorney Mark DeMarco or his clients or associates (Birnbaum 1989a). Critics of Woodland's tax policies are also quick to point out that Samuel Alloway, who was chairman of the Burlington County Board of Taxation when it heard the tax appeals, is related by marriage to the DeMarcos. Whatever the importance of this nepotistic fact, it stands as one of many examples of the associations between family ties and local politics that pervade Pinelands towns and many other rural locales.

An economic study funded by the Pinelands Commission (Government Finance Associates 1982) found that Woodland Township could potentially suffer serious fiscal stress as a result of the CMP's effects on the local tax base. For three other Pinelands towns studied, this was not found to be true. But the study's value is limited by its reliance on numbers and values of successful tax appeals as indicators of fiscal stress. This evidence can neither support nor refute critics' charges that the tax issue was engineered.

Woodland Township was the major beneficiary of New Jersey S.

1791, a state act that authorized payments to municipalities to offset property tax increases attributable to the Pinelands plan. S. 1791 provided leverage for the Pinelands effort because towns that had not by 1984 conformed with the CMP would no longer be eligible for funds. The act provided funding for only three years, but it also established a commission whose purpose is to seek long-term remedies for the tax shortfall problem. S. 1791's reimbursement formula gave Woodland more than a third of the $600,000 authorization for the tax year 1984. By 1985, this had fallen to $86,000. Still, the township received by far the largest single share of funds allocated under S. 1791. According to several key actors in Woodland's negotiations with the Pinelands Commission, this was a key factor in its reluctant decision to conform with the CMP.

A review of the conformance negotiations between the Pinelands Commission and Woodland Township reveals how much priority the commission placed on securing Woodland's compliance with the CMP. At the outset, Woodland officials resolved to accept planning funds offered by the Pinelands Commission only if they would not have to adhere to specific conditions of the CMP and would be allowed "meaningful input" in revising their master plan and ordinances. Woodland's resolution, passed early in 1981, stated that the township feared financial destruction through the confiscation of its tax base. The Pinelands Commission, worried that its approval of the resolution would prompt similar verbal assaults from other townships, would not agree to such language. More than a year passed before the matter was resolved and Woodland received its funds.

During this period, considerable negotiation took place between Woodland's representatives and the Pinelands Commission's staff and Conformance Subcommittee. Mark DeMarco, township solicitor, would bring proposals to the subcommittee and take replies back to the Woodland Township Committee. Woodland is one of a small number of towns to which the subcommittee and staff devoted extraordinary time and effort. Embarrassed by some of the publicity surrounding Woodland's 1983 tax problems, the commission sought to secure the town's conformance without major conflict. Therefore both parties, township and commission, possessed significant bargaining power. Many would interpret the resultant accord as more favorable to Woodland than other conformance deals were to the respective towns with which they were struck.

In addition to Chatsworth's designation as a Pinelands village,

Woodland's master plan includes several "special residential infill areas." Woodland's plan was the first to include such areas; others have since been created elsewhere in the preservation area. "Special agricultural production areas" totalling 20,900 acres were set aside—but only in Woodland's case were these designations made before plan certification. Also included are provisions for deed restriction of noncontiguous lands to fulfill Pinelands minimum lot-size requirements, and a special provision for accessory housing in the special agricultural production areas. Woodland also held out for a "neighborhood commercial" zone in Chatsworth and two "highway business" zones along Route 72. The latter permit a carefully regulated form of strip development that would serve the heavy commuter, shore, and local traffic on Route 72. Some observers point out that, in the end, Woodland's certified master plan and ordinances did not differ all that greatly from their pre-Pinelands forms.

Although the Pinelands Commission argues that all these provisions fall within the dicates of the CMP, they still represent an exceptional attempt to placate a Pinelands town. Some Woodland residents further allege that the commission has made certain exceptions in granting local development approvals. Such allegations are of course difficult, if not impossible, to substantiate. But the mere fact that they are made is noteworthy.

The most striking aspect of Woodland's entire Pinelands episode is the degree to which it divided the town. Woodland is home (or at least a base of operations) to several key actors in larger Pinelands issues. Garfield DeMarco was the first chairman of the Pinelands Environmental Council (Chapter 4); indeed, as an aide to Senator Barry Parker, he drafted legislation that created the council (Carpenter, 1984 interview). Gary Patterson and Mae Barringer, both important leaders in the Pinelands preservation crusade (Chapter 5), reside in Woodland. Patterson's and Barringer's political activism grew from their involvement in local battles. During the 1970s, they were active in Concerned Citizens of Woodland Township, a group that strongly opposed several proposals for large-scale residential developments. Concerned Citizens attended meetings, gave oral and written testimony, and, at one particularly heated meeting in 1977, conducted a funeral for a pine tree, all the while chanting "Save the Pines."

It appears that the Concerned Citizens' efforts may have persuaded the Planning Board not to approve at least one proposal. For a number of reasons (including the eventual jurisdiction of the Pine-lands Commission), none of the contentious projects ever came to fruition. But Concerned Citizens, which started out as a loosely organized group of citizens opposing specific projects, later became interested in broader regional issues. Those citizens followed the lead of many others in transforming their initially parochial environmental concerns into wider awareness and continuing action. Barringer experienced this evolution; Patterson, already knowledgeable and active as an environmental science professor at Glassboro College, expanded his sphere of activity into the political arena.

While it may be an exaggeration to say that these 1970s' issues were of foremost concern to most Woodland residents, they did create widespread interest and, at least at the "key actor" level, a rift between newcomers (little or no-growth advocates) and old-timers (allow controlled growth). Town elders *generally* supported proposals for residential development as long as they could exercise careful control over them; however, the record indicates that by no means were they fully united in their sentiments. The town elders were "elders" in a most meaningful sense: They were members of old Pine Barrens families. Much of the vocal opposition to development came from newer members of the community.

In 1977, as the Planning Board was deliberating over a master plan, the controversy heated up. Before that time, the township's guide was a 1969 master plan that had never been formally adopted (Woodland Township 1983). During the late 1970s and early 1980s, environmentalists (that is, preservationists) became the targets of considerable hostility. In part this can be attributed to some of the activities of Concerned Citizens, particularly their eventual support for Pinelands planning. But it is difficult to gauge the depth and breadth of local feeling about regional planning in the late 1970s. Some interviewees recall considerable opposition; others believe there was widespread "silent support" for Byrne's moratorium. The moratorium and subsequent development restrictions would keep Woodland as it was; clearly, this was what many residents wanted.

Implementation of the Pinelands plan brought serious problems to Woodland. First, sons and daughters of long-time residents were denied permission to build houses. This, like some of the early and aggressive actions of the Adirondack Park Agency (Chapter 2, "The Adirondack Park"), was no small provocation to local residents. Then there were the large tax increases of 1983. More than anything else, these generated opposition to the Pinelands program. And they helped foster some heated local political battles. One of the more colorful adversaries was Marvin Matlack. Matlack replaced Mae Barringer as a member of the Woodland School Board during the 1970s. Before this, Gary Patterson, Fran Gudauskis, and Mae Barringer—all proponents of Pinelands planning—were board members. Several residents allege that Garfield DeMarco used his influence to secure election of new board members opposed to Pinelands planning.

Vidich and Bensman (1968) underscore the importance of school and church in small-town politics. Indeed, in Woodland the school (Grades K-8) is a source of pride, a focus of family life, and a place where social contacts are made (Gudauskis, 1984 interview). The Pinelands issue drove a wedge between many people who had been united in friendship through their common interests in children and school. Yet the same was not true for parishioners of the United Methodist Church, Chatsworth's only church. Its membership of sixty-two (in 1984) is dominated by old Chatsworth families (Carter, 1984 interview). Many Woodland residents belong to other parishes, therefore attending church in other townships; many do not attend any church. The Chatsworth United Methodist Church, with its pine paneling and stained-glass windows representing Pine Barrens scenes, powerfully evokes a sense of community. It represents the old (pre-1970) Chatsworth; indeed, local residents worked together in the 1950s to create the piney interior. Because the church's congregation is neither so diverse nor so volatile as the population served by the school, the church did not became a flashpoint for conflict.

Returning to the school board episode, Mae Barringer's board seat went to Marvin Matlack, allegedly at Garfield DeMarco's behest. Matlack later had a falling out with DeMarco—some claim that this was because Matlack refused to do DeMarco's bidding. Matlack has been a consistent and fervent opponent of Pinelands planning. His politically conservative, individualistic character is represented in his home's decor: a large woodstove, eagle ornamentation, presidential portrait, Bibles, and copies of the New Jersey and U.S. Constitutions. Matlack considers himself a strict constitutional constructionist. He views Pinelands issues as a microcosm of the problems affecting America, including even the decline of the family! In concert variously with the Mid-Atlantic Legal Foundation (the eastern counterpart of the better-known Rocky Mountain and Pacific Legal Foundations), developers, the farm coalition, and municipalities, he has challenged—unsuccessfully—the Pinelands Development Credit program and the CMP itself. Matlack is perhaps the Pinelands' Anthony D'Elia, a disenfranchised developer and ardent Adirondack Park Agency opponent who wrote a book lambasting the agency's activities (D'Elia 1979). Matlack has yet to write the Pinelands book.

After his falling out with Garfield DeMarco, Matlack turned to local politics. He lost a heated 1983 Republican primary election to George Adams (DeMarco's candidate, according to Matlack), then switched to the Democratic party and ran against Adams in the general election. In a bitter and intensely fought campaign, Matlack ran against two things: Woodland's conformance with the CMP, and Garfield DeMarco. Among Matlack's litany of charges against DeMarco is that DeMarco, despite his vocal opposition, was always a *proponent* of Pinelands planning (Matlack, 1984 interview). Whatever the validity of Matlack's charge, the DeMarco family does indeed benefit from lowered taxes and holds a large number of Pinelands Development Credits (see Birnbaum 1989a, c). Their role in the conformance process, described earlier, may help explain those gains. Matlack and others also allege that DeMarco and friends were involved in various election irregularities. Although some six absentee ballots were nullified after the election, a lengthy investigation by the state Attorney General's Office cleared DeMarco and Election Board member Arthur Rago of wrongdoing. Matlack lost by only 28 votes (260–248), and the vote was not clearly split along newcomer/old-timer lines. Indeed, demographic and anecdotal evidence indicates that substantial numbers of long-time residents cast their ballots for Matlack. In 1985, Matlack was beaten by Robert Shinn (former Pinelands Commission vice-chair) in a primary bid for an Assembly seat; Matlack's main campaign issue was again the Pinelands plan. But by this time—in Woodland and elsewhere—the Pinelands were no longer such a salient issue. Woodland was receiving tax relief, and Pinelands planning had been grudgingly accepted by many, if not most, of its opponents. As one resident remarked: "If North Jersey wants to play, let them pay" (Stevenson, 1984 interview). With increased compensation, as well as the passage of time, many tensions and divisions seem to have healed. Indeed, even Matlack and former environmentalist adversaries Barringer, Patterson, and Gudauskis have made some amends. All are unhappy with Pinelands planning, each for different reasons.

What significance, then, do local politics and power relations in Woodland Township hold for regional planning? When the Pinelands plan was introduced, it represented a new layer in the relationship between the township and the interests of the mass society. Of course, Woodland has for many years looked outward rather than inward. Whereas goods and services, for example, used to be brought into the town, residents now make frequent excursions to surrounding urban and suburban areas for shopping, entertainment, and the like. Intracommunity linkages have not disintegrated; indeed, the school and the fire company, and to a lesser extent the Methodist church, are still foci of community activity. But the centrality of community has diminished—owing to increased societal control, both fiscal and cultural, and changing patterns of spatial organization, population composition, and daily activity. This transformation is in no way unique to Woodland. If anything, Woodland remains a remarkably tight-knit community, given its megalopolitan location.

In American small towns, land use and property taxes are preeminent concerns (Wolf 1981); Pinelands communities are no exception. Regional planning, therefore, is critically important to Woodland Township for three reasons: (1) its effects on local economic interests (especially the DeMarcos), (2) its effects on property taxes, and (3) its effects on individual futures—that is, will I be able to build a house for my daughter or son? Will I be able to sell my house and land when I retire?

Whereas the notion of Pinelands preservation attracts a statewide constituency, the aforementioned concerns do not. Only through the strength of Woodland's political and financial connections at the county and state levels have local interests been well represented. Had those links been weaker, Woodland might still have benefited from general concern about the plight of small-town residents. But in all likelihood, the town would have been less a focus of regional attention.

The Pinelands issue has been a divisive one for Woodland, a township whose traditional decision-making structure might best be described as monolithic (Clark 1968; Swanson, Cohen, and Swanson 1979). Municipal business was at one time—and probably is to some degree today—conducted by means of an informal meeting, where the agenda is set, and a formal meeting, where it is acted out. This common small-town phenomenon is described both by Vidich and Bensman (1968) and Swanson, Cohen, and Swanson (1979). Woodland is so small a township as to defy characterization in terms of an elitist (Hunter 1953) versus pluralist (Dahl 1961; Polsby 1963) theory of community governance. There are too few business leaders to test Hunter's theory of dominance by economic elites, and too few major decision outcomes to test Dahl's pluralist theory. Yet there is a considerable body of evidence to suggest that Woodland's politics have been dominated by a single economic–family interest: the DeMarcos. It appears that their control has been maintained principally through Garfield DeMarco's ability to secure jobs, at various levels of government, for township residents.

National environmentalist impulses of the 1970s came home to roost in Woodland Township. When concerns were first expressed at Planning Board meetings in 1970, no great conflicts were provoked. After all, many residents saw themselves as conservationists. Moreover, they felt they had been good stewards of the land—in some cases for several generations—and they wanted to continue in that role. Not until "environmentalists" began seriously to challenge business-as-usual did tension and divisions arise. By the mid 1970s, as pressure for development mounted and concern about its effects escalated, Woodland became a stage for acting out preservationist–conservationist battles reminiscent of larger-scale national struggles waged over the last century (see Nash 1982, 1990).

Some residents favored controlled development; others wanted none at all. But very few townsfolk were so detached from the community or driven by economic interest that they would have accepted development at any environmental cost. It seemed, though, that old-time residents were generally more willing to accept some change; newcomers wanted to "shut the door."

The controversy was fueled not just by individuals' concerns about the future character and population of the township but by economic concerns as well. The DeMarcos "lost" the war against Pinelands planning, but their interests often prevailed in subsequent battles over how to implement the CMP. Their interests coincide to a large degree with those of what I call the local "conservation" (as opposed to "preservation") camp. Freedom, individualism, and democracy (see Warren 1963) are the values most espoused, if not necessarily put into practice, by those in the conservation camp.

Preservationists may emphasize the same values, but they are willing to temper their enthusiasm and accept a greater measure of social control in the perceived common interest. Woodland's conservationists might be seen as mainly conservative in their politics, Jeffersonian in their outlook, and patriotic to a fault. Adirondack dissenters, in similarly zealous displays of patriotism, wave flags—even New York State's—that represent governments whose regulations they detest. Like their Adirondack counterparts, Pinelands conservationists must cope with these apparent contradictions. Marvin Matlack never deviated from his reverence for God and country, even in the midst of his embittered challenge to those who would invoke many of the same values in furtherance of their own dubious ends. Matlack's challenges may have prompted some collective soul searching, but in the end they did little to shift Woodland Township from its course. Powerful local interests adapted well to regional planning, in the process bending the Pinelands plan a little bit, and forcing the external interests represented by that plan to adapt to local concerns.

In Woodland, as elsewhere, local elites can be instrumental in influencing and sometimes profiting from environmental change. Large local landowning interests may not ordinarily be powerful enough to wield much influence over the broad sweep of events (e.g., imposition of a Pinelands plan). But their role in making accommodations to these changes after the fact is indeed important and is often underrecognized and poorly understood. While the Woodland case may be an exaggerated manifestation of this general phenomenon, it still stands as an illustration of the critical role played by local economic and political elites.

Those who would suggest that regional planning more fully accommodate local interests and concerns (Berger and Sinton 1985; Marsh 1981; Rubinstein 1983) need to be fully aware of the complexities and pitfalls involved in doing so. They correctly point out that over the years local interests have shaped the landscape, giving meaning and identity to the region's places. And both insiders and outsiders value the locally unique. Yet we must also consider the means by which this has been accomplished—the social, economic, and political relationships that have created, nurtured, and sometimes damaged those places. The basic question for planners is this: How does a sensitive form of regional planning that respects local interests reconcile itself to abuses and injustices at the local level?

Perhaps the simple answer is that it does not; however, the question rarely is raised. The Woodland case points to the importance of considering local political and economic influences not only in the local context but also in broader regional and statewide contexts.

Hamilton Township

Hamilton Township, located in the southern portion of the Pines (Map 5), was formed in 1813 from Great Egg Harbour and Weymouth townships. But the village of Mays Landing, now the seat of Atlantic County as well as the historic center of Hamilton Township, was prospering long before the township came into being. Mays Landing was an important supply point for the Revolutionary Army, and "The Landing" subsequently served as a center for bog-iron production, shipbuilding, charcoal burning, lumbering, and sawmills (Anonymous, n.d.). The Weymouth Forge prospered from 1802 until the 1860s, supporting a shipbuilding industry, producing ironware for export, and providing employment (lumbering, charcoaling, transport of products) through a large hinterland. In 1862, the Weymouth Forge was destroyed by fire. A paper mill was later built on the site, and it operated until 1887. It, too, suffered the fate of most of the Pinelands industries: It was plagued by a series of fires (McMahon 1973). Today, Atlantic County maintains the Weymouth ruins as a historic site.

With the coming of the Camden and Atlantic Railroad in the mid 1800s, growth was concentrated in a number of settlements along the right-of-way. These settlements still exist, though many are mere vestiges of what they once were. Marsh (1979) describes the southern Pine Barrens as an "ethnic archipelago," and Hamilton Township is set in the midst of this archipelago. Russians settled in Mays Landing, Mizpah began as a Jewish colony (it is now a largely black community), and the Pomona–Cologne area was settled by Germans. Although these communities are not nearly so ethnically distinct as they once were, early settlement patterns are still evident in today's population.

Occupying 105 mostly rural square miles, Hamilton ranks as New Jersey's largest township. It contains several small settlements, of which Mays Landing is the largest. Many of the township's 16,012 residents reside in these settlements, though growing numbers now live in newer "estates" and widely scattered single-family houses. Until very recently, the Atlantic County Race Track and scattered roadside developments constituted the bulk of Hamilton's commercial land uses. In 1985, agriculturally improved land totaled about 3,000 acres, and only 10.5 percent of the town's land base (inclusive of agricultural land) was developed (Hamilton Township 1985).

Hamilton Township's Master Plan (Hamilton Township 1985) articulates the desire to maintain a "rural ethic." Yet growth is seen as inevitable; its main sources and facilitators are Atlantic City casino-related housing demands, the high-speed rail system connecting Philadelphia and Atlantic City, and the town's network of arterial roadways. Hamilton's plan calls for careful management of that growth, so as to maintain as much as possible of the town's "rural fabric." Thus special emphasis is placed on open-space preservation, retention of agriculture, maintenance of a relatively undisturbed riverine environment (the Great Egg Harbor River), and promotion of low-intensity recreation opportunities. Historic preservation also ranks highly; the historic character of Mays Landing is described in the plan, and the intent seems to be to sustain the village's small-scale, walkable, knowable, quaint personality. At the same time, there is the desire to attract commercial development—"clean" development that would enhance the community's tax base. Generally, though, the overriding concern is with controlling the amount, quality, and timing of growth.

This consuming concern with controlling growth is a recent phenomenon. Before 1970, Hamilton was a Republican town. Democrats, who by the mid and late 1970s constituted a majority on the Township Committee, came into office on a pledge to clean up corruption; they were boosted in their efforts by the tide of post-Watergate reformism. It is alleged (Bird, 1985 interview) that the reformers themselves were corrupted and that their personal gains from public actions exceeded even the wrongs of their predecessors. At any rate, their attitude toward most development proposals was very accommodating—and the 1970s was indeed a period of growth for the township. Between 1970 and 1980, the population rose from 6,445 to 9,500.

But the receptive attitudes toward growth and new development were not to be sustained; indeed, they played an important part in undoing the 1970s political structure. In 1980, two Republican candidates were victorious; in their campaigns, they had capitalized on the development issue. But the Democrats held the majority on the five-member committee until Sharon Coady's 1981 election gave Republicans the edge. In 1982, two more Republicans, Arthur Bird and Barbara Sorrentino, were elected, giving the Republicans full control.

The Democratic committee had resolved, in solidarity with Atlantic County and the other municipalities in the county, to take no steps to cooperate with Pinelands planning efforts. But in 1981, the Hamilton Township Committee broke with the rest of the county when it voted to work toward conformance with the CMP. According to Mayor Bird (1985 interview), one of the Democratic committee members was persuaded to side with the Republicans on conformance. But the Planning Board was still Democratic, and little substantive progress was made in 1981.

This changed in 1982, after the Republicans gained a majority on the committee, as well as control of the Planning Board. The forces favoring strong growth controls initially saw the Pinelands plan as a good thing (Bird and Coady, 1985 interviews). They were enthusiastic about working with the Pinelands Commission and expected that their vision of Hamilton's future would fit with the environmental imperative of the Pinelands Commission. Hamilton's "new guard" wanted to preserve as much as possible of Hamilton's rural past; to keep it safe and uncluttered, and to maintain the quality of life (Bird, 1985 interview). Indeed, Mayor Bird's involvement in local politics grew from his opposition to a 1,000-acre, 2,500-apartment complex planned near his home. He subsequently became a regular planning meeting attendee, first as a concerned citizen and later as a member of the Planning Board.

Hamilton's changed attitude toward growth reflects a phenomenon that Babcock (1966, 79) elevates to the status of an "American objective": protection of the single-family home. Perin (1977), while objecting to "magnifying states of individual mind and emotion into states of social systems" (p. 25), nonetheless recognizes ownership of the single-family house as realization of the "American dream" (p. 77). To her way of thinking, there is no overriding mass psychology, but instead a shared set of propositions emanating from individual ideas, beliefs, assumptions, and definitions, which are in turn shaped and constrained by institutions. Jackson (1985) sees the availability of inexpensive housing and attitudes of racial prejudice as fundamental causes of mass suburbanization, while population growth and widespread belief in the "suburban ideal" have been necessary conditions for residential deconcentration. Irrespective of the relative importance of socioeconomic forces versus individual beliefs, the social and economic stratification achieved by suburbanization is regarded as desirable, or at least satisfactory, to a vast majority of suburbanites. Disruption of the status quo is resisted, often fiercely. Whether or not—or to what degree—these sentiments are shared by rural dwellers is a question that has received relatively little empirical attention.

It would be appropriate to regard Hamilton Township—at least Hamilton as it was before the advent of Pinelands planning—as largely rural. When the pace of change threatened to become too rapid and affect too many individuals, opposition coalesced and manifested itself in a change of government. To be sure, there are rural dwellers throughout the Pines stridently opposed to rapid residential growth. And there are those selectively opposed to growth in the form of multifamily housing. But it is not at all clear that opposition to multifamily housing is close to universal in rural Pinelands communities. Indeed, views on this issue differ not only among Hamilton Township's residents, but Woodland's as well. In Hamilton, however, opposition clearly is significant—and at least some of it comes from current apartment dwellers wishing to "shut the door."

It would be interesting to know how Hamilton would have reacted to a different Pinelands planning scenario, one that placed it in a more preservation than growth-oriented zone. The concerns of landowners who do not want their options restricted—in Hamilton as elsewhere—might have crystallized into opposition to Pinelands planning. At any rate, the 1981 Township Committee was willing to work toward conformance with the CMP and arranged with the Pinelands Commission for a planning assistance grant. In 1982, work got under way on revising the township's plan and ordinances, and a cooperative tone was established during a May 1982 meeting with the Pinelands Commission's Conformance Subcommittee.

But it was not until the spring of 1983 that the township completed its plan and ordinance revisions. During this period, Democrats gained full control in the township, and the township's sentiments shifted toward a cautious, restrictive attitude concerning growth. When Hamilton submitted its application to the Pinelands Commission in 1983, the response was a "conditional certification" pending the township's incorporation of a set of conditions that ran to more than fifty pages (New Jersey Pinelands Commission 1983e). Issues raised in that document include location of a proposed "adult bookstore zone," the extent of new commercial development to be allowed, number of units to be allowed in the forest area, transportation planning and capital improvements programs, density and bulk requirements for the township's regional growth area, and the township's extensive environmental impact statement requirements for new development. Of greatest concern to the Pinelands Commission were the latter two issues.

According to Mayor Bird (1985 interview), there had been only minimal communication with the Pinelands Commission before the first application for certification, and the discussions that did take place led him to believe—mistakenly, as it turns out—that at most only minor adjustments would be necessary for full certification. Township Committee member Sharon Coady (1985 interview) feels that the Pinelands Commission was arrogant and condescending; that they pictured the local residents as "barefoot and milking cows." Coady, a sociologist at Atlantic County Community College, local feminist leader, and world traveler, was incensed. Her sentiments were shared by others in local government, who felt they had been deluded by the Pinelands Commission. As a result, their visions of future environmental harmony went sour.

Thus began a long phase of negotiation, with each side working toward the best possible conformance deal. To the Pinelands Commission, Hamilton's conformance was key because it is one of three towns meant to absorb the bulk of the region's future growth; also, Hamilton's conformance would set a precedent for Egg Harbor and Galloway, the other two towns with large regional growth areas. Hamilton wanted to be in conformance so that it could again have some control over development review. What ensued was a series of meetings between the township's officials, planning consultant, and attorney; and the Pinelands Commission's Conformance Subcommittee. There were joint staff meetings as well. In addition to the issues listed above, a new one came to the table. Hamilton argued that the original population projections used to allocate regional growth needed to be revised in view of the slower than projected population growth. The commission was not, at the time, willing to consider such revisions. Indeed, neither party was willing to give very much on any of the issues discussed.

Each side's claims were backed by "findings," responses, reinterpretations, and consultants' reports. One of the most contentious issues was that of whether or not the township's bulk requirements would frustrate the aims of the Pinelands regional growth plan. Key actors on the township's side were local officials, especially Mayor Arthur Bird. Bird received some organized support from the Citizens Planning Association, headed by Katherine Layton. Layton also chairs the local historical commission, which is quite forthright in asserting its interests (some local officials refer to it as the "Hysterical Commission"). The historical commission has played an important role in planning for Mays Landing (Layton, 1985 interview). Hamilton's environmental commission, by contrast, has been rather inactive. For the most part, it reacts only to specific development proposals.

Development interests lobbied the Pinelands Commission extensively on Hamilton conformance issues. The New Jersey Builders Association, as well as representatives for the Mays Landing Country Club and Mays Landing Gulfstream, participated extensively in commission meetings with township representatives, had considerable staff contact with the commission, and gave much testimony to the commission. A frequent participant was John Madin, a Fellow of the Royal Society of Architects and head of the John Madin Design Group, which has offices in Switzerland and the United Kingdom. As planner for the proposed Mays Landing Country Club, Madin would fly in from Europe to attend Conformance Subcommittee meetings. This gives some impression of what was at stake. The development community urged that Hamilton's various applications for certification be rejected; they argued that since the CMP was already in place, it had to be strictly applied, at least in Hamilton's case. They wanted to ensure that Hamilton would not be allowed to negotiate away any of its development allocation or impose onerous restrictions on developers.

Some issues were settled during this period of negotiation. But not until late 1984 was there significant movement toward compromise on the most troublesome issues: residential densities and PURD (planned unit residential development) standards. The commission and township both became convinced of the need to expedite matters. Why things jelled precisely when they did is not entirely clear, but there was give and take on both sides. Peter Karabashian, the township's planning consultant, and John Stokes, Pinelands Commission assistant director, quickly developed and signed a proposed agreement in November 1984. It called for "minor" readjustments of regional growth boundaries; they in fact yielded a considerable reduction in the township's total dwelling-unit allocation. A further major reduction in residential allocation was achieved by redesignating 2,514 acres of the regional growth area as a "rural development/ reserve growth district." The township is allowed to zone this district at a low density, and higher-density zoning was to take effect automatically in 1991 unless Hamilton could demonstrate that there was no need for the higher density. Hamilton requested that the day of reckoning be postponed until 1993, and the commission acceded. Thus, the question has been conveniently deferred.

The proposed agreement was reached without resort to a third-party arbitrator; however, a procedural arrangement had been developed for arbitration of outstanding disputes. After considerable review and discussion, the proposed agreement was accepted by the township, the Conformance Subcommittee, and ultimately the Pinelands Commission. Questions were raised by members of the development community, but the Pinelands Commission stayed the course, responding that those concerns could be taken up directly with Hamilton Township. With an agreement ideal to none but tolerable to all, Hamilton came into conformance early in 1985.

By 1980, Hamilton Township had little choice but to accommodate itself to continued rapid residential growth—Pinelands plan or not. The basic questions facing Hamilton were those regarding the pace and kind of growth that would occur. The development community, given the constraints of the CMP, sought the most expeditious means of providing for development. Developers most acutely affected fought the hardest. Hamilton Township, by contrast, tried to stave off and control development. The Pinelands Commission was thrust into the unexpected role of mediator, though much of the mediation was indirect and subtle. Moreover, the commission had already had a major role in defining the rules of the game. Thus the commission did not function as the textbook environmental mediator: an impartial, third-party facilitator (Bingham 1986; Forester 1987; Lake 1986; Mernitz 1980).

Despite its advantages as gamemaster and referee, the Pinelands Commission seemed ill prepared for what it would face in Hamilton Township. Perhaps if the direct confrontation between regional and local interests had been better anticipated, a means of conflict resolution could have been set up earlier in the game. Given the importance attached to conformance, especially in a place where the stakes are as high as in Hamilton, it seems that the job could have been done in something less than two years. It would have behooved the commission to have found, early on, a means to identify and attempt to compromise on the "irreducible" conflicts. The approach finally taken did work, but not without considerable cost. It should have been possible to achieve a comparable resolution much earlier in the conformance process.

Manchester Township

Unlike Woodland and Hamilton, Manchester Township's conformance with the Pinelands plan was relatively quick and amicable. Manchester is located in Ocean County, near the Pinelands' northern fringes. This is prime territory for retirement-home developments. Indeed, Manchester's population consists principally of senior citizens.

Manchester, like other Pine Barrens towns, is really more than one place. Within it, we find remnants of former settlements as well as several distinct contemporary places. Manchester was established in 1865 by carving off a section of Dover Township. In the eighteenth century, two sawmills operated in the Manchester area, though there is some question as to whether one was actually within the current township boundaries (Dewey 1981). In the late 1700s and the 1800s, Manchester was known first as Federal Forge, then Federal Furnace (Dewey 1981; Salter 1890). At least two, perhaps three, ironworks operated there in the nineteenth century. In the mid 1800s, Nathan C. Whiting operated a sawmill in the part of Manchester now designated as Whiting. Located at the eventual junction of three rail lines—the Pennsylvania, Central (still in existence), and Tuckerton—the town of Whiting prospered. It supported a post office, church, and businesses, including the popular Pine Tavern (Beck 1937; Dewey 1981). The nearby town of Pasadena was home to more industry, including a gunpowder mill (moved from its original location in Whiting), terra cotta works, and sawmills (Beck 1936), as well as such short-lived ventures as a sanitarium, riding stable, and bowling and billiard hall (Beck 1937).

Dewey (1981) reports that area land values rose considerably in the mid 1800s, buoyed in part by the value of marl beds along one of the rail lines. In the early twentieth century, things became quieter, and the area's population remained fairly low and stable for decades. Land was cheap; indeed, parcels were given to northern New Jersey residents as inducements to subscribe to the *Newark Evening News* (Jados, 1985 interview). There were also some grandiose subdivision plans; Roosevelt City, for example, is a developer's failed dream whose imprimatur on the landscape is a ghostly grid of roads with only a few scattered dwellings.

This would all change by the 1960s and especially the 1970s. Whereas in 1890, Salter reported: "Probably fewer old persons, natives of the county, reside in Ocean in proportion to the population than in any other county in the state" (1980, 128–129), the county by the mid 1900s had become a magnet for retirement communities. Completion of the Garden State Parkway, the availability of large parcels of low-priced land, and proximity to New York and Philadelphia made the area very attractive to developers. Retirees, mostly from northern New Jersey, New York, and Pennsylvania, were lured by the closeness to metropolitan areas and the semi-rural setting, security, low costs, and services offered by the planned retirement communities (Heintz 1976). Ocean County and many of its municipalities (including Manchester) have actively courted the developers of these communities. Their principal objective is to keep tax rates low. Because seniors require relatively few municipal services, their tax dollars can, in effect, subsidize a certain amount of single and multifamily housing for nonretirees.

Manchester's senior citizen boom began a little later than those in other portions of Ocean County, presumably because Manchester is slightly less accessible. Manchester's population nearly doubled in the 1960s, growing from 3,779 in 1960 to 7,550 in 1970. But it really soared in the 1970s, reaching 27,987 in 1980. The first retirement community was built in 1962, and it was soon followed by a second. Both were small. In the late 1960s and early 1970s, the large Crestwood Village and Leisure Technology developments came on line. They are located, respectively, in the Whiting–Roosevelt City and Pine Lake Park–Ridgeway vicinities, areas where the township sought to encourage development. In the 1970s, both developments expanded considerably, and they were followed by some small, non-senior citizen developments attracted by the low tax rate (Alan

Mallach Associates 1980). By 1984, there were 13,816 senior citizen dwelling units—the bulk of them accounted for by a number of Crestwood Villages and 3,064 single-family dwellings (Manchester Township, n.d.). Little commercial or industrial development is found in Manchester, though an exhausted ilmenite mine occupies a considerable area. That land is eventually to be reclaimed and made available for development. Though the former mine land is in the Pinelands National Reserve, it is outside the Pinelands planning area. The New Jersey Division of Coastal Resources, which has jurisdiction over the land, informed the Pinelands Commission in 1990 that it was planning to change the designation for 7,500 developable acres from "extensive growth" to "limited growth"—the most restrictive designation it can impose.

That matter aside, the CMP had already imposed a general lid on future development for Manchester, thus frustrating hopes for retirement community expansion on the order once envisioned. Seventy-two percent of the Township's 82.5 square miles is within the Pinelands planning area; this is subdivided into preservation district (45 percent), forest area (25 percent), military and federal installation area (13 percent), Whiting Village (12 percent), and regional growth area (5 percent) (New Jersey Pinelands Commission 1983a). The growth area cannot be developed to its full potential until a planned sewerage interceptor is completed.

Initially, the township opposed by resolution Governor Byrne's 1979 executive order, which imposed a Pinelands building moratorium. But as it turned out, Manchester's conformance experience was generally amicable. One key issue was the Whiting Village designation. Village designation allows for infill development, but that development is normally meant to be contained within a fairly restricted area. But Whiting, due to extensive and dispersed development that preceded the Pinelands plan, is far larger than other Pinelands villages. A bit of "old Whiting" remains, but it is set within a mosaic of large developments. This situation is without parallel in the Pinelands, and the Pinelands Commission recognized this. While there was considerable discussion and negotiation between the Conformance Subcommittee and township representatives in drawing village boundaries, it was by and large amicable. Representatives of environmental organizations have expressed some concern about Whiting's boundaries, but they have not made this a major issue.

Manchester was conditionally certified in January 1983 and fully certified in July 1983. The process was relatively quick and painless, and this may be attributed principally to three factors. First, the population consists largely of senior citizens. Heintz's 1976 study of New Jersey retirement communities (one of them in Manchester Township) found little evidence to suggest that age-homogeneous environments foster political action or organization. She also found that there were no formal movements to affect the kind or extent of local growth; that 18.4 percent of residents attended planning board meetings (she feels this is "low," which is arguable), most of them seeking personal zoning relief; and that 72.1 percent of residents favor additional growth in their communities.

In Manchester's case, the Pinelands issue was not a politically charged one in any overt way. There was little opposition to Pinelands planning (Tolischius, 1985 interview), but also little vocal support. Because retirees presumably have the time to be interested, one might think that they would be more interested than other citizens in planning issues. This generally does not seem to be the case (Heintz 1976; Jackson 1981). A landfill controversy in the mid 1980s did arouse interest and prompt letter-writing campaigns by various seniors' groups in Manchester (Lynch, 1985 interview), but such was not the case with Pinelands planning. Typically, people do not become actively involved unless or until they are immediately affected by an issue. Since few Manchester residents are profoundly affected at a personal level by Pinelands regulations, there is little inducement for activism. While the Pinelands plan curtails the township's development potential, this is of little consequence to most senior citizens—they do not want to build houses. Moreover, the effect on taxes should be minimal, since the existing ratio of senior citizens to younger residents is not likely to shift dramatically. Other factors may alter the local population's age structure, but the Pinelands plan is not likely to exert major influence.

The second factor that helps explain Manchester's amicable conformance is the standoffish stance taken by developers. Those most affected by Pinelands planning are the developers of senior citizen housing; this is especially true of Crestwood. Developers did indeed oppose the Pinelands plan, but their opposition was not particularly adamant or vocal. Perhaps they viewed the regional plan as a fait accompli, thinking that little could be accomplished by opposing it at the local level. This same general perception may also have stifled the initiative of some old-time residents—who in any case constitute a small minority—concerned about infringements on individual rights.

Finally, township administrator Joseph Portash gave his total support to Pinelands planning (Portash, 1985 interview)—this despite his earlier (pre-CMP) expectations that Manchester's policy of courting large-scale senior citizen development would go on indefinitely (Alan Mallach Associates 1980). Portash apparently exercised considerable influence in Manchester—he was mayor for thirteen years (1964–1977), he appointed most of the Planning Board members who worked on Pinelands conformance, and in the words of one credible observer who shall remain anonymous, "If he said they'd conform, they would." Manchester's mayor and zoning officer held less than favorable opinions of the Pinelands Commission and its actions (Lynch, 1985 interview), yet their concerns seemed to hold little official sway. Portash had many regional-level contacts, and, in his own words, a "good rapport" with Pinelands Commission Executive Director Terrence Moore (Portash, 1985 interview). In short, Portash had the makings of an excellent conformance facilitator.

But there is a dark side to the Joseph Portash story. In the 1970s, Portash was executive director of the Pinelands Environmental Council—until he resigned in 1976 after being convicted of accepting a $30,000 bribe from an Ocean County developer. He also resigned as mayor of Manchester, but became township administrator a year later. Though Portash's conviction was overturned on appeal, he would be linked with a much larger scandal in 1990. It seems that Portash and friends embezzled at least $2 million in municipal funds; possibly as much as $10 million by some estimates (LeDuc 1990; Sullivan 1990). Portash amassed an impressive real estate and investment portfolio and frequented the high-stakes tables at Atlantic City and Las Vegas. Shortly after voters ousted him from office, he died of a heart attack at his Maine vacation home, leading some Manchester residents to proclaim that reports of his death were exaggerated!

Portash's actions went unnoticed for so many years because he was an apparently competent administrator, responsive to his constituents' needs. Not until the late 1980s did his misdeeds begin to catch up with him. Soaring local tax rates prompted urgent concern, shaking residents from the complacency described earlier. Stop Tax Oppression Promptly (STOP) became a powerful force for change.

STOP pushed for a referendum to change the form of government to mayor–council, and the measure's passage led to Portash's undoing. His legacy to Manchester is painfully evident in the enormous fiscal and legal consequences with which the town must cope.

These three case studies reflect the diversity of issues encountered in regional Pinelands planning. Indeed, subregional social and political diversity has made itself manifestly clear during the course of the Pinelands plan's implementation. One approach for the Pinelands Commission might have been simply to recognize these differences. This is not, however, a strategy overtly favored by the commission; nor would a mere division of the Pinelands into a number of different yet equal (in terms of the planning resources devoted to them) subunits likely have worked. Woodland, Hamilton, and Manchester's experiences underscore this point. Woodland and Hamilton townships consumed an exceptional share of the commission's time and attention, while Manchester's conformance required only a minimal greasing of wheels.

Woodland and Hamilton townships were granted significant concessions by the Pinelands Commission. The strength and salience of local concerns, combined with the regional importance to Pinelands planning of "succeeding" in these two towns, gave them a fair measure of bargaining power. It might be argued that the special attention given these towns reflects a general flexibility on the part of the commission; a concern for uniquely local interests. The record would seem to indicate otherwise. Indeed, only meager attention has been spared for local concerns not forcefully and influentially expressed (see Berger and Sinton 1985).

Despite their uneven treatment by Pinelands planning, the fact remains that local concerns, when sufficiently important to local residents, are not easily suppressed. That the Pinelands Commission had to accommodate some of these concerns does not mean that the ensuing benefits were fairly distributed. Indeed, local elites, in Woodland at least, seemed to be the greatest Pinelands beneficiaries. Elsewhere, in Hamilton and Manchester, the benefiting constituencies are a bit harder to define. While it may eventually come to light that Manchester's Joseph Portash turned Pinelands planning to his personal benefit, insufficient evidence is available at present to support such a contention.

Perhaps the most valuable lesson to be learned is that local uniqueness cannot be managed by bureaucratic formula. Nor is the regional planning agency well situated to deal with local corruption and injustice. Yet obviously it must contend with the facts of political life. One option—seemingly not considered by the Pinelands Commission—might be to enlist the support of "well-governed" towns in censuring those that are badly governed. I would propose that the agency's role be merely that of facilitator, not judge. Interestingly enough, the Pinelands Preservation Alliance (Chapter 5, "Citizen Organizations and Public Institutions") seems willing to take on this role of uncovering local injustices, though how successful they will be in doing so remains to be seen. Perhaps the towns themselves need to be enlisted in this critical examination of local governance. If the Pine Barrens region is to be defined as a political entity, then maybe it is the place to try creating a "United Nations" of towns.

7

A Successful Bureaucracy

In February 1991, the Pinelands Commission and friends sponsored a tenth-anniversary festival of self-adulation that was attended by a large crowd of supporters and well-wishers. There was much to celebrate. The Pinelands program had come through a decade of trying political times with flying colors. Because the national reserve concept was unprecedented, and because New Jersey had no other critical-area protection program comparable to that for the Pinelands, the Pinelands effort had to pass critical tests during its early years. And, indeed, early successes ensured its long-term entrenchment within a labyrinthine political, legal, and administrative landscape. Many of the Pinelands Commission's early eggs were put in the conformance basket. The results—forty-five of fifty-two municipalities and all seven counties in conformance as of 1991—are indeed impressive. Pinelands planning also withstood potentially destructive legal and political challenges. Only in more recent years, secure in its place as guardian of one-fifth of New Jersey's land base, has the Pinelands Commission turned more of its attention to research, education, and even self-assessment. This chapter describes commission strategies and draws attention to some of the broader issues that have been neglected, or at least temporarily set aside, during the first few years of Pinelands planning and management.

Conformance

One of the Pinelands Commission's preeminent concerns during its first three years was to secure the conformance of municipal and county plans and ordinances with the Comprehensive Management Plan (CMP) for the Pinelands. This is confirmed in various ways: Executive Director Terrence Moore's informal statement that "what it took the Adirondack Park Agency ten years to do, we've done in one and a half years"; the very large share of the Pinelands Commission's three-year progress report (New Jersey Pinelands Commission 1983a) dealing with conformance; and former Commissioner John Sinton's (Berger and Sinton 1985; Sinton 1984) observation that Franklin Parker, commission chair, had used the number of conforming towns as the chief measure of the CMP's success. That the commission attaches so much importance to conformance is not surprising; indeed, it is a very visible measure of achievement. The conformance process, which consumed a great deal of the commission's early time and energies, was one of the key objectives, if not *the* key objective, during the commission's early years.

What is especially important, though, is the great success the Pinelands Commission has enjoyed in securing local conformance with the CMP. Regardless of whether or not one accepts the premise that conformance is an indicator of larger program successes, this is an extraordinary achievement in and of itself. As early as 1985, all but a fifth of the towns had conformed with the Pinelands plan and four of seven counties were in conformance. By 1991, only seven towns were not in compliance. This success has not come without prolonged negotiations and intense struggles in several towns and counties; some of these cases are considered later.

In terms of municipal conformance, the Pinelands program does indeed compare very favorably with other regional land use planning programs. But many of those programs had to struggle with towns that had no planning structure at all. The Pinelands were not quite such a "planning frontier," since New Jersey's Land Use Law required that all towns have master plans and zoning ordinances. For this reason, and because different programs have different conformance requirements, it is not entirely fair to make comparisons. But the Pinelands plan's success rate is so outstanding as to overwhelm these qualifications.

Popper's (1981) review of land use programs in Florida, Vermont, New York (Adirondack Park), California (coastal zone), Maryland (Power Plant Siting Act), and Pennsylvania (Surface Mining Conservation and Reclamation Act) reveals that these programs have had generally limited success in stimulating even the writing of land use plans and ordinances. DeGrove's (1984) analysis of programs in Hawaii, Vermont, Florida, California (coastal zone), Oregon, Colorado, and North Carolina (coastal zone) yields similar findings; while Carol (1987) affirms that the Pinelands local conformance rate compares favorably with those in the Adirondacks and Oregon. Within a time frame comparable to that of the Pinelands program, only California's Coastal Commissions had even begun to achieve a respectable rate of compliance of plans and ordinances, and that rate lagged as the program progressed.

Why the overwhelming success with Pinelands conformance? First, opposition has not been sufficiently organized or effective. What opposition there was to the Pinelands legislation, as well as adoption of the CMP, did not coalesce as a unified regional noncooperation effort after the plan took effect. The South Jersey Secession Movement, organized around Pinelands and other issues, quietly receded. Key interest groups and individuals that might have chosen to organize an anticonformance campaign did not in fact do so. Development and agricultural interests did, however, remain active in their concern and sometimes vehement in their opposition to Pinelands planning. Members of these communities also participated in lawsuits challenging the CMP. But farmers tended more toward making noise than engaging in substantive actions. The development community—that is, the Coalition for the Sensible Preservation of the Pinelands and later the New Jersey Builders Association and the Builders League of South Jersey—was more interested in gaining concessions than thwarting the planning process. These organizations have at times been powerful rhetorical opponents of Pinelands planning, but their true role might best be described as that of the loyal (quasi-loyal, at least) opposition (Bauman 1981; Fisher, 1985 interview). Indeed, it has usually been in their interest to get on with conformance—especially, for the development community, in towns slated to absorb a large share of regional growth (see the discussion of Hamilton Township in Chapter 6).

In the municipalities and counties themselves, opposition to conformance was considerable. This is substantiated to a degree by my 1982 survey of local officials, planners, and planning consultants in eleven municipalities and three counties. This survey was not comprehensive, and since it relied entirely on personal interviews, the responses, especially from politicians, were often riddled with ambiguity. Still, it is possible to extract from the responses of six of the eleven townships a clear sense of discontent with either the objectives of Pinelands planning or the way it was being implemented. Officials from four of the townships felt Pinelands planning might be necessary, but not for their town. The concerns of the key actors who were interviewed may not accurately reflect the attitudes of the local citizenry, who in many cases may be more ambivalent than their elected representatives. All told, however, the interview results seem to suggest that discontent with Pinelands planning was fairly widespread. But as a general rule, the discontent did not translate into concerted action—with some very notable exceptions. Most notable are Ocean County and Atlantic County and its municipalities.

Ocean County

The population of Ocean County has grown very rapidly over the past several decades, as the figures below indicate:

1950	56,609
1960	108,241
1970	208,470
1980	346,038
1990	433,203

In 1980, 31.8 percent of the population was fifty-five years of age or older (U.S. Department of Commerce 1982). Indeed, much of Ocean County's growth over the past thirty to forty years can be attributed to an influx of retirees (see description of Manchester Township in Chapter 6). This is the kind of residential growth the county anticipates for the remainder of the century, though at a rather slower pace (New Jersey Pinelands Commission 1983d).

Ocean County's vision of the future differed in some substantial ways from that of the Pinelands plan. The county envisioned considerable growth and sought to accommodate that growth in an orderly, planned fashion. By many accounts, their pre-Pinelands planning was sophisticated and sound, though geared to accommodating extensive residential development, principally in the form of large retirement communities. Although county planning functions in New Jersey are limited primarily to the areas of transportation and utilities, this infrastructure facilitates and guides growth. The towns then work within this framework to grow in a manner compatible with local interests.

Although many points were at issue in Ocean County, the key countywide questions concerned the location, rate, and timing of residential growth. More specifically, the county and Pinelands Commission clashed over (1) the need–demand–desire for development (including airport and road expansion) in the western portion of Berkeley Township, and the associated redesignation of Pinelands management areas that would be needed to accommodate the growth; (2) the question of alignment and size of a sewer interceptor to serve existing developments in Berkeley, as well as the interceptor's effect on future growth; and (3) the allocation of new development within three critical watershed subbasins in the Berkeley area (New Jersey Pinelands Commission 1983d). There was a great deal of discussion on these issues between the commission's Conformance Subcommittee and representatives of Ocean County and Berkeley Township.

Ocean County was conditionally certified in April 1983, which meant that the Pinelands Commission continued to handle development review, pending resolution of issues identified by the commission. Following the conditional certification, negotiations continued in earnest, with the commission striving to reach some sort of compromise with the county. For a time, attention focused on the effects of the county's development proposals on the northern pine and corn snakes. Robert Zappalorti, of Herpetological Associates, was commissioned by the county to prepare a report on critical snake habitats. Radio transmitters were attached to snakes and their movements recorded. William Tucker, who sees much environmentalism as a pretense used by the privileged classes, comments on Herpetological Associates:

Working out of his home, Zappalorti was soon making consulting fees of $10,000 for spending two to three weeks scouring proposed construction sites to help suburban communities locate endangered species that could block unwanted projects . . . this . . . only represents upper-middle-class people using their professional and legal skills to twist and turn environmental concerns to their own purposes. (1982, 184)

In Ocean County, Zappalorti's work was used to show that development could coexist with snake habitat. This prompted critiques by Pinelands Commission staff and by a panel of scientists assembled by the Rutgers University Division of Pinelands Research. They concluded that the Zappalorti study should not be used as a basis for any decision making that might affect the snakes (New Jersey Pinelands Commission 1983d). Thus, attention was for a time focused on a very narrow issue. The snake issue may not have been entirely without merit, but the point is that two public, professional organizations were using their money, time, and talents to bicker over an issue that obscured the much larger confrontation between the local power structure and regional and statewide interests. Such confrontations over narrowly defined issues that act as proxies for deeper conflicts are, of course, quite common in the United States: the snail darter in Tennessee, the spotted owl in the Pacific Northwest, Hudson River striped bass in the case of New York City's proposed Westway.

At one point in the negotiations, Pinelands Commission staff and Ocean County planners reached agreement on the "need" for about 3,500 new residential units above and beyond what the Pinelands plan allowed for Berkeley Township. And in 1985, after long and intense work with Pinelands Commission staff that began in November 1983 (New Jersey Pinelands Commission 1985c), Berkeley Township came into conformance with the CMP. Berkeley wanted to conform with the CMP despite Ocean County's resolute resistance. But after a 1986 appellate court ruling voided the forest area reclassification that would have accommodated the agreed-upon growth needs, the commission had to "decertify" Berkeley and renegotiate. Ocean County finally came into conformance in 1987; what seemed to move the county off the dime was the prospect of receiving funds from the 1985 Infrastructure Bond Act. Conformance, of course, was a precondition for eligibility.

Atlantic County

Atlantic County was the other opposition stronghold. The initial policy of the county and its towns was one of noncooperation with the Pinelands Commission. But in reality, Atlantic County's residents are deeply concerned about future development—indeed, the threat of overdevelopment—of their towns. Many local leaders who agreed in principle with the need for and value of a Pinelands preservation program opposed it in practice. Widespread resentment stemmed from the general perception that the Pinelands plan is an inflexible zoning scheme, forced on local residents by a distant bureaucracy (Conover, 1984 interview; Marsh, 1983 interview; Sinton, 1982 interview). Many Atlantic County officials take the view that their county is sufficiently removed from the core of the Pinelands that it should be treated differently; some believe that it should simply be left to its own resources. Of course, the CMP does treat much of Atlantic County differently from the core preservation area. Only a small portion of the county is in the preservation area; the rest is subject to the less restrictive protection area regulations.

Nevertheless, many local leaders are offended at the manner in which the CMP was developed and the way it is being implemented. Because the CMP was produced within such tight time constraints, Pinelands planning began as, and to a large extent remains, a "top-down" process. This has prompted charges of elitism and arrogance. They come not only from unwavering advocates of local autonomy, but also from individuals who are generally supportive of regional planning. These include Stockton State College professor John Sinton (Sinton 1984) and former Stockton professor Elizabeth Marsh (1983 interview). The Pinelands Commission's failure to consider variations in local conditions and concerns has been a common target of its critics. Imposition of the same water-quality standard in the protection and preservation areas is one of the actions that inflamed Atlantic County and some of the municipalities.

Former County Executive Charles Worthington may have been the driving force behind the loosely organized, but initially quite effective, boycott on dealing with the Pinelands Commission (Conover, 1984 interview). Two county representatives to the Pinelands Commission—first Philip Nanzetta and later John Sinton—had hoped to see changes in the way the plan was administered. In this regard, they argued for greater flexibility and sensitivity on the commission's part. Both felt frustrated in their efforts. Sinton's successor was Joel Jacovitz, former leader of the South Jersey Secession Movement (see VanKoski 1983). Jacovitz, a southern New Jersey builder, often took center stage at commission meetings, questioning or dissenting on most of the commission's actions, which had by that time become quite routine. He even played tapes of one closed-session meeting to the *Atlantic City Press*. Worthington (1984 interview) described him as "crazy"; just as crazy, in fact, as the environmentalists.

By the mid 1980s, the writing was on the wall for Atlantic County. Jacovitz was replaced on the commission by a quieter presence, and several of the county's towns were coming into conformance with the Pinelands plan. The boycott was over. In 1989, the county was certified by the Pinelands Commission, thus making it eligible for $14 million in grants and loans to build a sewer line.

Conformance's Overall Success

Atlantic and Ocean counties represent exceptions to the commission's general success in securing local conformance with the CMP. At the regional level, successful opposition was never mobilized. Undoubtedly, a majority of Pinelands mayors, if not vehemently opposed to Pinelands planning, at least had serious reservations about it. Yet the Pinelands Municipal Council, an advisory organization of Pinelands mayors created by the state Pinelands legislation, never was able to achieve a quorum at any of its meetings. Nor was it ever granted funds—as are some of today's community groups that oppose hazardous waste sites, landfills, and other unwanted facilities (LULUs, or locally unwanted land uses) required by state or local law. The council lacked the savvy and dedication of many of today's anti-LULU groups. Indeed, it never captured the same kind of constituent respect and public interest that the similarly constituted Adirondack Park Local Government Review Board garnered in the 1970s and beyond. Most Pinelands mayors, while willing to negotiate with the Pinelands Commission regarding their own town's fate, felt a general sense of futility regarding their ability to affect regional and statewide matters. Most are part-time officials and as a rule could not justify spending their scarce time going to what they saw as inconvenient, unproductive meetings.

What other factors argue for the success of the conformance process and, as a corollary, the lack of an effective opposition to it?

First, the economic climate of the early 1980s was rather forgiving to a regulatory program that limits and redirects various kinds of development. It was a recessionary period, accompanied by reduced housing starts and mortgage activity in New Jersey and much of the rest of the country (Biddle 1983). Thus, initial effects of the Pinelands plan were masked by broader economic trends, so that in some cases where the CMP might have been blamed for restricting development, it was not—or at least not to the extent it might have been under different economic circumstances. Indeed, several local officials interviewed in 1982 opined that the real test of Pinelands planning was yet to come. They were reserving their final judgment on the plan's effects pending an upturn in the general economic climate. By the time judgment day arrived, newer and more pressing matters were undoubtedly foremost in many of their minds.

The CMP also withstood numerous legal challenges (Rielley, Larsen, and Weaver 1984) and administrative threats in its early years. The plan was forged, and has been implemented, with a keen eye to legal defensibility. Not only has the CMP survived challenges based on the "taking question" (Randle 1982) and on its constitutionality (actually, the courts refused to hear them); it has also survived a host of other, lesser challenges, including those to the Pinelands Development Credit program. This reinforces the impression that Pinelands planning is there to stay. It also allows Pinelands commissioners and staff to "save face" in potentially embarrassing public situations; they can justify certain actions merely by saying, "It is the Plan [law]. . . . We have to be able to defend our actions."

The Pinelands Commission witnessed some administrative changes as a result of the 1981 election of Republican Governor Thomas Kean, as well as political shifts within Pinelands counties. In response to the sentiment that led to the South Jersey Secession Movement (VanKoski 1983), Kean pledged during his campaign to look after the interests of southern New Jersey. But this was not a rejection of regional planning; indeed, Kean asserted his support for the Pinelands program very shortly after his election. Although his passion for Pinelands protection did not match that of Brendan Byrne, he continued to provide the strong executive leadership that is so crucial to the success of regional land use programs. The importance of gubernatorial leadership is confirmed by DeGrove (1984), who stresses its value to all state land use programs (with the sole exception of California) he analyzed. Liroff and Davis

(1981) make a similar observation in the Adirondack context, and Pinelands Commission Executive Director Terrence Moore (1983) emphasizes the same point with respect to the Pinelands.

Governor Kean did make some changes. Early on, he replaced the commission's two most ardent preservationists (Gary Patterson, Floyd West) with two commissioners (Stephen Lee, James Hyres) inclined to be more receptive to municipal and county concerns. There was little threat, however, of undoing the plan, and its provisions for local conformance remained intact. Some local officials had been holding off on conformance until they learned more about the Kean administration's Pinelands intentions. But any hopes they might have harbored for a gutting of the Pinelands program were quickly dashed. Thus it was time for those towns to resume progress toward conformance, and ultimately reclaim at least some control over local development review. The urge to regain a measure of local control was in clear evidence in some towns, while officials of other towns did not see this as a compelling factor. The latter viewed local control as nominal only, since their plans and ordinances had to be thoroughly revised to comply with the provisions of the CMP. In a sense, their skepticism was confirmed in 1984 when the Pinelands Commission denied the formerly automatic right of uncertified municipalities to appeal Pinelands development approval decisions to an administrative law judge. Although that action probably had only a very limited effect in inducing recalcitrant towns to conform with the CMP, it did produce a hue and cry that was heard in the governor's office, and the commission was eventually forced to modify its policy.

The Pinelands Commission created a special vehicle to help move the conformance process: the Conformance Subcommittee. This group would meet as often as needed with local officials, planners, and consultants to negotiate details of conformance agreements. The relaxed, nonadversarial setting of the commission's New Lisbon offices was the venue for most meetings. Situated in the front of the nineteenth-century house that serves as the commission's headquarters, the meeting room is quiet and comfortable; state-issued furnishings detract only slightly from its welcoming character. Moreover, the setting is appropriately rural; New Lisbon's location in the northwestern fringes of the Pines adds to the ambience. The general conviviality (including the executive director's quick wit) helped create the cooperative tone that typified most meetings. Once a good working relationship is established, it becomes difficult for critics, now part and parcel of the process, to be too severe in their criticism. They are especially likely to refrain from direct attacks on those with whom they have worked. But the degree to which group dynamics actually influenced the underlying attitudes and values of local actors is difficult, if not impossible, to ascertain. The net result for Pinelands planning, though, would seem to be this: At a minimum, the negotiating process expedited the proceedings in cases where local representatives were predisposed toward cooperation.

The Pinelands Commission staff has the legal and administrative capability to make life more pleasant for towns that conform with the plan. For example, uncertified towns lack the ability to regulate certain kinds of development not covered by the CMP. Once in conformance, the town can usually reassert that regulatory power. Although this particular aspect of the conformance process may not have directly affected many towns, it was extremely important in specific cases—for example, exploration for natural gas storage in Stafford Township and a 1,000-foot-high transmitter tower in Waterford Township. Despite intense local opposition, the commission could do little to halt these projects because they were not specifically regulated by the CMP.

Some municipalities claimed that desired development approvals came more quickly and easily after certification. This approach was never officially employed, and there is no firm evidence that it was informally employed. Yet speculation abounds. In 1983, Cape May County Planning Director Elwood Jarmer stated that "Pinelands Executive Director Terrence Moore has indicated that unless the county conforms, there could be problems for any major county project within the Pines. He made clear the planned county landfill would be just such a project" (Post 1983). The landfill received a waiver from the commission, and the county is now in conformance.

Interviews with local officials brought forth another interesting point. Several not only indicated their opposition to regional planning, but also expressed their deep conviction that the law of the land must be enforced. Van Abs (1986) concurs on this point. As Alexis de Tocqueville (1945) observed nearly one-hundred fifty years ago, obedience in America is not to public officials, but to the law. State and regional regulators may be despised, but the law is the law. Once convinced of the irreversibility of Pinelands regulations, many local officials worked hard to make them effective.

Interest-group activity also played an important part in the conformance process. Development interests, for example, had a hand in expediting—to the extent that they could—Hamilton Township's conformance (see Chapter 6). Environmental organizations monitored the conformance process quite closely, although only the Association of New Jersey Environmental Commissions (ANJEC) and the New Jersey Conservation Foundation consistently observed the proceedings. The presence of members of the environmental community at meetings and hearings probably helped keep the proceedings from flagging and prevented commission members and staff from negotiating away too much of what those members most valued. While environmentalists were not usually very vocal or adamant at the conformance meetings, their unspoken presence seemed to act as something of a control rod, keeping the negotiations from straying too far from the CMP's preservation objectives.

A strong fiscal inducement for conformance came in 1985 when New Jersey voters approved a $30-million bond issue to provide funds for infrastructure capital projects in Pinelands regional growth areas. The statewide vote was 930,250 in favor and 532,114 against, with a similar voting ratio prevailing through much of southern New Jersey (New Jersey Department of State 1985). The bond issue provides grants and loans for transportation, wastewater treatment, water supply, and other infrastructure projects. This money is made available only to towns and counties in conformance with the CMP—and for a town to receive money, not only must the town itself be in conformance, but so must the county within which it is located. Supported by a recommendation enshrined in the CMP, the Pinelands Commission had urged for some time that steps be taken to provide capital for regional growth areas, but the commission did not specifically push for the bond referendum. It was a legislative initiative, and the commission expressed its support after the fact. Above and beyond its significance in spreading statewide some of the costs imposed on Pinelands localities by the CMP, the bond issue provided a powerful lever for securing the conformance of reluctant municipalities and counties.

The Postconformance Era

Conformance was exceedingly important to the Pinelands Commission in its first few years; it was the unifying theme for many of the commission's activities. By 1984, with the bulk of the conformance work behind it, the commission moved toward a new central focus: its three-year plan review, which itself took about five years (fortunately, the second review does not begin at a three-year interval). As described (Chapter 5, "Citizen Organizations and Public Institutions"), the plan review procedure was enormously cumbersome. In the end, it yielded relatively few significant changes; the major plan amendments involve historic resource protection, stricter regulation of commercial forestry, and streamlined application requirements. By plan review time, Pinelands planning was working well; the CMP's basic integrity faced few threats. Thus, at least from a bureaucratic point of view, it would have been foolish to risk upsetting the equilibrium. Berger and Sinton (1985) had already stated, before the fact, that the plan review would yield no major changes to the CMP; their prediction was in large part borne out.

A series of other activities, routine and nonroutine, have consumed the remainder of the commissioners' and staff's energies in the postconformance era. Key among them is the business of administrative and legal caretaking. The commission tracks the development review process in certified towns and continues to carry it out in those not certified. Legal defense of the Pinelands plan has been carried on with great success, but not without cost. Examples of individual cases that consumed great time and effort include defenses of the commission's denial of a waiver allowing construction of 4,500 units in a forested section of Manchester Township and the commission's granting of waivers to build 1,411 units in Berkeley Township and 483 units in Stafford Township's forest area (all in Ocean County).

In recent years, the commission has attempted to step up its "public programs" effort. But, even by its own admission, this still consists mainly of attempts to secure greater understanding and acceptance of its activities (New Jersey Pinelands Commission 1983a). The public programs staff deals with telephone and personal inquiries, writes news releases, tracks and tries to influence media coverage of Pinelands activities, informs legislators, arranges for dissemination of brochures and slide shows, maintains contacts with schools and colleges, and organizes public hearings and meetings with special-interest groups. Criticism or suggestions for fundamental changes to the CMP or Pinelands planning are not solicited; self-criticism is not encouraged. Public participation is not actively solicited; instead, interested parties must come to the com-mission's offices and subcommittee meetings. Funding and staff are not available to do much more than this, nor does there seem to be a great deal of interest in doing more. Indeed, to do so would risk upsetting the status quo. In 1990, the commission *did* solicit comments from various interest groups. As in the past, the most active groups tended to be the plan's natural supporters: the en-vironmental interest groups that already enjoyed some degree of comfort and familiarity with commission workings. One significant outcome of the solicitation, however, was a decision to vary the times and locations of the commission's monthly meetings. Prior to this time, they had always been held on Friday mornings.

Among the issues neglected to some degree during the early Pine-lands years were the economic and cultural implications of Pinelands management. Political pressures to deal with economic concerns are of course considerable, while "cultural resources" attract little in the way of a constituency. Thus, of the two, economic issues had higher priority.

The Pinelands Commission maintains that because the CMP re-inforces existing patterns of development, it is not likely to have major regional economic effects. Yet the commission acknowledges that economic consequences may be variable at the subregional level (New Jersey Pinelands Commission 1983b). Given the former premise, it is not surprising that commission studies conclude that most of the CMP's economic effects are either minimal or that there is not enough information to draw inferences (Government Finance Associates 1982; New Jersey Pinelands Commission 1983b, 1985b; see also Conant and Pizor 1988).

An early analysis of land transactions showed that the CMP had no overall effect (New Jersey Pinelands Commission 1983b). But a later analysis indicated that it might have had a dampening effect on land sales and might be responsible for a trend toward larger acreage transactions in the preservation area (New Jersey Pinelands Commission 1985b). The studies revealed that land prices had risen in regional growth areas and dropped in the preservation area (New Jersey Pinelands Commission 1983b, 1985b). Pinelands planning seems to have had the effect of depressing housing sales during the 1979 building moratorium. But since the CMP's enactment, devel-opment apparently has been moving away from restricted areas and into regional growth areas and outside the Pinelands. No increase in housing values is attributed to the CMP. Nor, apparently, has the CMP had significant effects on regional employment, mining, or agriculture (New Jersey Pinelands Commission 1983b, 1985b).

A study of municipal impacts in four Pinelands townships (Government Finance Associates 1982) indicated only minor effects in three of them. But in Woodland Township, a drop in vacant land values had shifted the property tax burden onto homeowners (see Chapter 6, "Woodland Township"). Generally, the effects on municipalities, with the exception of Woodland Township, are seen as minor (New Jersey Pinelands Commission 1983b, 1985b).

The economic analyses contain few surprises. But the data bases used and the time elapsed between enactment of the CMP and completion of the studies were not sufficient to draw strong conclusions. In some instances, this allowed a bit of leeway for making qualified generalizations and predictions based on limited data. The commission, while careful to qualify any such statements, took advantage of opportunities to cast partial results in a light that reflects favorably on the CMP and commission actions. Economic monitoring became an ongoing activity in the mid 1980s, after the commission brought an economist on staff.

Although the Comprehensive Management Plan is meant to be both an ecological and cultural management plan, regional ecology has had the lion's share of the attention. The commission has, however, made belated efforts to incorporate cultural concerns into its planning and management activities. Barry Brady, an archeologist, was brought on staff and worked with government officials, planners, historians, and architects to develop a *Cultural Resources Management Plan* (New Jersey Pinelands Commission 1986b). This well-crafted, informative document spells out the commission's cultural policies for historic sites. Based on the former Heritage Conservation and Recreation Service's RP 3 model ("Resource Protection Planning Process"), it classifies Pinelands material culture into agricultural, industrial, and architectural study units. Municipalities are given guidelines for treatment of historic period sites. Depending on a site's "significance," some level of documentation, mitigation of development impacts, or avoidance of the site altogether is advised. In 1988, the Pinelands Commission (1988a, 1988b) issued a model historic preservation ordinance and historic area delineations for towns and villages. In 1990, the commission adopted revisions to the 1986 *Cultural Resources Management Plan*. The revisions were aimed at simplifying the identification, evaluation, and protection of local historic sites (New Jersey Pinelands Commission 1990b).

Amendments to the CMP made municipal treatment of cultural resource impacts a mandatory part of the development review process. This has opened the door to a time-consuming, expensive process that some developers and residents perceive as monumental waste in search of a few arrowheads. Indeed, the question of what constitutes a "significant" cultural resource was, for a time, a point of contention between the Pinelands Commission and the National Park Service. The commission favored a broad definition of cultural significance that would allow considerable scope for review and regulation, even though in many cases that power might never be exercised. Park Service representatives argued for a more narrow definition, one that would restrict from the outset the circumstances under which development review power is exercised. The recommendations contained in the *Cultural Resources Management Plan* are the product of a series of compromises. Noteworthy, though, is the commission's emphasis on the "regulable" aspects of culture and history.

The Pinelands Commission also has sought to bolster its research and education activities in the postconformance era. In 1984, the Pinelands Educational Advisory Council was created to direct the commission's education programs. In the same year, the Pinelands Research and Management Council was established. Representatives from the state and federal governments, the Rutgers University Division of Pinelands Research, and Stockton State College advise the commission on research priorities and help develop funding strategies. Most council recommendations fall squarely within the realm of Pinelands ecology (Council on Pinelands Research and Management 1986).

Among specific recent studies authorized or conducted by the Pinelands Commission are assessments of the Pinelands Development Credit Program (Kehde 1987; New Jersey Pinelands Commission 1988a), an infrastructure master plan (Roy F. Weston, Inc. 1986) and financing plan (New Jersey Pinelands Commission 1987b), evaluations of innovative septic systems (New Jersey Pinelands Commission 1986a, 1990a), development of wetlands delineation models (New Jersey Pinelands Commission 1985a, 1990c), and development of a management plan for the pygmy pine forest, 3,800 acres of which were designated a state natural area in 1989.

The commission has directed considerable recent attention to both surface and groundwater issues. It works with county health departments to compile surface-water data. In parts of Camden County, Pinelands water is being exported in the form of sewage; it is drawn from the Kirkwood and Cohansey aquifers and discharged into the Delaware River Basin, outside the Pinelands. In response to concerns about this practice, the commission adopted CMP amendments that reduce residential development densities allowed in Camden County growth areas. Additional concerns about water withdrawals both within the Pines and from portions of critical aquifers that extend beyond the Pines have prompted calls for a major new study of the Kirkwood–Cohansey system. In conjunction with the U.S. Geological Survey, the Pinelands Commission is seeking funding for a five-year, $6.1 million study of the effects of large-scale water withdrawals. In short, existing legislation prohibiting export of Pinelands water has hardly put contentious hydrologic issues to rest.

Most of the studies with which the Pinelands Commission is involved employ the talents of biologists, ecologists, hydrologists, soil scientists, and—more recently—economists. The commission had only a very limited role in recent studies of Pinelands folklife (Hufford 1986; Moonsammy, Cohen, and Williams 1987); it had a larger part in the Pinelands Interpretation Study (Pinelands Interpretation Committee 1984) and the Pinelands Cultural Resource Plan (New Jersey Pinelands Commission 1986b). For the most part, though, the commission has provided little in the way of inspiration, funding, or technical expertise for social, cultural, or historic studies. Its limited contributions have dealt mostly with prehistory. Still, by the mid 1980s, the Pinelands Commission had begun to show a modicum of interest in Pine Barrens residents that went beyond the realm of development review.

By the mid 1980s, much Pinelands Commission business had become essentially a series of routine activities. Monthly commission meetings brought little in the way of surprises or excitement. Under Governor Kean, the commission had become more localist and politically conservative in its orientation. As a result, commission staff operated within narrower constraints than was the case during the earliest Pinelands years, when they were able to make decisions and regulate the timing and flow of information to the commissioners with the expectation of receiving most commissioners' support (Batory, 1982 interview). Indeed, inasmuch as they control the flow of information, the planning staff have power (Foresta 1981; Forester 1982; Koebel 1979). Pinelands Commission staff have perhaps made greatest use of this power as a means to delay dealing with particular problems; in essence, as a means of conflict reduction or avoidance. But staff interests have been changing. Although much of the commission's staff still consists of relatively young "ecological enthusiasts," this is changing to some degree. For example, an engineer now works alongside the biologists and ecologists on the development review staff.

Like other players in the Pinelands game, commission staff adapted well to the changing political circumstances of the 1980s. In fair measure, the staff retained its ability to anticipate and shape the responses of the commissioners to specific issues. Some commissioners have made it known that they are well aware of this, and quite concerned about it. Michael Hogan, of Burlington County, has challenged the executive director and other staff members on specific issues, and it was he who suggested that the commissioners hold retreats and that they assume a more contemplative posture, independent of the staff. The first retreat was held in 1987.

For some time, environmentalists have been concerned about the Pinelands Commission's apparent complacency. Several environmentalists complained that the first plan review demonstrated that the commission was an entrenched bureaucracy (Jackson and Walnut, 1985 interviews). Clearly, the environmental community's influence is not what it once was; indeed, the commission's lone remaining "environmentalist" in 1985 (and some of the more orthodox preservationists might question this characterization) was Candace McKee Ashmun, one of Governor Byrne's original appointees. Nonetheless, the commission's day-to-day activities still center around vegetation and water-quality matters. And this emphasis is well represented in recommendations made by the Council on Pinelands Research and Management (1986). Moreover, as part of its latest plan review and amendment cycle, the commission was working in 1991 to tighten requirements for granting "waivers of strict compliance" from the CMP's performance standards for development. Environmental organizations are still strong, even if some of their turf has been yielded to economic development interests. Though the political adjustments continue, the environmental spirit of Pinelands planning is not likely to be broken.

The first several years of the Pinelands program were years of lost opportunities—at least in terms of developing creative and equitable approaches to reconciling metropolitan interests with rural concerns. The bulk of the time and resources went first to securing local conformance and later to a burdensome and not very productive review of the planning effort. Throughout, the legal defense of the CMP was a concern of the first order. Only toward the conclusion of the plan review process did the Pinelands Commission begin seriously to consider broader questions such as historic preservation, interpretation, primary and secondary education, and economic development. The Pinelands management infrastructure was securely in place by the mid 1980s; thus the commission was able to tackle these questions without feeling as threatened as it might have in earlier years. But the responses to the newly raised questions quickly became programmatical and mechanical, and commissioners grew increasingly complacent. The business at hand would be dispensed with expeditiously, and the new or unexpected would be quickly routinized.

Most local opposition had been quieted by the mid 1980s, and additional measures aimed at mollifying landowners were put in place in the late 1980s and early 1990s. Plans for a $5 million visitors' complex that might have brought unwanted "national park" status to the Pines were deleted from Senator Bill Bradley's 1988 Pinelands bill; the Pinelands Commission adopted a program in 1990 to identify for public acquisition small parcels of land rendered virtually worthless by the CMP (Congress had authorized $1 million of Bradley bill acquisition funds for this purpose); two staff "liasons" were assigned in 1990 to work with development applicants and property owners; and the commission began in 1990 to alter the times and places of its monthly meetings, making it easier for Pinelands residents to attend. Indirectly, perhaps, these actions spoke to the concerns of the Pinelands Landowners Society, which was formed in 1987 to represent small landowners. Whatever the intent of the various accommodations, opposition to Pinelands planning remained rather muted. So, too, did environmental support (see Chapter 5), at least for a time. Public debate was generally viewed as acrimonious and counterproductive to the Pinelands effort. One could, of course, argue that this allowed the Pinelands Commission to get on with the job of "preserving, protecting, and enhancing" the Pinelands. In response, two questions might be raised: Was the

Pinelands program achieving its goals? And if it was, was it doing so in the best possible manner?

As a matter of bureaucratic convention, the Pinelands Commission is virtually bound to answer the first question in the affirmative and try to elude the second. But even the most impassioned preservationist would probably be hard pressed to argue that the absence of a strong, centralized Pinelands planning program would have meant the total destruction of the ecological resource. Given the growing sophistication of local planning, the ever-present threat of stronger regional controls (even if they are not actually imposed), the ability of state and federal governments to pursue environmental objectives by selectively controlling purse strings, and economic and social trends that would seem to have favored a slow pace of development in large areas of the Pines, it may well be that the role of Pinelands planning in effecting desirable environmental outcomes is overestimated. But the Pinelands program has put the machinery in place for long-term protection of Pinelands resources, whatever definition one may wish to accept for protection. Of course, that planning machinery may be manipulated. It is always possible to assert that the program's goals have been achieved, or at least partly achieved, simply because the goals are so loosely defined that there is wide latitude for interpretation (Bogden and Taylor 1975; Floden and Weiner 1978). In this scenario, only the most glaring abrogation of the original intent of the Pinelands protection legislation could clearly be labeled a failure. And larger questions of efficiency and equity can be bypassed altogether. Indeed, at their February 1991 tenth-anniversary party, the Pinelands Commission and friends engaged in a festival of self-aggrandizement, averting many of the more searching social and political questions.

8

Pinelands Planning in Perspective

In the face of many obstacles, the Pinelands program not only has endured but has prospered (Babcock and Siemon 1985; Moore 1986; Rielley, Larsen, and Weaver 1984). It has weathered various legislative, administrative, and legal storms—many gentle, others quite threatening. By many reckonings, this alone indicates success. But there are broader considerations. In addressing them, this chapter speaks to major concerns raised at the book's outset: the Pinelands as a place, equity in regional management, and politics of regional plan implementation.

The principal impetus for regional planning came from outside the region, from interest groups and political impulses favoring ecological preservation. Local residents and interest groups, by contrast, believe that most environmental planning should be done at the local level. They tend to give far greater weight to human concerns than do their more ecocentric counterparts based outside the Pines.

Though its genesis and early evolution tended toward the ecocentric, the Pinelands Commission has since had to go to considerable lengths to accommodate local concerns about property values, taxes, economic development, and self-determination. Indeed, local citizens, politicians, and entrepreneurs have not been merely passive, if unhappy, subjects of commission rule; they have influenced the planning process in important ways (though not necessarily in ways that can be interpreted as fair or equitable). In this concluding chapter, I consider some of the broad social, political, and economic implications of these environmental conflicts—and their accommodation.

The Pinelands as a Place—or Places

Is there a Pinelands region beyond those defined by physical criteria or administrative fiat? Are notions of Piney culture and Pine Barrens wilderness mere abstractions, part of a created dichotomy between city and countryside (Birnbaum 1991; Fitzsimmons 1989; Smith 1984)? In other words, are the Pinelands essentially a social construct?

Few could disagree that both scholarly and popular interest in Pine Barrens ecology and folklore have surged in recent years. And to the extent that even the most vague, generalized name recognition of the Pinelands–Pines–Pine Barrens has increased over the past several years, we could argue that the notion of the Pinelands as a coherent region has gained wider acceptance. Changing popular perceptions have not only helped the Pinelands emerge in name; they have gone a long way toward creating a more informed and compassionate "regional idea." Earlier notions about degenerate, incestuous Pineys have given way to greater interest in the region's physical and cultural attributes. Among the factors responsible are general growth in environmental awareness over the past two decades, John McPhee's writings about the Pine Barrens (McPhee 1967, 1974), and all the attention generated by recent planning issues and activities.

Yet the end result of all the consciousness raising may be a highly romanticized view of a charming folk culture, replete with natives living in rustic cabins, making their livings gathering berries and pinecones. True, the Pines possess some special cultural qualities— made possible by their unusual physical character and made visible by their "isolation" in the midst of the nation's most densely populated megalopolis. But the existence of a clearly distinguishable, regional folk culture is questionable. Still, this need not constrain us from "inventing" one, just as traditions have been invented in various other cultural contexts (Hobsbawm and Ranger 1983).

Often, representations of traditional Pine Barrens activities are not qualified by a realistic portrait of contemporary life in the Pines. Even the New Jersey State Museum's 1987 exhibit on Pinelands culture and traditions—in most respects a thoughtful, sensitive portrayal of Pinelands history—overemphasized the past in the context of the present. Clearly, society as a whole can benefit by preserving traditional knowledge, understanding its past, creating opportunities for those who wish to engage in traditional activities, and even cultivating a sense of heritage among those who do not (see Lowenthal 1968; Lowenthal and Binney 1981). But at the same time, we must understand that the everyday lives of Pine Barrens residents are—and in fact always have been—thoroughly woven into the surrounding metropolitan cultural and economic fabrics. Many a contemporary Piney (leaving aside for a moment the contentiousness of that label), who treasures the physical and cultural assets of the Pines in ways not always immediately obvious to outsiders, cannot understand why this sentiment should condemn him or her to a lifestyle of limited economic and cultural opportunities. Similar sentiments abound in New York State's Adirondack Park. Like the Pineys, many an Adirondacker has fears about becoming museumized: classified, in essence, as an endangered species to be carefully managed along with the rest of the region's flora and fauna.

The distinction between insiders and outsiders, between local and extralocal interests, is not always easy to make. Not all Pinelands-based interest groups, for example, have as their main constituencies local residents. An example is the Whitesbog Preservation Trust. Its historic preservation work is carried on from offices in the Pine Barrens, yet it chiefly represents preservationist interests based outside the region. Conversely, an important part of the mission of the New Jersey Builders Association, which operates mainly outside the Pines, is to represent forcefully those vocal Pine Barrens sentiments that coincide with the interests of the housebuilding community. The New Jersey Farm Bureau, a statewide farmers' group, takes positions on Pinelands issues more in accord with those of local Pinelands politicians than with larger statewide agricultural concerns. And then there are the unlikely alliances, respecting few traditional spatial or political boundaries, that coalesce around specific issues such as facility siting (landfills, utility lines, transmission towers, and the like) or local growth management.

Enigmatic issues of spatial definition notwithstanding, it is safe to say that "metropolitan interests" have predominated in Pinelands management. For this reason, the Pinelands National Reserve might be considered an instrument of urban expansion, especially if open space and ecological protection are seen as products of that expansion. The restructuring of space to satisfy urban needs and desires defines—in fact, "creates"—places like the Pinelands. Although shared images and perceptual boundaries elude rigorous definition, our communal conceptions of locales such as the Pine Barrens nonetheless are immensely important in shaping our thinking about nature and culture. What was formerly a lot of pine trees is now seen as a largely unspoiled, though threatened, wilderness—this despite the fact that the Pines have been thoroughly exploited for their resources for three centuries. Culture and traditions are invented, or at least transformed and magnified in the popular imagination, to create the idea of a simple and harmonious relationship between people and environment. Perhaps this helps fulfill a deep societal need (Birch 1990; Marx 1964; Nash 1982; Oelschlaeger 1991; Schmitt 1969; Short 1991; Williams 1973), a yearning sustained and nurtured by the environmentalism of the 1970s.

The Pinelands experience, as I have presented it, suggests that before attempting to reconcile competing conceptions of the region, land use planners should become as familiar as they can with the bases for those differing conceptions. The Pinelands "ecological region," for example, is not the same spatial entity as the elusive Pinelands "culture region." The former, at least, can be delineated with some certainty; the latter is conceptually questionable. Indeed, there are really multiple physical and cultural regions. In the physical realm, we can define various hydrologic, vegetation, and soil regions. Then there are the much more evasive political, cultural, and economic regions—or, more appropriately I would argue—subregions. Finally, we have to consider all these regions—most of them already eluding clear definition by any "objective" measure—as perceived, as social constructs. Although the descriptive section of the Pinelands plan reveals an awareness of the multiplicity of approaches to regionalization, that awareness is not carried through to the plan's regulations and their implementation.

Regional planners must first be good regional analysts; they should try to understand the complex physical, political, cultural, and economic textures of their planning areas. That knowledge then becomes integral to the various planning rationales put forth. Indeed, from different ecological, economic, cultural, and other rationales should emerge different planning boundaries and planning processes. If there is to be a comprehensive plan, it should either be dedicated to some single purpose or sufficiently flexible to accommodate the requisite diversity of purposes. The latter would imply that the planning area be seen as many places, with many needs. The Pinelands experience shows us that we have a great deal to learn about reconciling contemporary societal needs with our desires to understand and preserve (in whatever form) valued physical environments and traditional ways of life.

Equity in Regional Management

Benefits and costs of Pinelands planning are unevenly distributed within the Pinelands, outside the Pinelands, and across the elusive boundary that separates inside from outside. Indeed, equity is a central issue that precedes and accompanies any regional planning scheme. Yet many of the benefits and costs are intangible; they are difficult to describe in even the most general terms. Moreover, one individual's or organization's cost is another's benefit, even, at times, when the parties in question are immediate neighbors.

Although it is difficult to draw simple, unambiguous conclusions about the overall distribution of costs and benefits, it seems fair to conclude that interests from outside the Pines have reaped much of the immediate benefit. They, particularly those concerned with ecological protection, have set the terms for regional management and have succeeded in removing a good deal of local control to the state–federal level. This loss of local control has generated widespread resentment inside the region, inflicting wounds that may be very slow to heal. For more than two centuries, the Pines have been plundered for their natural resources—not, perhaps, as thoroughly as Appalachia (Caudill 1962; Erikson 1976), but extensively nonetheless. When the interests of the mass society shifted toward ecological protection, external dominance of the region took on new form and vigor. In part, at least, that increased dominance is the product of a universal trend toward decreased local autonomy

(Vidich and Bensman 1968); in recent decades, increased state and federal financing and oversight of programs have preempted a good deal of local decision-making authority. But the remainder of the explanation, and the most important part of it, has to do with circumstances specific to the Pinelands.

It is not surprising that in populous states like New York, New Jersey, and California, we find widespread general support for critical area protection and planning. Yet in the affected areas themselves, opposition to state oversight often is intense (see Elazar 1984; Hays 1987). In the statehouse or governor's mansion, though, that opposition may be heard as little more than an annoying whisper. A great many citizens are in favor of environmental protection; only a few are opposed. Still, the deafening roar of statewide approval does not always drown out cries of local opposition. A conservative legislature may be sympathetic to local views—and any legislature engages in vote trading. Opponents of state regulation may be willing to trade a lot to get their way; indeed, in their districts local autonomy and control over one's land are often among the most pressing political issues.

Hahn and Dyballa (1981), in their analysis of regional land use programs in New York State, argue that one key ingredient for success is strong statewide support. In the Adirondacks, this support was present in the early 1970s. One reason that proposals for a Catskills Commission were defeated in the 1970s was that statewide support, though strong, was not strong enough—at least not over a sufficient period—to enable passage of the necessary legislation. In New Jersey, statewide support for Pinelands protection, if not necessarily overwhelming, certainly has been sufficient to sustain a strong program. Rather than Hahn and Dyballa's robust backing, though, it appears that abundant statewide sentiment ranging between indifference and "motherhood and apple pie" support permitted Pinelands planning to move forward.

But more insidious forces may be driving regional land use control. The Pinelands offer important assets: open space, vast reserves of pure groundwater, and the prospect of an exclusive and accessible exurban residential refuge. Are planning and management agendas being set by influential capitalist interests based outside the Pine Barrens? Before the 1989 establishment of the Pinelands Preservation Alliance, the Pinelands had no equivalent to the Adirondack Council, an organization whose directorship is dominated by wealthy, influential landowners whose principal residences are outside the Adirondacks. Nor is membership of the Pinelands Commission so constructed. One could, however, look critically at the membership of the New Jersey Conservation Foundation (NJCF). The NJCF, consisting in its first incarnation of wealthy landowners opposed to a jetport in northern New Jersey's Great Swamp, is at present active in Pinelands issues—indeed, it spearheaded the effort that led to creation of the Pinelands Preservation Alliance. But the NJCF is only one among several key Pinelands players (Chapter 5), and the influence it wields over regional planning is not comparable to that wielded by the Adirondack Council. Time will tell how influential the Pinelands Preservation Alliance becomes, and what interests it truly represents. To date, though, the most active individuals and organizations in the Pinelands have been those whose status lends itself to "local," not national or international, influence.

In parts of the region—near Atlantic City, and to a much lesser degree in Ocean County—powerful oligopolistic interests have stakes in the organization and use of Pinelands space. But these are not critical stakes. In the Adirondacks and various other critical areas, it can be argued that big capital has significant stakes in both resource protection and resource exploitation (see Heiman 1983, 1988; Plotkin 1987; Walker and Heiman 1981). But the stakes are generally smaller in the Pinelands. The concerns of Atlantic City–based capitalist interests lie principally within the city and its immediate surroundings. And many Ocean County developers, though their financial holdings are substantial, are best characterized as regional players. Further, there seems to be little reason for large capital interests to promote planning for an area the size of the Pinelands. If anything, a smaller regional planning authority would suit their purposes well—one, for example, that managed growth only in Atlantic County (Mason 1986). This is the part of the Pinelands where expansionist forces of capitalism have, in several localities, collided with exclusionary property rights (Plotkin 1987). The case study of Hamilton Township (Chapter 6) provides a prime example. In 1990, Governor Florio created a state–city council to promote Atlantic City revitalization (Jenkins 1990). But commercial and industrial development is being promoted, not only in the city, but also in the Atlantic County growth nodes of the Pinelands. A high-priority project is the Atlantic City International Airport in Egg Harbor Township, in the Pines.

The critical Pinelands resource that may ultimately serve industrial and urban needs is its vast supply of pure groundwater. As described in Chapter 4, Joseph Wharton was thwarted in his efforts to divert Pinelands waters to neighboring Philadelphia when the New Jersey legislature in 1884 unanimously approved legislation prohibiting export of state waters. In that same decade, concerns about destructive logging practices led to creation of the Adirondack Forest Preserve. An important distinction between the Adirondacks and the Pines is in the nature and comprehensiveness of early state regulation: Whereas the Adirondack Forest Preserve was created in 1885, New Jersey voters turned down an option to purchase the Wharton Tract in 1915. Not until 1950 did the state acquire the land.

Today, any export of water more than ten miles beyond Pinelands boundaries is prohibited by state law. Yet the region remains rife with conspiracy theories about northern New Jersey's future designs on that water. It is not at all inconceivable that at some point in the future—perhaps the very near future—Pinelands water might be mined to serve the urban–industrial needs of the surrounding megalopolis. Indeed, Pine Barrens aquifers, and as a probable consequence Pine Barrens ecology, are already affected by groundwater withdrawals beyond Pinelands boundaries, as well as permitted water withdrawals for consumptive purposes (that is, those uses where water is not returned to its immediate hydrologic source). But one would be rather hard pressed to argue that creation of a megalopolitan water preserve was part of the grand design of Pinelands planning. Only diehard conspiracy thinkers, most of them from southern New Jersey, are prepared to make this case. Fueled by deep resentment sustained by decades of political domination from the north, many residents of South Jersey have convinced themselves beyond doubt that this is the sole reason, or at least a major underlying reason, for the establishment of the Pinelands National Reserve. In the Adirondacks, the evidence is much more conclusive: The Adirondack Forest Preserve was established first and foremost as a water and timber preserve (Graham 1978; Heiman 1983, 1988; Liroff and Davis 1981; Terrie 1981). In the Pinelands, by contrast, there is scant evidence of legislative or political intent to create a water preserve to be tapped for future megalopolitan drinking water or industrial use.

Rather than grand conspiracies or designs, we encounter in Pine-

lands planning and management a mosaic of relatively small con-
tests—each of them, however, immensely important to those deeply
engaged in them. What has inspired and guided much of Pinelands
planning is the desire to preserve and protect a large ecological
laboratory. In its implementation, this vision has been considerably tempered by the political and financial concerns of powerful
local interests. Nationally, the phenomenon that has most influenced Pinelands events, and in particular played a major part in the
timing of the Comprehensive Management Plan, appears to be environmentalism of the 1970s. What this has meant for the 1980s,
and in turn will mean for the 1990s and beyond, is discussed next.

The Politics of Accommodation

I have already described the ways in which key Pinelands interests have adapted to a shifting political landscape. In employing
the strategies that it did, the Pinelands program is not alone; indeed, no state-level or regional environmental protection program
has been sustained without at least some compromises. Quiet Revolution programs have had to reconcile themselves to the fact that
they cannot usurp too many local planning functions. Indeed, that
realization yielded numerous legal, administrative, and procedural
compromises (DeGrove 1984, 1986, 1989; Popper 1981, 1988),
some of which are described in Chapter 2. With the benefit of hind-
sight, the Pinelands Commission could take advantage of many of
these Quiet Revolution experiences. And to a considerable degree,
it has. When it adopted its first set of substantive plan amendments,
the Pinelands Commission followed the Quiet Revolution's lead by
simplifying development application requirements. But the Pinelands Commission had the benefit of Quiet Revolution experience
from the outset; as a result, its requirements generally were not so
onerous and time-consuming to begin with. The procedural streamlining might better be characterized as fine-tuning than a major
overhaul.

Quiet Revolution prophets Richard Babcock and Charles Siemon
(1985) present an example—by no means an isolated case—of
brazen revolutionary arrogance on the part of California's North
Central Coastal Commission. Despite the considerable education
provided the Pinelands program by such Quiet Revolution failings,

one of the most commonly articulated complaints about the Pinelands Commission, as evidenced in a majority of the interviews
conducted at the township level, is that Pinelands Commission staff
are arrogant. But this resentment has never grown into the widespread, at times approaching violent, opposition experienced in
New York State's Adirondack Park. Perhaps this is because the Pinelands staff, cognizant of the Adirondack Park Agency's experiences
(the staffs of the two agencies have consulted with each other),
realized that regulatory might must be carefully tempered from the
outset. Moreover, Pinelands residents, intensely concerned as they
are, may not be quite so strongly motivated about land use issues
as are Adirondackers. Because the Pinelands are less physically (if
not economically and politically) isolated from the megalopolitan
core, there may be a somewhat greater merging of interests and
sentiments with those of nearby urban areas.

The passage of time tends to soften local hostility toward regional planning. Indeed, until very recently, it seemed that enough
time had gone by and enough changes had been made for regional
planning to gain the grudging acceptance of most Adirondackers.
But in an apparent reversal of the trend toward accommodating
local Adirondack interests, Governor Mario Cuomo in 1989 created
the Commission on the Adirondacks in the Twenty-First Century.
Concerned about subdivision of large parcels of forested land, as
well as excessive development permitted under current regulations,
the commission presented to the governor a highly controversial
set of recommendations (Commission on the Adirondacks in the
Twenty-First Century 1990). Among other things, the commission recommended that New York State acquire 655,000 acres of
lands (initially, in large part, through purchase of easements); that
only one principal structure be permitted on parcels up to 2,000
acres in size and one structure for each 2,000 acres thereafter in
the "resource management" zones; that more stringent siting and
performance standards be adopted; and that a one-year subdivision
and development moratorium be applied to resource management,
rural use, and shoreline zones. At the same time, the commission
called for subsidies for economic development (especially in the
forestry and tourism industries), affordable housing programs, and
new health-care and education programs.

The report met with intense local resistance (Mason 1991). And
in a matter of months, the Governor's Office and environmental sup-

porters tempered their zeal for new legislation and land-acquisition programs. Furthermore, their efforts were set back when the state's voters rejected a 1990 bond issue that would have provided funds for land acquisition. At any rate, an economic recession combined with a major state fiscal crisis did not bode well for major new legislative initiatives. Heightened national environmental concern of the late 1980s and early 1990s had little effect in boosting the cause of land use regulation in the Adirondacks. Although the final outcome remains uncertain, the entire process—with its strong environmental initiatives tempered in the face of intense local opposition—bears considerable resemblance to the course of events during the 1970s. Only in this case the time frame is greatly compressed.

The recent tactical retreat in the Adirondacks excepted, most legislative and regulatory accommodations (reported in Chapter 2) occurred in the mid to late 1970s. During those years, the Quiet Revolution was on the wane, and the nation was beset with economic recession, oil crises, and Watergate and its repercussions. The Pinelands program was conceived toward the end of this period of reassessment and consolidation, and it prospered during the much more environmentally conservative Reagan era. But even in the absence of major federal initiatives, the 1980s witnessed some reaffirmation and strengthening of earlier state-level programs (DeGrove 1984, 1986, 1989; Popper 1988), as well as the introduction of a variety of new ones. Many of the new programs are highly centralized in structure, but more spatially constricted and specialized in purpose than the programs of the 1970s. Their objectives include energy, industrial, and waste-facility siting; farmland preservation; groundwater protection; and regulation of wetlands, floodplains, and other sensitive areas (Popper 1988).

But the Pinelands program—with its regional critical-area orientation, multiple purposes, wide-ranging vision, and regulatory might—is much more in keeping with the spirit of the Quiet Revolution. Its remarkable success in "reforming" local planning practices—something Quiet Revolution programs generally failed to accomplish—has been facilitated in part by New Jersey's predispositions toward land use planning and environmental protection. Still, as I have argued, the Pinelands program has taken many cues from the Quiet Revolution, benefiting not only from its successes but also its shortcomings.

Why, then, did the Pinelands Commission and the State of New

Jersey still have to make significant concessions to local elites? In part, their actions may be explained by the need to adjust to shifting political winds of the 1980s. More significant, though, may have been the need to leave negotiating space: If too many concessions had been granted early on, not only would environmental supporters have been alienated, but the commission and legislature would have foreclosed future bargaining options.

Although the promotion of greater inter- and intraregional equity is one of the effects of these adjustments, it would be hard to argue that the redistribution is a very fair one; certainly it has little in common with the social-welfare aspirations of earlier regional planning endeavors (Chapter 2). Nonetheless, the tax reimbursement and infrastructure bond programs should assist some communities in bearing the costs imposed on them by the Pinelands plan, and the buyouts of some small property owners will provide additional relief. The transfer of development rights scheme (Chapter 4) may in theory also promote greater inter- and intraregional equity, but its lack of vigor through much of the 1980s limited its effectiveness. In some cases, the costs of Pinelands planning may be more psychological than economic (see Chapters 5, 6); in this regard, the effect of recent measures may be more one of equalizing satisfaction (or lessening some of the worst dissatisfaction) with the Pinelands plan than equalizing economic welfare. Future analyses may assist in sorting out these issues, but they, too, will surely have their biases favoring the politically appropriate responses to difficult questions.

Summary and Prospect

One of the most potent observations that can be made about Pinelands planning is that it has worked. But success has a high price: The plan, to a degree even greater than the Quiet Revolution programs of the 1970s, has usurped a good deal of local initiative. Through this book, I have argued for a different scenario, one in which regional environmental planning gives fitting respect and weight to local concerns and desires. Yet there are dilemmas inherent in doing so. Respect for local interests may well imply acceptance of corrupt local officials and unjust practices. Is this price worth paying—or, perhaps, is the regional planning authority obligated to try to correct what it sees as dishonest and unfair? Should we assume that regional or state agencies are themselves beyond moral and ethical reproach?

The high price of preserving local self-determination may be one worth paying. Moreover, local governments may not be as environmentally irresponsible as many a preservationist would have us believe. Pinelands planning notwithstanding, Healy and Rosenberg (1979) found that local government's role was indeed better recognized in the post–Quiet Revolution era of land use management. Popper (1981) points out that local planning itself had changed by the 1970s, with environmental concerns increasingly evident in local planning decisions. There seems little basis for the assumption so widely shared among environmental planning advocates that all small-town planners, or at least the vast majority, are ignorant, selfish, or inept.

Berger and Sinton (1985) argue for a more locally based approach to Pinelands planning. So did Congressmen Forsythe and Hughes in 1978 when they proposed the establishment of "ecological management units" in the Pines (Chapter 4, "The Federal Role"). Although it is beyond the scope of this book to examine specific subregional schemes rigorously, it is abundantly clear that subregionalization is in keeping with the human ecological character of the Pines. Geographical areas that residents understand and know, and within which there is some degree of social homogeneity, are the subregions of the Pine Barrens, not the large and diverse area that constitutes the Pinelands planning area. But delineating such subregions is no trivial task. Moreover, even if a subregional approach were favored, local opposition might still be considerable. There would surely be charges of discrimination, inequity, and intent to divide and conquer. Berger and Sinton's 1985 attempt at subregionalization (Map 2), while founded on solid precepts, would need extensive "field testing" and refinement before it might actually be accepted by the residents it is meant to serve. Regrettably, Pinelands planning has gone well beyond the point where such an approach might be seriously considered, let alone put into place.

While Pinelands planning has succeeded administratively, it has not been especially sensitive to local human needs. Essentially, a large zoning map was superimposed on the region and made to work through legal and administrative fiat. The formal planning process lasted about one year, hardly enough time for serious consultation with localities. Pinelands planners argue that however desirable such consultation might have been, it would have consumed too much time: precious time that the plan's opponents would have used to undo the program entirely. Moreover, there was the looming threat—though hardly foreseen as early as 1978—of a hostile federal administration. Had the plan not been sealed and delivered by early 1981, local opponents might have used this development to their advantage.

These factors cannot be discounted. At the same time, we need to remember that these threats loom especially large when nurtured by widely held negative perceptions of local government. Indeed, many environmentalists and other advocates of regional planning feel that most local officials are neither technically competent nor sufficiently motivated to deal with regional concerns, perhaps not even to represent their own constituents in these matters. There are few exceptions to this planning gospel. One notable one, though, is New York State's Tug Hill program (Dyballa, Raymond, and Hahn 1981; Marsh 1981). Here, support for regional planning—albeit planning of a far less comprehensive nature than that in the Pines—was built virtually from the bottom up. Regional planners worked closely with local residents, and "circuit riders" traveled from town meeting to town meeting. Other possible, though imperfect, models for the bottom-up approach to regional planning include the renewed attempt of a humbled National Park Service (following an initial spectacular failure) at recreational planning along the Upper Delaware River (Pontier 1987), and planning for lands adjacent to national estuarine reserves (Clark and McCreary 1987). These examples stand in contrast to the Pinelands experience and the many Quiet Revolution programs that employ top-down approaches to planning.

In recent years, the Pinelands program has conceded much more to locally based interests than it did during its first few years. But this was not the result of any overt change of administrative heart on the Pinelands Commission's part; rather, it was a response to political realities. New Jersey's solid commitment to comprehensive regulation of its critical environmental areas—embraced by its environmental organizations and widely supported (or at least met with indifference) by the general public—was not powerful enough to subsume the concerns of local governments and entrepreneurs. Not surprisingly, the local political and economic interests that lobbied for Pinelands concessions are among the greatest beneficiaries (Birnbaum 1989a, b, c; 1991). Benefits to Pine Barrens residents not politically well connected tend to be largely coincidental.

The case studies in Chapter 6 portray a Pine Barrens populace holding deep convictions about environmental protection, accompanied by varying degrees of resistance to increased governmental control (especially nonlocal). Is it possible to create land use planning programs that achieve regional environmental protection while responding to such local sentiments? The Pinelands experience would suggest that it probably is, but that such ventures are likely to be costly, difficult, and fraught with their own setbacks and inequities. At any rate, future land use programs will have to contend with more and better-articulated local concerns. Vigilant citizens will watch over them more closely than ever. Land use controls might in some cases even be demanded by local stakeholders who have traditionally opposed regional planning. But in contrast with the Quiet Revolution model, these controls would be very specific in purpose and circumscribed in spatial extent.

Environmental concern appears once again to be on the ascendancy in America. But it is accompanied, at least within local contexts, by continuing mistrust of government and corporate intentions. This may also imply wider distrust of local government and entrepreneurial interests than has been evident in the recent past. If there is to be another "revolution" in land use planning, it is almost certain to be more genuinely localist and grass roots than the first. And while this does not mean that all Quiet Revolution impulses will grind to a halt, it suggests that they will be forced to adapt to diverse and constantly changing—and as a result highly unpredictable—political currents. This is precisely what political economists such as Walker and Heiman (1981) and Plotkin (1987) argue that the Quiet Revolution sought to avert.

Given these constraints, one of the more politically palatable forms of land management may be outright acquisition, either by governments or by private land trusts. Of course, acquisition is expensive. It also requires willing sellers—or, alternatively, that eminent domain powers be invoked. If we assume only the former, and downplay any threat of the latter, then it is fair to say, as Foresta (1981) does, that the occasional outright acquisition of land usually arouses much less hostility than does land use regulation. This is supported by interview results from Pinelands towns and by Wolf's 1981 remark that there is more opposition to the regulation of one's land than to environmental protection. But land acquisition is no panacea; not only are funding prospects generally rather bleak, but in a highly charged climate of local suspicion, even a modest acquisition program may prompt considerable protest. Indeed, the 1990 report of the Commission on the Adirondacks in the Twenty-First Century, with its ambitious proposal for eventual state acquisition of 655,000 acres, prompted a firestorm of local opposition. Besides, massive acquisition programs are not what the framers of the greenline planning concept had in mind.

Whatever the specific mix of management techniques, perhaps the most effective accommodation with local concerns is achieved when clear, immediate, and affordable benefits accompany regional planning. Such benefits have been offered in the Pinelands, for example, in the way of local tax reimbursements and infrastructure funding. Even such "bribes," however, are likely to meet with increasing skepticism, scrutiny, and resistance. Once again, the Adirondacks illustrate this point. A proposed package of state-funded subsidies and incentives has done little, if anything, to lessen the hostility created by the report of the Commission on the Adirondacks in the Twenty-First Century.

The question of how to accommodate increasingly complex, sophisticated, and unpredictable localist sentiment will be fundamental to future local and regional land use endeavors. But this will not be planners' only concern. In closing, I reiterate the broad outlines of three other overarching issues that pervade Pinelands planning. First, what is preservation? Does it imply only minimal human presence? If we assume that wilderness indeed occupies some vital place in our national thinking and welfare (see Birch 1990; Marx 1964; Nash 1982; Oelschlaeger 1991; Schmitt 1969; Short 1991; Williams 1973), then does this mean the unspoken assumption in protecting valued areas is that people, at least in moderate or large numbers, are to be kept out? In part, Pinelands planning has been built on this premise. While the issue may have been more central in the early years, it remains very much alive today.

The second question involves the politics of place. What constitutes a region, and how important is it that we see our lands through the regional lenses of physiography, culture, politics, or economics? While the concept of region can encompass anything from the subtle and permeating to the striking and incontrovertible, regional consciousness remains an elusive affair: It is neither very tangible nor measurable even in a crude way. Still, it can be an essential force in shaping an area's social, political, and economic character, and in turn it is shaped by larger societal forces. Should region be used as an organizing concept in comprehensive planning for valued areas? Even though this issue is central to Pinelands planning, it has not been resolved, or even very thoroughly considered, by the Pinelands Commission. Instead, emphasis has been on defining and protecting the natural region; most social and cultural programs have amounted to little more than added baggage.

This leads to the third question: What are "cultural resources," and if they are valued by some segments of society, what can and should be done to "preserve" or "enhance" them? Perhaps the question seems absurd; the idea of managing culture sounds totalitarian. Yet Berger and Sinton (1985) speak of providing opportunities for cultural self-preservation in the Pine Barrens. This may be plausible and defensible if there is indeed a self-interest in cultural preservation. Unfortunately, the impetus is more likely to originate in romantic yearnings outside the region. Indeed, those seeking to preserve local culture may be longing for regional character and traditions that never, even at their historical peak, lived up to latter-day images. Ample testimony is offered by "Piney Power" bumper stickers displayed by non-Pineys proud to have spent a day in the area. At its most conspicuous excess, in places like Pennsylvania's Amish region, cultural imagery can become a vibrant growth industry. Nothing comparable has happened in the Pines, nor is it likely to. But this should not obscure the larger, seemingly obvious point: We need first to ask what it is we are setting about to save or enhance before we even begin trying to do so. This question never has been squarely faced in the Pinelands.

I am convinced that the Pinelands experience informs us, first and foremost, about local planning and politics. But it also reflects the larger ways in which we think about natural environments, cultural heritage, and self-determination. Many of the questions raised in the preceding pages invite us to think broadly about political trends, residential preferences, recreational needs, and even popular culture. The Pinelands, not long ago an almost forgotten area, are now the focus of local, statewide, national, and international attention. This alone may be the most revealing observation; indeed, it informs much of this book. As we continue to think about how we might best manage our valued places, the Pinelands experience compels us to ask ourselves who "we" are and what it is that we truly value.

References

PRINT AND FILM MATERIALS

Adams, John H., et al. 1985. *An Environmental Agenda for the Future.* Washington, D.C., and Covelo, Calif.: Island Press.

Advisory Commission on Intergovernmental Relations. 1973. *Substate Regionalism and the Federal System.* Vols. 1 and 2. Washington, D.C.: U.S. Government Printing Office.

Alan Mallach Associates. 1980. *Case Study Materials on Pinelands Growth Factors.* Trenton, N.J., and Philadelphia, Pa.: Alan Mallach Associates.

Alexander, Ames. 1990. "Environment Laws Get Mixed Reviews." *Asbury Park Press,* April 17.

Anderson, F. 1973. *NEPA in the Courts.* Baltimore: Johns Hopkins University Press.

Andrews, Richard N. L. 1980. "Class Politics or Democratic Reform: Environmentalism and American Political Institutions." *Natural Resources Journal* 20:221–241.

———. 1985. "Agency Responses to NEPA: A Comparison and Implications." *Natural Resources Journal* 25:122–143.

Anonymous. n.d. "A Brief History of Hamilton Township." Mimeographed.

Archer, Jack H., and Robert W. Knecht. 1987. "The U.S. National Coastal Zone Management Program: Problems and Opportunities in the Next Phase." *Coastal Management* 15:103–120.

Arnstein, Sherry R. 1969. "A Ladder of Citizen Participation." *Journal of the American Institute of Planners* 35:216–224.

AT&T Employees Credit Union. 1989. "The Pine Barrens." *Credit Lines,* Winter.

Ayres, Tom. 1979. "The Pinelands Cultural Society: Folk Music Performance and the Rhetoric of Regional Pride." In *Natural and Cultural Resources of the New Jersey Pine Barrens: Inputs and Research Needs for Planning. Proceedings and Papers of the First Research Conference on the New Jersey Pine Barrens*, edited by John W. Sinton, 225–233. Pomona, N.J.: Stockton State College Center for Environmental Research.

———. 1981. "Home in the Pines: Folk Music Performance and Regional Pride." *New Jersey Folklore* 21:22–27.

Babcock, Richard F. 1966. *The Zoning Game: Municipal Practices and Policies*. Madison: University of Wisconsin Press.

Babcock, Richard F., and Fred P. Bosselman. 1973. *Exclusionary Zoning: Land Use Regulation and Housing in the 1970's*. New York: Praeger.

Babcock, Richard F., and Charles L. Siemon. 1985. *The Zoning Game Revisited*. Cambridge, Mass.: Lincoln Institute of Land Policy.

Batisse, Michel. 1982. "The Biosphere Reserve: A Tool for Environmental Conservation and Management." *Environmental Conservation* 9:101–111.

———. 1985. "Action Plan for Biosphere Reserves." *Environmental Conservation* 12:17–27.

Bauman, Gus (litigation counsel, National Association of Home Builders). 1981. Letter to Philip Cacuzza, Executive Vice President, New Jersey Builders Association, March 3.

Beale, Calvin L. 1982. "The Population Turnaround in Rural and Small Town America." *Policy Studies Review* 2:43–54.

Beck, Henry Charlton. 1936, 1961. *Forgotten Towns of Southern New Jersey*. New Brunswick, N.J.: Rutgers University Press.

———. 1937, 1963. *More Forgotten Towns of Southern New Jersey*. New Brunswick, N.J.: Rutgers University Press.

———. 1947. "Jersey Devil and Other Legends of the Jersey Shore." *New York Folk Quarterly* 3:102–106.

———. 1956. *The Roads of Home*. New Brunswick, N.J.: Rutgers University Press.

Berger, Jonathan. 1980. "Planning the Use and Management of the Pinelands: An Historical, Cultural, and Ecological Perspective." Prepared for the New Jersey Pinelands Commission, New Lisbon, N.J.

———. 1982. "Oh, How I Miss My Jersey Home: People, Place, and Planning in the Pine Barrens." In *History, Culture, and Arche-*

ology of the Pine Barrens: Essays from the Third Pine Barrens Research Conference, edited by John W. Sinton, 235–260. Pomona, N.J.: Stockton State College Center for Environmental Research.

Berger, Jonathan, and John W. Sinton. 1985. *Water, Earth, and Fire: Land Use and Environmental Planning in the New Jersey Pine Barrens.* Baltimore and London: Johns Hopkins University Press.

Biddle, Chris W. 1983. "N.J. Housing Market Is Booming Right Now." *Burlington County Times*, March 20.

Bingham, Gail. 1986. *Resolving Environmental Disputes: A Decade of Experience.* Washington, D.C.: Conservation Foundation.

Birch, Thomas. 1990. "The Incarceration of Wildness: Wilderness Areas as Prisons." *Environmental Ethics* 12:3–26.

Birnbaum, Shira. 1989a. "Town's Policy Goes Easy on Tax Defaulters." *Courier-Post* (South Jersey), January 8.

———. 1989b. "Woodland Feels Pinch of Pineland Laws." *Courier-Post* (South Jersey), January 9.

———. 1989c. "Woodland a Political Battleground." *Courier-Post* (South Jersey), January 10.

———. 1991. "A Critique of Environmental Reform: Remaking New Jersey's Pine Barrens." Masters' thesis, Rutgers University, New Brunswick, N.J.

Blacksell, Mark, and Andrew Gilg. 1981. *The Countryside: Planning and Change.* Winchester, Mass.: Allen and Unwin.

Bogden, Robert, and Steven J. Taylor. 1975. *Introduction to Qualitative Research Methods: A Phenomenological Approach to the Social Sciences.* New York: Wiley.

Booth, Richard. 1987. "New York's Adirondack Park Agency." In *Managing Land-Use Conflicts: Case Studies in Special Area Management*, edited by David J. Brower and Daniel S. Carol, 140–184. Durham, N.C.: Duke University Press.

Borrelli, Peter, ed. 1988. *Crossroads: Environmental Priorities for the Future.* Washington, D.C.: Island Press.

Boschken, Herman L. 1982. *Land Use Conflicts: Organizational Design and Resource Management.* Urbana: University of Illinois Press.

Bosselman, Fred P. 1986. "State and Local Plans in Hawaii: Lessons for Florida." In *Perspectives on Florida's Growth Management Act of 1985*, edited by John M. DeGrove and Julian Conrad Juergensmeyer, 1–14. Cambridge, Mass.: Lincoln Institute of Land Policy.

Bosselman, Fred P., and David Callies. 1971. *The Quiet Revolution in*

Land Use Control. Washington, D.C.: U.S. Government Printing Office.

Bouchier, David. 1987. *Radical Citizenship: The New American Activism.* New York: Schocken.

Boyd, Howard P. 1991. *A Field Guide to the Pine Barrens of New Jersey: Its Flora, Fauna, Ecology and Historic Sites.* Medford, N.J.: Plexus.

Boyer, M. Christine. 1981. "National Land Use Policy: Instrument and Product of the Economic Cycle." In *The Land Use Policy Debate in the United States,* edited by Judith I. deNeufville, 109–125. New York: Plenum Press.

Boyte, Harry C. 1980. *The Backyard Revolution.* Philadelphia: Temple University Press.

Boyte, Harry C., Heather Booth, and Steve Max. 1986. *Citizen Action and the New American Populism.* Philadelphia: Temple University Press.

Boyte, Harry C., and Frank Riessman, eds. 1986. *The New Populism: The Politics of Empowerment.* Philadelphia: Temple University Press.

Brower, David J., and Daniel S. Carol, eds. 1987. *Managing Land-Use Conflicts: Case Studies in Special Area Management.* Durham, N.C.: Duke University Press.

Bryant, Christopher R. 1989. "Entrepreneurs in the Rural Environment." *Journal of Rural Studies* 5:337–348.

Buchholz, Kenneth, and Ralph E. Good, eds. 1983. *Compendium of Archaeological, Cultural and Historical Literature of the New Jersey Pine Barrens.* New Brunswick, N.J.: Rutgers University Center for Coastal and Environmental Studies.

Burch, Philip H. 1975. "Interest Groups." In *Politics in New Jersey,* edited by Richard Lehne and Alan Rosenthal, 109–136. New Brunswick, N.J.: Rutgers University Eagleton Institute of Politics.

Burke, Edmund M. 1968. "Citizen Participation Strategies." *Journal of the American Institute of Planners* 34:287–294.

Buttimer, Anne. 1978. "Charism and Context: The Challenge of La Geographie Humaine." In *Humanistic Geography: Prospects and Problems,* edited by David Ley and Marwyn S. Samuels, 58–76. London: Croom Helm.

Callies, David L. 1984. *Regulating Paradise: Land Use Controls in Hawaii.* Honolulu: University of Hawaii Press.

Carney, Leo H. 1985a. "Lakehurst Called 'Monster' Dump." *New York Times,* April 18.

———. 1985b. "Wilderness Area Proposed for Pinelands." *New York Times*, April 21.

Carol, Daniel S. 1987. "New Jersey Pinelands Commission." In *Managing Land-Use Conflicts: Case Studies in Special Area Management*, edited by David J. Brower and Daniel S. Carol, 185–219. Durham, N.C.: Duke University Press.

Carson, Rachel. 1962. *Silent Spring*. Boston: Houghton Mifflin.

Carter, Luther J. 1974. *The Florida Experience: Land and Water Policy in a Growth State*. Baltimore: Johns Hopkins University Press, for Resources for the Future.

Caudill, Harry. 1962. *Night Comes to the Cumberlands: A Biography of a Depressed Area*. Boston: Little, Brown.

Cavanaugh, Cam. 1978. *Saving the Great Swamp: The People, the Power Brokers, and an Urban Wilderness*. Frenchtown, N.J.: Columbia Publishing.

Clark, John R., and Scott T. McCreary. 1987. "Special Area Management at Estuarine Reserves." In *Managing Land-Use Conflicts: Case Studies in Special Area Management*, edited by David J. Brower and Daniel S. Carol, 49–93. Durham, N.C.: Duke University Press.

Clark, Terry N., ed. 1968. *Community Structure and Decision-Making*. San Francisco: Chandler.

Coalition for the Sensible Preservation of the Pinelands. 1980a. *Report to the Pinelands Commission on the Preservation Area*. Prepared by Sterns, Herbert & Weinroth.

———. 1980b, c, d. *Report to the Pinelands Commission on the Protection Area* (prepared by Sterns, Herbert & Weinroth). Vol. 1, *Technical Issues* (Gerald E. Speitel Associates). Vol. 2, *Economic Analysis* (Frederick O'R. Hayes Associates). Vol. 3, *An Alternative Land Capability and Management Plan for the Protection Area* (Rogers Wells, Inc.).

Cohen, David Steven. 1982. *Folklife in New Jersey: An Annotated Bibliography*. Trenton: New Jersey Historical Commission.

———. 1985. "The Origin of the Pineys: Local Historians and the Legend." In *Folklife Annual 1985*, edited by Alan Jabbour and James Hardin, 40–59. Washington, D.C.: Library of Congress.

Collins, Beryl Robichaud, and Emily W. B. Russell, eds. 1988. *Protecting the New Jersey Pinelands: A New Direction in Land-Use Management*. New Brunswick, N.J.: Rutgers University Press.

Commission on the Adirondacks in the Twenty-First Century. 1990. *The Adirondack Park in the Twenty-First Century*. Albany: State of

New York.

Conant, James K., and Peter J. Pizor. 1988. "Economic and Fiscal Support Programs." In *Protecting the New Jersey Pinelands: A New Direction in Land-Use Management*, edited by Beryl Robichaud Collins and Emily W. B. Russell, 232–258. New Brunswick, N.J.: Rutgers University Press.

Conservation Foundation. 1985. *National Parks for a New Generation: Visions, Realities, Prospects.* Washington, D.C.: Conservation Foundation.

———. 1987. *State of the Environment: A View toward the Nineties.* Washington, D.C.: Conservation Foundation.

———. 1988. *Protecting America's Wetlands.* Washington, D.C.: Conservation Foundation.

Constantini, Edward, and Kenneth Hanf. 1973. *The Environmental Impulse and Its Competitors: Attitudes, Interests, and Institutions at Lake Tahoe.* Davis: University of California at Davis Institute of Governmental Affairs.

Corbett, Marjorie R., ed. 1983. *Greenline Parks: Land Conservatism Trends for the Eighties and Beyond.* Washington, D.C.: National Parks and Conservation Association.

Council on Environmental Quality. 1979. *Environmental Quality 1979.* Washington, D.C.: U.S. Government Printing Office.

———. 1990. *Environmental Quality: Twentieth Annual Report.* Washington, D.C.: U.S. Government Printing Office.

Council on Pinelands Research and Management. 1986. *A Long Term Research and Management Plan for the New Jersey Pinelands.* New Lisbon, N.J.: New Jersey Pinelands Commission.

Cronan, William. 1983. *Changes in the Land: Indians, Colonists, and the Ecology of New England.* New York: Hill and Wang.

Dahl, Robert A. 1961. *Who Governs?* New Haven: Yale University Press.

Daniels, Thomas L., and Arthur C. Nelson. 1986. "Is Oregon's Farmland Preservation Program Working?" *Journal of the American Planning Association* 52:22–32.

Danielson, Michael N. 1976. *The Politics of Exclusion.* New York: Columbia University Press.

Davies, Christopher S. 1983. "The Imprint of Federal Policy on Evolving Urban Form." In *United States Public Policy: A Geographical View*, edited by John W. House, 263–309. Oxford: Clarendon Press.

Davis, Charles E. and James P. Lester. 1989. "Federalism and Environmental Policy." In *Environmental Politics and Policy: Theories and Evidence*, edited by James P. Lester, 57–84. Durham, N.C.: Duke University Press.

DeGrove, John M. 1984. *Land, Growth & Politics*. Washington, D.C., and Chicago: American Planning Association.

———. 1986. "Creative Tensions in State/Local Relations." In *Growth Management: Keeping on Target?* edited by Douglas L. Porter, 169–172. Washington, D.C.: ULI–The Urban Land Institute with the Lincoln Institute of Land Policy.

———. 1989. "Growth Management and Governance." In *Understanding Growth Management: Critical Issues and a Research Agenda*, edited by David J. Brower, David R. Godschalk, and Douglas R. Porter, 22–42. Washington, D.C.: ULI–The Urban Land Institute and the Center for Urban and Regional Studies of the University of North Carolina at Chapel Hill.

DeGrove, John M., and Julian Conrad Juergensmeyer, eds. 1986. *Perspectives on Florida's Growth Management Act of 1985*. Cambridge, Mass.: Lincoln Institute of Land Policy.

D'Elia, Anthony N. 1979. *The Adirondack Rebellion*. Onchiota, N.Y.: Onchiota Books.

deNeufville, Judith I., ed. 1981. *The Land Use Policy Debate in the United States*. New York: Plenum Press.

Devall, Bill, and George Sessions. 1985. *Deep Ecology: Living as If People Mattered*. Salt Lake City: Peregrine Smith.

Dewey, William S. 1981. *Early Manchester and William Torrey*. Publisher unknown.

Dickinson, Robert E. 1964. *City and Region: A Geographical Interpretation*. London: Routledge and Kegan Paul.

Didato, Barry. 1990. "The Paths Less Traveled: A Wrapup on the Nation's Greenways." *Planning* 56(11):6–10.

Downs, Anthony. 1967. *Inside Bureaucracy*. Boston: Little, Brown.

———. 1972. "Up and Down with Ecology—the 'Issue-Attention Cycle.'" *Public Interest* 28:38–50.

Dunlap, Thomas. 1980. "Conservationists and Environmentalists: An Attempt at Definition." *Environmental Review* 4:29–31.

Dyballa, Cynthia D. 1979. *Regionalism in the Catskills: A Political Analysis*. Ithaca, N.Y.: Center for Environmental Research.

Dyballa, Cynthia D., Lyle S. Raymond, Jr., and Alan J. Hahn. 1981. *The Tug Hill Program*. Syracuse, N.Y.: Syracuse University Press.

Eagleton Institute of Politics. 1981. "Eagleton Poll 43." New Brunswick, N.J.: Rutgers University Eagleton Institute of Politics.

Edel, Matthew. 1981. "Land Policy, Economic Cycles, and Social Conflict." In *The Land Use Policy Debate in the United States*, edited by Judith I. deNeufville, 127–139. New York: Plenum Press.

Elazar, Daniel J. 1984. *American Federalism: A View from the States*. 3d ed. New York: Harper & Row.

Environmental Defense Fund et al. 1984. *A Task Force Report to the Pinelands Plan Review Subcommittee on the Comprehensive Management Plan*. New York: EDF.

Erikson, Kai T. 1976. *Everything in Its Path: Destruction of Community in the Buffalo Creek Flood*. New York: Simon and Schuster.

Etzioni, Amitai. 1960. "Two Approaches to Organizational Analysis." *Administrative Science Quarterly* 5:257–278.

Fairbrothers, David E. 1979. "Endangered, Threatened, and Rare Vascular Plants of the Pine Barrens and Their Biogeography." In *Pine Barrens: Ecosystem and Landscape*, edited by Richard T. T. Forman, 395–405. New York: Academic Press.

Feinstein, Miles Roger. 1963. "The Origins of the Pineys of New Jersey." B.A. thesis, History Department, Rutgers University, New Brunswick, N.J.

Fischer, Michael L. 1985. "California's Coastal Program: Larger-Than-Local Interests Built into Local Plans." *Journal of the American Planning Association* 51:312–321.

Fite, Gilbert C. 1981. *American Farmers: The New Minority*. Bloomington: Indiana University Press.

Fitzsimmons, Margaret. 1989. "The Matter of Nature." *Antipode* 21:106–120.

Floden, Robert E., and Stephen S. Weiner. 1978. "Rationality to Ritual: The Multiple Roles of Evaluation in Governmental Processes." *Policy Sciences* 9:9–18.

Fogleman, Valerie, Dierdre K. Hirner, and James D. Mertes. 1985. "Greenline Parks: An Anglo-American Comparison with Emphasis on National Recreation Areas, National Seashores and National Recreational and Scenic Rivers in the United States." Manuscript.

Foresta, Ronald A. 1981. *Open Space Policy: New Jersey's Green Acres Program*. New Brunswick, N.J.: Rutgers University Press.

———. 1984. *America's National Parks and Their Keepers*. Washington, D.C.: Resources for the Future.

————. 1986. "The Administrative Face of Natural and Historic Preservation." *Applied Geography* 6:309–324.

Forester, John. 1982. "Planning in the Face of Power." *Journal of the American Planning Association* 48:67–80.

————. 1987. "Planning in the Face of Conflict: Negotiation and Mediation Strategies in Local Land Use Regulation." *Journal of the American Planning Association* 53:303–314.

Forman, Richard T. T. 1979. "The Pine Barrens of New Jersey: An Ecological Mosaic." In *Pine Barrens: Ecosystem and Landscape*, edited by Richard T. T. Forman, 569–585. New York: Academic Press.

Foster, Charles H. W. 1984. *Experiments in Bioregionalism: The New England River Basins Story*. Hanover, N.H., and London: University Press of New England.

Fowler, Michael. 1982. "Rural Industrial Communities in the Pinelands: Paper Manufacturing at Harrisville, New Jersey." In *History, Culture, and Archeology of the Pine Barrens: Essays from the Third Pine Barrens Research Conference*, edited by John W. Sinton, 156–165. Pomona, N.J.: Stockton State College Center for Environmental Research.

Friedmann, John, and Clyde Weaver. 1979. *Territory and Function: The Evolution of Regional Planning*. Berkeley and Los Angeles: University of California Press.

Furuseth, Owen J., and J. T. Pierce. 1982. "A Comparative Analysis of Farmland Preservation Programmes in North America." *Canadian Geographer* 26:191–206.

Gale, Richard P. 1972. "From Sit-In to Hike-In: A Comparison of the Civil Rights and Environmental Movements." In *Social Behavior, Natural Resources, and the Environment*, edited by William R. Burch, Neil H. Cheek, Jr. and Lee Taylor, 280–305. New York: Harper & Row.

Gallant, Alisa L. 1989. *Regionalization as a Tool for Managing Environmental Resources*. EPA/600/3-89/060. Corvallis, Oreg.: NSI Technology Services Corporation and United States Environmental Protection Agency.

Galloway, Thomas D., ed. 1982. *The Newest Federalism: A New Framework for Coastal Issues*. Wakefield, R.I.: Wilson.

Geisler, Charles C. 1980. "The Quiet Revolution in Land Use Control Revisited." In *The Rural Sociology of the Advanced States: Critical Perspectives*, edited by Frederick Buttel and Howard Newby,

489–529. Montclair, N.J.: Allanheld Osmun.

Gillespie, Angus. 1979. "Folk and Hillbilly Music in the Pines: Gladys Eayre and the Pineconers' Repertoire." In *Natural and Cultural Resources of the New Jersey Pine Barrens: Inputs and Research Needs for Planning. Proceedings and Papers of the First Research Conference on the New Jersey Pine Barrens*, edited by John W. Sinton, 234–260. Pomona, N.J.: Stockton State College Center for Environmental Research.

Gillespie, Angus K., and Tom Ayres. 1979. "Folklore in the Pine Barrens: the Pinelands Cultural Society." *New Jersey History* 97:221–243.

Glikson, Arthur. 1971. *The Ecological Basis of Planning*. Edited by Lewis Mumford. The Hague: Martinus Nijhoff.

Goddard, Henry Herbert. 1912. *The Kallikak Family*. New York: Macmillan.

Goldstein, Joan. 1981. *Environmental Decision Making in Rural Locales: The Pine Barrens*. New York: Praeger.

Good, Ralph E., Norma F. Good, and John W. Anderson. 1979. "The Pine Barren Plains." In *Pine Barrens: Ecosystem and Landscape*, edited by Richard T. T. Forman, 283–295. New York: Academic Press.

Gordon, William R., Jr. 1984. "The Coastal Barrier Resources Act of 1982: An Assessment of Legislative Intent, Process, and Exemption Alternatives." *Coastal Zone Management Journal* 12:257–286.

Gould, Stephen Jay. 1981. *The Mismeasure of Man*. New York: Norton.

Government Finance Associates, Inc. 1982. *Report to the New Jersey Pinelands Commission: An Analysis of the Fiscal Impact of the Pinelands Comprehensive Management Plan on Selected Municipalities*. Princeton, N.J.: Government Finance Associates, Inc.

Governor's Pinelands Review Committee. 1979. *Planning and Management of the New Jersey Pinelands*. Trenton: State of New Jersey.

Graham, Frank J., Jr. 1978. *The Adirondack Park: A Political History*. New York: Knopf.

Gray, L. C., et al. 1924. "Utilization of Our Lands for Crops, Pasture and Forests." In U.S. Department of Agriculture, *Agriculture Yearbook 1923*, 415–506. Washington, D.C.: U.S. Government Printing Office.

Green, Bryn. 1981. *Countryside Conservation*. London: Allen and Unwin.

Grove, Noel. 1990. "Greenways: Paths to the Future." *National Geographic* 177(6):77–99.

Guttenberg, Albert Z. 1973. *The Land Use Movement of the 1920's: A Bibliographic Essay*. Exchange Bibliography no. 462. Monticello, Ill.: Council of Planning Librarians.

Hahn, Alan J., and Cynthia D. Dyballa. 1981. "State Environmental Planning and Local Influence: A Comparison of Three Natural Resource Management Agencies." *Journal of the American Planning Association* 47:324–335.

Halpert, Herbert Norman. 1947. "Folktales and Legends from the New Jersey Pines: A Collection and a Study." Ph.D. dissertation, University of Indiana, Indianapolis.

Hamilton Township. 1985. *Hamilton Township Comprehensive Management Plan*. Atlantic City, N.J.: Peter Karabashian Associates, Inc.

Hardin, Garret. 1968. "The Tragedy of the Commons." *Science* 162:1243–1248.

Harper, Stephen C., Laura L. Falk, and Edward W. Rankin. 1990. *The Northern Forest Lands Study of New England and New York*. Rutland, Vt.: U.S. Department of Agriculture, Forest Service.

Harshberger, J.W. 1916. *The Vegetation of the New Jersey Pine Barrens: An Ecologic Investigation*. Philadelphia: Christopher Sower.

Hart, John Fraser. 1975. *The Look of the Land*. Englewood Cliffs, N.J.: Prentice-Hall.

Hartshorne, Richard. 1939. *The Nature of Geography: A Critical Survey of Current Thought in the Light of the Past*. Lancaster, Pa.: Association of American Geographers.

Hartzog, Sandra. 1982. "Pine Barren's Prehistory: Current Directions." In *History, Culture, and Archeology of the Pine Barrens: Essays from the Third Pine Barrens Research Conference*, edited by John W. Sinton, 3–5. Pomona, N.J.: Stockton State College Center for Environmental Research.

Hays, Samuel P. 1959. *Conservation and the Gospel of Efficiency: The Progressive Conservation Movement, 1890–1920*. Cambridge, Mass.: Harvard University Press.

———. 1987. *Beauty, Health, and Permanence*. Cambridge, England: Cambridge University Press.

Healy, Robert G. 1983. "Hallmarks of a New Decade in Land Use." *Planning* 49:20–23.

Healy, Robert G., and John S. Rosenberg. 1979. *Land Use and the States*. 2d ed. Baltimore: Johns Hopkins University Press, for Resources for the Future.

Healy, Robert G., and Jeffrey A. Zinn. 1985. "Environment and Development Conflicts in Coastal Zone Management." *Journal of the American Planning Association* 51:299–311.

Healy, Robert G., et al., eds. 1978. *Protecting the Golden Shore: Lessons from the California Coastal Commissions*. Washington, D.C.: Conservation Foundation.

Heeter, David G. 1976. "The Vermont Experience." In Daniel R. Mandelker, *Environmental and Land Controls Legislation*, 323–391. Indianapolis: Bobbs-Merrill.

Heiman, Michael K. 1983. "Regional Planning and Land Use Reform for Conservation and Development in New York State." Ph.D. dissertation, University Microfilms International, Ann Arbor, Mich.

———. 1988. *The Quiet Evolution: Power, Planning, and Profits in New York State*. New York: Praeger.

———. 1989. "Production Confronts Consumption: Landscape Perception and Social Conflict in the Hudson Valley." *Environment and Planning D: Society and Space* 7:165–178.

Heintz, Katherine McMillan. 1976. *Retirement Communities: For Adults Only*. New Brunswick, N.J.: Rutgers University Center for Urban Policy Research.

Herbert H. Smith Associates. 1963. *The New Jersey Pinelands Region*. West Trenton, N.J.: Herbert H. Smith Associates.

———. 1964. *Future Development Plans: The New Jersey Pine Barrens Region*. West Trenton, N.J.: Herbert H. Smith Associates.

Hess, David E. 1983. "Institutionalizing the Revolution: Judicial Reaction to State Land Use Laws." In *Land Use Issues of the 1980s*, edited by James H. Carr and Edward E. Duensing, 99–112. New Brunswick, N.J.: Rutgers University Center for Urban Policy Research.

Hiemstra, Hal, and Nancy Bushwick. 1986. "How States Are Saving Farmland." *American Land Forum* 6(2):60–65.

Hirner, Dierdre K. 1985. "Public Parks on Private Lands: Greenline Parks Protecting Landscapes of National Significance." Ph.D. dissertation, University Microfilms, Ann Arbor, Mich.

Hiss, Tony. 1988. "Reflections: Encountering the Countryside." *New Yorker*, August 21, 40–69; August 28, 37–63.

Hobsbawm, Eric, and Terrence Ranger, eds. 1983. *The Invention of Tradition*. New York: Cambridge University Press.

Hoskins, David W. 1984. *Land Use, Water Quality and Ecosystem Integrity in the New Jersey Pinelands*. New York: Environmental Defense Fund.

House, John W. 1983. "Regional and Area Development." In *United States Public Policy: A Geographical View*, edited by John W. House, 34–79. Oxford: Clarendon House.

Houston, Lawrence O. 1984. "No Town Is an Island." *New Jersey Reporter* 14:37–39.

Hufford, Mary. 1986. *One Space, Many Places: Folklife and Land Use in New Jersey's Pinelands National Reserve*. Washington, D.C.: American Folklife Center, Library of Congress.

Hughes, Robert M. 1989. "Ecoregional Biological Criteria." In Environmental Protection Agency, *Water Quality Standards for the 21st Century*. Washington, D.C.: Environmental Protection Agency.

Hughes, Robert M., and David P. Larsen. 1988. "Ecoregions: An Approach to Surface Water Protection." *Journal of the Water Pollution Control Federation* 57:912–915.

Hunter, Floyd. 1953. *Community Power Structure: A Study of Decision Makers*. Chapel Hill: University of North Carolina Press.

Ingram, Helen M., and Dean E. Mann. 1989. "Interest Groups and Environmental Policy." In *Environmental Politics and Policy: Theories and Evidence*, edited by James P. Lester, 135–157. Durham, N.C., and London: Duke University Press.

Irwin, Barbara Smith. 1978. "New Jersey Pine Barrens Folklore: A Selective Bibliography." *New Jersey Folklore* 2:16–20.

Jackson, Kenneth T. 1985. *Crabgrass Frontier: The Suburbanization of the United States*. New York: Oxford University Press.

Jackson, Richard H. 1981. *Land Use in America*. New York: Wiley.

Jenkins, Patrick. 1990. "State to Join Forces with Atlantic City to Reignite the Resort's Comeback." *Star-Ledger* (Newark), August 3.

Jones, Suzi. 1976. "Regionalization: A Rhetorical Strategy." *Journal of the Folklore Institute* 13:105–120.

Kehde, Karl. 1987. *Pinelands Development Credit Evaluation Report*. New Lisbon, N.J.: New Jersey Pinelands Commission.

Kenski, Henry C., and Margaret Corgan Kenski. 1984. "Congress

Against the President: The Struggle Over the Environment." In *Environmental Policy in the 1980s: Reagan's New Agenda*, edited by Norman J. Vig and Michael E. Kraft, 97–120. Washington, D.C.: CQ Press.

Kern, Don, ed. 1990. "Grassroots!" *Inner Voice* 2(2).

King, Leslie, and Glenn Harris. 1989. "Local Responses to Rapid Rural Growth: New York and Vermont Cases." *Journal of the American Planning Association* 55:181–191.

Kinsey, David N. 1985. "CZM from the State Perspective: The New Jersey Experience." *Natural Resources Journal* 25:73–102.

Kite, Elizabeth S. 1913. "The Pineys." *Survey* 31:7–13, 38–40.

Klimm, Lester. 1953. "The Empty Areas of the Northeastern United States." *Geographical Review* 44:325–345.

Koebel, Charles Theodore. 1979. "Planning Techniques and Process in a Bargaining Framework." Ph.D. dissertation, University Microfilms, Ann Arbor, Mich.

Kraft, Michael E. 1984. "A New Environmental Policy Agenda: The 1980 Presidential Campaign and Its Aftermath." In *Environmental Policy in the 1980s: Reagan's New Agenda*, edited by Norman J. Vig and Michael E. Kraft, 29–50. Washington, D.C.: CQ Press.

Kraft, Michael E., and Norman J. Vig. 1984. "Environmental Policy in the Reagan Administration." *Political Science Quarterly* 99:415–439.

Kusler, Jon A. 1983. "Regulating Sensitive Lands: An Overview of Programs." In *Land Use Issues of the 1980s*, edited by James H. Carr and Edward E. Duensing, 128–153. New Brunswick, N.J.: Rutgers University Center for Urban Policy Research.

Lake, Laura, ed. 1986. *Environmental Mediation: The Search for Consensus*. Boulder, Colo.: Westview.

Lake, Robert W., ed. 1987. *Resolving Locational Conflict*. New Brunswick, N.J.: Rutgers University Center for Urban Policy Research.

Lawrence, Dorthea Dix. 1953. "People of the Pine Barrens." *Geographical Magazine* 25:534–538.

League of Conservation Voters. 1990. *National Environmental Scorecard*. Washington, D.C.: League of Conservation Voters.

LeDuc, Daniel. 1990. "The Town Joe Portash Left Broke." *Philadelphia Inquirer*, October 14.

Leonard, H. Jeffrey. 1983. *Managing Oregon's Growth: The Politics of Development Planning*. Washington, D.C.: Conservation Foundation.

Lichter, Daniel T., Glenn V. Fuguitt, and Tim B. Heaton. 1985. "Components of Nonmetropolitan Population Change: The Contribution of Rural Areas." *Rural Sociology* 50:88–98.

Linowes, R. Robert, and Don T. Allensworth. 1975. *The States and Land-Use Control*. New York: Praeger.

————. 1976. *The Politics of Land-Use Law: Developers vs. Citizens Groups in the Courts*. New York: Praeger.

Liroff, Richard A. 1985. "NEPA Litigation in the 1970s: A Deluge or a Dribble?" *Natural Resources Journal* 25:162–177.

Liroff, Richard A., and G. Gordon Davis. 1981. *Protecting Open Space: Land Use Controls in the Adirondack Park*. Cambridge, Mass.: Ballinger.

Little, Charles E. 1983. "The National Perspective: Greenline Parks." In New York State Department of Environmental Conservation, *Proceedings: Greenline and Urbanline Parks Conference*, 3–5. Albany, N.Y.

————. 1990. *Greenways for America*. Baltimore and London: Johns Hopkins University Press.

Little, Silas. 1974. "Wildflowers of the Pine Barrens and Their Niche Requirements." *New Jersey Outdoors* 1:16–18.

————. 1979. "Ecology and Silviculture of the Pine Barrens Forests." In *Natural and Cultural Resources of the New Jersey Pine Barrens: Inputs and Research Needs for Planning. Proceedings and Papers of the First Research Conference on the New Jersey Pine Barrens*, edited by John W. Sinton, 105–118. Pomona, N.J.: Stockton State College Center for Environmental Research.

Long, L., and Diana DeAre. 1988. "U.S. Population Redistribution: A Perspective on the Nonmetropolitan Turnaround." *Population and Development Review* 14:433–449.

Lowe, Philip D., and Michael W. Worboys. 1980. "Ecology and Ideology." In *The Rural Sociology of the Advanced Societies: Critical Perspectives*, edited by Frederick Buttel and Howard Newby. Montclair, N.J.: Allenheld, Osmun; London: Croom Helm.

Lowenthal, David. 1968. "The American Scene." *Geographical Review* 58:61–88.

Lowenthal, David, and Marcus Binney, ed. 1981. *Our Past Before Us: Why Do We Save It?* London: T. Smith.

Lowenthal, David, and Hugh C. Prince. 1964. "The English Landscape." *Geographical Review* 54:309–346.

————. 1965. "English Landscape Tastes." *Geographical Review*

55:186–222.

Lowi, Theodore J. 1969. *The End of Liberalism: Ideology, Policy, and the Crisis of Public Authority.* New York: Norton.

Lyday, Noreen. 1976. *The Law of the Land: Debating National Land Use Legislation 1970–75.* Washington, D.C.: Urban Institute.

McClaughry, John. 1975. "The New Feudalism." *Environmental Law* 5:675–702.

McCloy, James F., and Ray Miller, Jr. 1976. *The Jersey Devil.* Wallingford, Pa.: Middle Atlantic Press.

McCormick, Jack. 1970. *The Pine Barrens: A Preliminary Ecological Inventory.* Trenton: New Jersey State Museum.

McCormick, Jack, and Richard T. T. Forman. 1979. "Introduction: Location and Boundaries of the New Jersey Pine Barrens." In *Pine Barrens: Ecosystem and Landscape*, edited by Richard T. T. Forman, xxxv–xlii. New York: Academic Press.

McCormick, Jack, and L. Jones. 1973. *The Pine Barrens: Vegetation Geography.* Trenton: New Jersey State Museum.

McCormick, Richard P. 1975. "An Historical Overview." In *Politics in New Jersey*, edited by Richard Lehne and Alan Rosenthal, 83–108. New Brunswick, N.J.: Rutgers University Eagleton Institute of Politics.

MacEwen, Malcolm, and Ann MacEwen. 1982. *National Parks: Conservation or Cosmetics?* Winchester, Mass.: Allen and Unwin.

McGarvey, Robert G. 1972. "The Pine Barrens: Isolation and Images." Master's thesis, Temple University, Philadelphia.

McHarg, Ian. 1969. *Design with Nature.* Garden City, N.Y.: Doubleday.

McIntyre, Joy. 1980. "In Burlington County, DeMarco Is the King." *Burlington County Times.*

MacKaye, Benton. 1928. *The New Exploration: A Philosophy of Regional Planning.* New York: Harcourt, Brace.

McMahon, William. 1964. *Historic South Jersey Towns.* Atlantic City, N.J.: Press Publishing.

———. 1973. *South Jersey Towns: History and Legend.* New Brunswick, N.J.: Rutgers University Press.

———. 1980. *Pine Barrens Legends, Lore and Lies.* Wallingford, Pa.: Middle Atlantic Press.

McPhee, John. 1967. *The Pine Barrens.* New York: Farrar, Straus, and Giroux.

———. 1974. "People of the New Jersey Pine Barrens." *National Geographic* 45:52–77.

MacPherson, C. B. 1977. *The Life and Times of Liberal Democracy.* Oxford, England: Oxford University Press.

Maize, Kennedy P., ed. 1988. *Blueprint for the Environment: Advice to the President-Elect from America's Environmental Community.* Washington, D.C.: Blueprint for the Environment.

Mallowe, Mike. 1985. "In Search of the Jersey Devil." *Reader's Digest*, January, 115–119.

Manchester Township. n.d. "Some Pertinent Facts and Figures."

Mandelker, Daniel R. 1976. *Environmental and Land Controls Legislation.* Indianapolis: Bobbs-Merrill.

Markusen, Ann. 1981. "Introduction to the Political Economy Perspective." In *The Land Use Policy Debate in the United States*, edited by Judith I. deNeufville, 103–107. New York: Plenum Press.

Marsh, Elizabeth. 1979. "The Southern Pine Barrens: An Ethnic Archipelago." In *Natural and Cultural Resources of the New Jersey Pine Barrens: Inputs and Research Needs for Planning. Proceedings and Papers of the First Research Conference on the New Jersey Pine Barrens*, edited by John W. Sinton, 192–198. Pomona, N.J.: Stockton State College Center for Environmental Research.

———. 1981. *Cooperative Rural Planning: A Tug Hill Case Study.* Watertown, N.Y.: Temporary State Commission on Tug Hill.

———. 1982. "The South Jersey House." In *Natural and Cultural Resources of the New Jersey Pine Barrens: Inputs and Research Needs for Planning. Proceedings and Papers of the First Research Conference on the New Jersey Pine Barrens*, edited by John W. Sinton, 185–192. Pomona, N.J.: Stockton State College Center for Environmental Research.

Marx, Leo. 1964. *The Machine in the Garden: Technology and the Pastoral Ideal in America.* New York: Oxford University Press.

Mason, Robert J. 1986. "Environmental Conflict and Accommodation: An Evaluation of Regional Land Use Management in the New Jersey Pinelands." Ph.D. dissertation, University Microfilms, Ann Arbor, Mich.

———. 1991. "Local Responses to Proposed New Land-Use Controls in New York's Adirondack Park." In *Proceedings, Joint Meeting of the New England–St. Lawrence Valley Geographical Society and the Middle States Division of the Association of American Geographers*, edited by Dean M. Hanink, Elizabeth Hovinen, and Gary Hovinen, 7–15.

Mason, Robert J., and Mark T. Mattson. 1990. *Atlas of United States Environmental Issues.* New York: Macmillan.

Mason, Robert J., William D. Solecki, and Enid L. Lotstein. 1987. "Comments on 'On "Bioregionalism" and "Watershed Consciousness." '" *Professional Geographer* 39: 67–68.

Mayer, W. F. 1859. "In the Pines." *Atlantic Monthly* 3:560–569.

Mendell, Carl, and Anne Yedinsky. 1981. "Sam Hunt: Personality of the Pines." *New Jersey Folklore* 2:43–48.

Mernitz, Scott. 1980. *Mediation of Environmental Disputes: A Source-book*. New York: Praeger.

Merrill, Leland G., Jr., et al. 1978. *A Plan for A Pinelands National Preserve*. New Brunswick, N.J.: Rutgers University Center for Coastal and Environmental Studies.

Meyner, Robert B., et al. 1983. *Three Decades of the Governor's Office: A Panel Discussion*. Trenton: New Jersey Historical Commission.

Mitchell, James K. 1986. "Coastal Management Since 1980." In *Ocean Yearbook 6*, edited by Elisabeth Mann Borgese and Norton Ginsburg, 319–345. Chicago: University of Chicago Press.

Mitchell, John G. 1978. "The Re-greening of Urban America." *Audubon* 80:29–52.

Mitchell, Robert Cameron. 1984. "Public Opinion and Environmental Politics in the 1970s and 1980s." In *Environmental Policy in the 1980s: Reagan's New Agenda*, edited by Norman J. Vig and Michael E. Kraft, 51–74. Washington, D.C.: CQ Press.

Moakley, Maureen, and Gerald Pomper. 1975. "Party Organizations." In *Politics in New Jersey*, edited by Richard Lehne and Alan Rosenthal, 83–108. New Brunswick, N.J.: Rutgers University Eagleton Institute of Politics.

Mogulof, Melvin. 1975. *Saving the Coast: California's Experiment in Intergovernmental Land Use Control*. Lexington, Mass.: Lexington Books.

Moonsammy, Rita, David S. Cohen, and Mary T. Hufford. 1987. "Living with the Landscape: Folklife in the Environmental Sub-regions of the Pinelands." In *Pinelands Folklife*, edited by Rita Zorn Moonsammy, David S. Cohen, and Lorraine E. Williams, 65–225. New Brunswick, N.J.: Rutgers University Press.

Moonsammy, Rita Zorn, David S. Cohen, and Lorraine E. Williams, eds. 1987. *Pinelands Folklife*. New Brunswick, N.J.: Rutgers University Press.

Moore, Terrence D. 1983. "The New Jersey Pinelands." In *Proceedings: Greenline and Urbanline Parks Conference*, edited by Charles C. Morrison, 29–31. Albany: New York State Department of Environmental Conservation.

———. 1986. "Saving the Pinelands." In *Growth Management: Keeping on Target?* edited by Douglas R. Porter, 131–135. Washington, D.C.: ULI–The Urban Land Institute.

Morandi, Larry, Gordon Meeks, Jr., and Douglas M. Sacarto. 1983. *Land Management: Sustaining Resource Values*. Denver: National Conference of State Legislatures.

Morrison, Charles C., ed. 1983. *Proceedings: Greenline and Urbanline Parks Conference*. Albany: New York State Department of Environmental Conservation.

Morrison, Denton E., Kenneth E. Hornback, and W. Keith Warner. 1972. In *Social Behavior, Natural Resources, and the Environment*, edited by William R. Burch, Neil H. Cheek, Jr. and Lee Taylor, 259–279. New York: Harper & Row.

Moss, Elaine, ed. 1977. *Land Use Controls in the United States: A Handbook on the Legal Rights of Citizens*. New York: Dial Press.

Myers, Phyllis. 1974. *So Goes Vermont: An Account of the Development, Passage, and Implementation of State Land Use Legislation in Vermont*. Washington, D.C.: Conservation Foundation.

———. 1976. *Zoning Hawaii: An Analysis of the Passage and Implementation of Hawaii's Land Classification Law*. Washington, D.C.: Conservation Foundation.

Nash, Roderick. 1982. *Wilderness and the American Mind*. 3d ed. New Haven and London: Yale University Press.

———. 1990. *American Environmentalism: Readings in Conservation History*. 3d ed. New York: McGraw-Hill.

Nelson, Holly, and Alan J. Hahn. 1980. *State Policy and Local Influence in the Adirondacks*. Ithaca, N.Y.: Cornell University Press.

Nelson, Robert H. 1977. *Zoning and Property Rights: An Analysis of the American System of Land-Use Regulation*. Cambridge, Mass. and London: MIT Press.

New Jersey Department of State. Ca. 1985. *Results of the General Election Held November 5, 1985*. Trenton.

New Jersey Folklife. 1987. Special issue (vol. 11) by Pinelands Folklife Project folklorists.

New Jersey Pinelands Commission. 1980. "Comprehensive Management Plan for the Pinelands National Reserve and Pinelands Area." New Jersey Pinelands Commission, New Lisbon, N.J. Photocopy.

———. 1983a. "Comprehensive Management Plan: A Progress Report on the First Three Years of Implementation." New Jersey Pinelands Commission, New Lisbon, N.J. Photocopy.

————. 1983b. "Economic & Fiscal Impacts of the Pinelands Comprehensive Management Plan." New Jersey Pinelands Commission, New Lisbon, N.J. Photocopy.

————. 1983c. "Discussion of Growth Projections in Ocean County." New Jersey Pinelands Commission, New Lisbon, N.J. Typescript.

————. 1983d. "Report on Conformance of Ocean County Master Plan and Subdivision and Site Plan Resolution." New Jersey Pinelands Commission, New Lisbon, N.J. Typescript.

————. 1983e. "Report on Conformance, Township of Hamilton." New Jersey Pinelands Commission, New Lisbon, N.J. Typescript.

————. Ca. 1984. "Administering America's First National Reserve." New Jersey Pinelands Commission, New Lisbon, N.J. Photocopy.

————. 1985a. "Buffer Delineation Model for New Pinelands Wetlands." New Jersey Pinelands Commission, New Lisbon, N.J. Photocopy.

————. 1985b. "Economic & Fiscal Impacts of the Pinelands Comprehensive Management Plan: First Biennial Update." New Jersey Pinelands Commission, New Lisbon, N.J. Photocopy.

————. 1985c. "Report on Conformance of Municipal Master Plan and Land Use Ordinances, Township of Berkeley: Findings of Fact." New Jersey Pinelands Commission, New Lisbon, N.J. Typescript.

————. 1985d. "Report on the Township of Hamilton's Response to the Commission's Conditional Certification of October 7, 1983." New Jersey Pinelands Commission, New Lisbon, N.J. Typescript.

————. 1985e. "Reviewing the Comprehensive Management Plan: Draft Report to the Pinelands Commission." New Jersey Pinelands Commission, New Lisbon, N.J. Photocopy.

————. 1986a. "Effectiveness of Standard and Alternative Design Septic Systems in Renovating Domestic Wastewater in Pinelands Soils." New Jersey Pinelands Commission, New Lisbon, N.J. Photocopy.

————. 1986b. "Pinelands Cultural Resource Management Plan for the Historic Period Sites." New Jersey Pinelands Commission, New Lisbon, N.J. Photocopy.

————. 1987a. "Continuing the Pinelands Acquisition Program." New Jersey Pinelands Commission, New Lisbon, N.J. Photocopy.

———. 1987b. "Pinelands Infrastructure Financing Plan." New Jersey Pinelands Commission, New Lisbon, N.J. Photocopy.

———. 1988a. "The Pinelands Development Credit Program." New Jersey Pinelands Commission, New Lisbon, N.J. Photocopy.

———. 1988b. "Pinelands Model Historic Preservation Ordinance." New Jersey Pinelands Commission, New Lisbon, N.J. Photocopy.

———. 1988c. "Pinelands Villages and Towns: Historic Area Delineations." New Jersey Pinelands Commission, New Lisbon, N.J. Photocopy.

———. 1990a. "An Assessment of the Nitrogen Removal Efficiency and Performance of RUCK Septic Systems in the New Jersey Pinelands." New Jersey Pinelands Commission, New Lisbon, N.J. Photocopy.

———. 1990b. "Comprehensive Municipal Inventory Guidelines Pursuant to the Pinelands Cultural Resource Management Plan for Historic Period Sites." New Jersey Pinelands Commission, New Lisbon, N.J. Photocopy.

———. 1990c. "New Jersey Pinelands Commission Manual for Identifying and Delineating Pinelands Area Wetlands." New Jersey Pinelands Commission, New Lisbon, N.J. Photocopy.

———. 1991. "1990 Annual Report." New Jersey Pinelands Commission, New Lisbon, N.J. Photocopy.

New Jersey Senate. Energy and Environment Committee. 1978. *Public Hearing on Proposed Central Pine Barrens Water Quality Standards.* Vol. 1. Trenton.

———. 1979. *Public Hearing on S. 3091 and S. 3138: Pinelands Protection Act.* Vols. 1–4. Trenton.

———. 1980. *Public Hearing on Implementation of the "Pinelands Protection Act."* Trenton.

New Jersey State Planning Commission. 1988. *Communities of Place: The New Jersey Preliminary State Development and Redevelopment Plan.* Trenton: New Jersey State Planning Commission.

New York Times. 1969a. "Mr. Meyner Turns Left." August 30.

———. 1969b. "Jersey Nominees Clash on Jetport." September 6.

———. 1981. "Congressional Fight on Pinelands Looms." February 1.

Norton, Bryan G. 1986. "Conservation and Preservation: A Conceptual Rehabilitation." *Environmental Ethics* 8:195–220.

Ocean County Nature and Conservation Society. n.d. "Pinelands Environmental Council." Mimeographed.

Oelschlaeger, Max. 1991. *The Idea of Wilderness: From Prehistory to the Age of Ecology*. New Haven, Conn., and London: Yale University Press.

O'Hare, Michael. 1977. "Not on My Block, You Don't." *Public Policy* 25:407–458.

O'Hare, Michael, Lawrence Bacow, and Debra Sanderson. 1983. *Facility Siting and Public Opposition*. New York: Van Nostrand.

O'Riordan, Timothy. 1981. *Environmentalism*. 2d ed. London: Pion.

Owens, David W. 1985. "Coastal Management in North Carolina: Building a Regional Consensus." *Journal of the American Planning Association* 51:322–329.

Panzer, Shayna. 1980. "A History of Efforts to Regulate the Pinelands." *New York Times*, July 20.

Parsons, James J. 1985. "On 'Bioregionalism' and 'Watershed Consciousness.'" *Professional Geographer* 37:1–6.

Pelham, Thomas G. 1979. *State Land-Use Planning and Regulation: Florida, the Model Code, and Beyond*. Lexington, Mass.: Lexington Books.

Pepper, David. 1984. *The Roots of Modern Environmentalism*. London: Croom Helm.

Perin, Constance. 1977. *Everything in Its Place: Social Order and Land Use in America*. Princeton: Princeton University Press.

Petulla, Joseph M. 1988. *American Environmental History*. 2d ed. Columbus, Ohio: Merrill.

Pierce, Arthur D. 1957. *Iron in the Pines*. New Brunswick, N.J.: Rutgers University Press.

Pierson, George. 1979. "The Wood-Using Industries of the Pinelands." In *Natural and Cultural Resources of the New Jersey Pine Barrens: Inputs and Research Needs for Planning. Proceedings and Papers of the First Research Conference on the New Jersey Pine Barrens*, edited by John W. Sinton, 119–131. Pomona, N.J.: Stockton State College Center for Environmental Research.

Pinelands Advisory Committee. n.d. *Report of the Pinelands Advisory Committee*. n.p.

Pinelands Agricultural Study Commission. 1985. *Report of the Pinelands Agricultural Study Commission*. Trenton: New Jersey Department of Agriculture.

Pinelands Environmental Council. 1975. *Plan for the Pinelands*.

Browns Mills, N.J.: Pinelands Environmental Council.

Pinelands Interpretation Committee. 1984. *New Directions to Pinelands Interpretation: The Report of the Pinelands Interpretation Committee* (Draft). Philadelphia: U.S. Department of the Interior, National Park Service, Mid-Atlantic Regional Office.

Platt, Rutherford H. 1985. "Congress and the Coast." *Environment* 27:12–17, 34–40.

———. 1991. *Land Use Control: Geography, Law, and Public Policy.* Englewood Cliffs, N.J.: Prentice-Hall.

Platt, Rutherford H., George Macinko, and Kenneth Hammond. 1983. "Federal Environmental Management: Some Land-Use Legacies of the 1970s." In *United States Public Policy: A Geographical View*, edited by John W. House, 125–166. Oxford: Clarendon House.

Plotkin, Sidney. 1980. "Policy Fragmentation and Capitalist Reform: The Defeat of National Land-Use Policy." *Politics and Society* 9:409–445.

———. 1987. *Keep Out: The Struggle for Land Use Control.* Berkeley: University of California Press.

Polsby, Nelson W. 1963. *Community Power and Political Theory.* New Haven: Yale University Press.

Pontier, Glenn. 1987. "Impasse on the Upper Delaware." In *Managing Land-Use Conflicts: Case Studies in Special Area Management*, edited by David J. Brower and Daniel S. Carol, 231–243. Durham, N.C.: Duke University Press.

Popper, Frank J. 1981. *The Politics of Land-Use Reform.* Madison: University of Wisconsin Press.

———. 1985. "The Environmentalist and the LULU." *Environment* 27(2):7–11, 37–40.

———. 1988. "Understanding American Land Use Regulation Since 1970: A Revisionist Interpretation." *Journal of the American Planning Association* 54:291–301.

Porter, Douglas L., ed. 1986. *Growth Management: Keeping on Target?* Washington, D.C.: ULI–The Urban Land Institute with Lincoln Institute of Land Policy.

Portney, Paul R., ed. 1990. *Public Policies for Environmental Protection.* Washington, D.C.: Resources for the Future.

Post, Kevin. 1983. "Pinelands Juggernaut Is Compelling Conformance." *Gazette-Leader* (Wildwood, N.J.), September 29.

President's Commission on Americans Outdoors. 1987. *Americans Outdoors: The Legacy, the Challenge.* Washington, D.C.: Island Press.

Randle, Ellen. 1982. "The National Reserve System and Transferable Development Rights: Is the New Jersey Pinelands Plan an Unconstitutional 'Taking'?" *Boston College Environmental Affairs Law Review* 10:183–241.

Reilly, William K., ed. 1973. *The Use of Land: A Citizens' Policy Guide to Urban Growth. A Task Force Report Sponsored by the Rockefeller Brothers Fund.* New York: Crowell.

Renew America. 1990. *The State of the States.* Washington, D.C.: Renew America.

Rhodehamel, Edward C. 1979. "Hydrology of the New Jersey Pine Barrens." In *Pine Barrens: Ecosystem and Landscape*, edited by Richard T. T. Forman, 147–167. New York: Academic Press.

Rielley, Kevin J., Wendy U. Larsen, and Clifford L. Weaver. 1984. "Partnership in the Pinelands." In *Land Reform, American Style*, edited by Charles C. Geisler and Frank J. Popper, 129–148. Totowa, N.J.: Rowman and Allenheld.

Ripley, Elmer. n.d. "A Brief History of Hamilton Township." Mimeographed.

Robichaud, Beryl, and Murray F. Buell. 1973. *Vegetation of New Jersey: A Study of Landscape Diversity.* New Brunswick, N.J.: Rutgers University Press.

Rohrer, Wayne C., and Louis H. Douglas. 1969. *The Agrarian Transition in America: Dualism and Change.* Indianapolis: Bobbs-Merrill.

Rosenbaum, Nelson. 1976. *Land Use and the Legislatures: The Politics of State Innovation.* Washington, D.C.: Urban Institute.

Rostow, Walter W. 1960. *The Stages of Economic Growth: A Non-Communist Manifesto.* Cambridge, England: Cambridge University Press.

Roy F. Weston, Inc. 1986. "Pinelands Infrastructure Master Plan." Prepared for the New Jersey Pinelands Commission.

Rubinstein, Nora J. 1983. "A Psycho-Social Impact Analysis of Environmental Change in New Jersey's Pine Barrens." Ph.D. dissertation, University Microfilms, Ann Arbor, Mich.

Rudel, Thomas K. 1984. "The Human Ecology of Rural Land Use Planning." *Rural Sociology* 49:491–504.

Runte, Alfred. 1979. *National Parks: The American Experience.* Lincoln: University of Nebraska Press.

Russell, Emily W. B. n.d. "Planning the Pinelands National Reserve." Manuscript.

Sabatier, Paul, and David Mazmanian. 1979. *Can Regulation Work: The Implementation of the 1972 California Coastal Initiative.* Davis and Claremont, Calif.: University of California, Davis, Institute of Government Affairs and Pomona College Program in Public Policy Analysis.

Sale, Kirkpatrick. 1985. *Dwellers in the Land: The Bioregional Vision.* San Francisco: Sierra Club Books.

Salomon, Mary Kealy. 1982. "State Land Use Controls in New York and New Jersey: The Adirondacks and the Pinelands." Master's thesis, Cornell University, Ithaca, N.Y.

Salter, Edwin. 1890. *A History of Monmouth and Ocean Counties, Embracing a Genealogical Record of Earliest Settlers in Monmouth and Ocean Counties and Their Descendents.* Bayonne, N.J.: E. Gardner & Son. Reprinted by Ocean County Historical Society, 1980.

Samuelson, Sue. 1986. "Changes in Regional Identities in South Jersey: The Impact of the Pinelands National Reserve." *New Jersey Folklife* 11:14–20.

———. 1987. "Celebrations and Festivities in the Pinelands National Reserve." *New Jersey Folklife* 12:32–37.

Saunders, Peter, et al. 1978. "Rural Community and Rural Community Power." In *International Perspectives in Rural Sociology*, edited by Howard Newby, 55–84. Chichester: Wiley.

Schiff, Stanley D. 1986. "The Pine Barrens: Vast, Vital, Vulnerable." *Amicus Journal* 8(1):28–33.

Schmitt, Peter J. 1969. *Back to Nature: The Arcadian Myth in Urban America.* New York: Oxford University Press.

Schnaiberg, Allan. 1977. "Politics, Participation and Pollution: The 'Environmental Movement.'" In *Cities in Change: Studies on the Urban Condition*, edited by John Walton and Donald E. Carns, 464–480. 2d ed. Boston: Allyn and Bacon.

Scott, Randall, ed. 1975. *Management & Control of Growth: Issues, Techniques, Problems, Trends.* Washington, D.C.: Urban Land Institute.

Selznick, Philip. 1953. *TVA and the Grass Roots: A Study in the Sociology of Formal Organization.* Berkeley and Los Angeles: University of California Press.

Sheppard, Carroll Anne. 1989. "Where Are the Pineys?" *New Jersey Folklife* 14:21–29.

Short, John Rennie. 1991. *Imagined Country: Society, Culture and Environment*. London and New York: Routledge and Kegan Paul.

Shrom, Ralph. 1982. "In DeMarco's World, Individuality's a Virtue." *Burlington County Times*, June 20.

Siemon, Charles L., and Wendy U. Larsen. 1985. "Florida: Grappling with Growth II." *Urban Land* 44(9):36–37.

Sierra Club, New Jersey Chapter. 1985. "Pine Barrens Wilderness." A Sierra Club White Paper. Princeton, N.J.

Sills, David L. 1975. "The Environmental Movement and Its Critics." *Human Ecology* 3:1–41.

Simmons, I. G. 1978. "National Parks in England and Wales." In *International Experience with National Parks and Related Reserves*, edited by J. G. Nelson, R. D. Needham, and D. L. Mann, 383–409. Waterloo, Ontario: Department of Geography, University of Waterloo.

Simon, Herbert A. 1976. *Administrative Behavior*. 3d ed. New York: Free Press.

Sinton, John W. 1980. "An Inventory of Historic and Cultural Resources of the New Jersey Pinelands." Prepared for the New Jersey Pinelands Commission.

———. 1981. "Cultural Self-Preservation: Planning for Local Cultures in the New Jersey Pine Barrens." *New Jersey Folklore* 2: 39–42.

———, ed. 1979. *Natural and Cultural Resources of the New Jersey Pine Barrens: Inputs and Research Needs for Planning. Proceedings and Papers of the First Research Conference on the New Jersey Pine Barrens*. Pomona, N.J.: Stockton State College Center for Environmental Research.

———, ed. 1982. *History, Culture, and Archeology of the Pine Barrens: Essays from the Third Pine Barrens Research Conference*. Pomona, N.J.: Stockton State College Center for Environmental Research.

———. 1984. Letter to the Editor. *New York Times*, July 22.

Sinton, John W., and Geraldine Masino. 1979. "A Barren Landscape, A Stable Society: People and Resources of the Pine Barrens in the Nineteenth Century." In *Natural and Cultural Resources of the New Jersey Pine Barrens: Inputs and Research Needs for Planning. Proceedings and Papers of the First Research Conference on the New Jersey Pine Barrens*, edited by John W. Sinton, 168–191. Pomona,

N.J.: Stockton State College Center for Environmental Research.

Sinton, John W., and Bill Wills, Jr. 1978. "Hunting Clubs in the Pine Barrens." *New Jersey Folklore* 1:25–29.

Smith, Herbert H. 1979. *The Citizen's Guide Planning*. Chicago and Washington, D.C.: American Planning Association.

Smith, J. David. 1985. *Minds Made Feeble: The Myth and Legacy of the Kallikaks*. Rockville, Md.: Aspen.

Smith, Neil. 1984. *Uneven Development*. Oxford, England: Basil Blackwell.

Sorensen, Jens. 1978. *State-Local Collaborative Planning: A Growing Trend in Coastal Zone Management*. Washington, D.C.: U.S. Department of Commerce, Office of Coastal Zone Management and Office of Sea Grant.

South Jersey Resource Conservation and Development Council. 1979. "South Jersey Resource Conservation and Development Area Plan. Mimeographed.

Stalley, Marshall, ed. 1972. *Patrick Geddes: Spokesman for Man and the Environment*. New Brunswick, N.J.: Rutgers University Press.

Stansfield, Charles A., Jr. 1983. *New Jersey: A Geography*. Boulder, Colo.: Westview.

Steiner, Michael C. 1983. "Regionalism in the Great Depression." *Geographical Review* 73:430–446.

Strong, Douglas H. 1984. *Tahoe: An Environmental History*. Lincoln and London: University of Nebraska Press.

Sullivan, Joseph F. 1990. "Multimillion Fraud Shakes New Jersey Haven for Aged." *New York Times*, September 3.

Sullivan, Ronald. 1969. "As New Jersey Goes . . . Governorship Election Ramifications Are Expected to Reach Washington." *New York Times*, September 27.

Sussman, Carl, ed. 1976. *Planning the Fourth Migration: the Neglected Vision of the Regional Planning Association of America*. Cambridge, Mass.: MIT Press.

Swanson, Bert E., Richard A. Cohen, and Edith P. Swanson. 1979. *Small Towns and Small Towners: A Framework for Survival and Growth*. Beverly Hills, Calif.: Sage.

Tedrow, John C. F. 1979. "Development of Pine Barrens Soils." In *Pine Barrens: Ecosystem and Landscape*, edited by Richard T. T. Forman, 61–79. New York: Academic Press.

Terrie, Philip. 1981. "The Adirondack Forest Preserve: The Irony of Forever Wild." *New York History* 62:261–288.

————. 1985. *Forever Wild: Environmental Aesthetics and the Adirondack Forest Preserve*. Philadelphia: Temple University Press.

Thomas, Charlotte E. 1985. "The Cape Cod National Seashore: A Case Study of Federal Administrative Control Over Traditionally Local Land Use Decisions." *Boston College Environmental Affairs Law Review* 12:225–272.

Thompson, Grant P. 1985. "The Environmental Movement Goes to Business School." *Environment* 27:6–11, 30.

Tobias, Michael, ed. 1985. *Deep Ecology*. San Diego: Avant.

Tocqueville, Alexis de. 1945. *Democracy in America*. Edited by Phillips Bradley. New York: Vintage Books.

Trela, John and Lowell Douglas. 1979. "Soils, Septic Systems and Carrying Capacity in the Pine Barrens." In *Natural and Cultural Resources of the New Jersey Pine Barrens: Inputs and Research Needs for Planning. Proceedings and Papers of the First Research Conference on the New Jersey Pine Barrens*, edited by John W. Sinton, 37–58. Pomona, N.J.: Stockton State College Center for Environmental Research.

Tucker, William. 1982. *Progress and Privilege: America in the Age of Environmentalism*. New York: Anchor/Doubleday.

Turner, Frederick Jackson. 1920. *The Frontier in American History*. New York: Holt, Rinehart and Winston.

U.S. Congress. House. 1977a. Remarks by Representative James J. Florio on "Preservation of Pine Barrens National Ecological Reserve." *Congressional Record* 123 (April 20): 11474–11478.

————. 1977b. Remarks by Representative Edwin B. Forsythe on H.R. 9535, "Pinelands Preservation Act." *Congressional Record* 123 (October 13): 33711–33714.

————. Subcommittee on Fisheries and Wildlife Conservation and the Environment of the Committee on Merchant Marine and Fisheries. 1978. *Hearings on Pinelands National Wildlife Refuge (Pomona, NJ)*, November 28, 1977.

U.S. Senate. 1977. Remarks by Senator Harrison Williams on S. 2306, "National Reserves System Act of 1977." *Congressional Record*, November 4, 37249–37251.

————. Committee on Interior and Insular Affairs, Subcommittee on Parks and Recreation. 1975. *Green-line Parks: An Approach to Preserving Recreational Landscapes in Urban Areas*. 94th Cong., 1st sess.

————. Subcommittee on Parks and Recreation of the Committee

on Energy and Natural Resources. 1979. *Hearings on S. 2706, S. 2848, H.R. 12536*, August 4, 1978.

U.S. Department of Commerce. Bureau of the Census. 1982. *1980 Census of Population. General Population Characteristics*. Washington, D.C.: U.S. Government Printing Office.

U.S. Department of the Interior. 1980. Final Environmental Impact Statement: *Proposed Comprehensive Management Plan for the Pinelands National Reserve*. Philadelphia, Pa.: Heritage Conservation and Recreation Service.

U.S. Department of the Interior, National Park Service. n.d. "Pine Barrens of New Jersey." Study Report. Mimeographed.

————. 1972. *Part Two of the National Park Service Plan: Nature*. Washington, D.C.: U.S. Government Printing Office.

————. 1976. "New Jersey Pine Barrens: Concepts for Preservation." Mimeographed.

————. Mid-Atlantic Regional Office. 1984. "The New Jersey Pinelands: A Progress Report on the Nation's First National Reserve." Mimeographed.

U.S. Environmental Protection Agency. 1987. *Unfinished Business: A Comparative Assessment of Environmental Problems: Overview Report*. EPA/230/2-87/025a. Washington, D.C.: U.S. Environmental Protection Agency.

————. 1988. *Future Risk: Research Strategies for the 1990s*. SAB-ED-88-040. Washington, D.C.: U.S. Environmental Protection Agency.

————. 1990. *Reducing Risk: Setting Priorities and Strategies for Environmental Protection*. SAB-EC-90-021. Washington, D.C.: U.S. Environmental Protection Agency.

U.S. Man and the Biosphere Program. 1989. "Biosphere Reserves: What, Where and Why?" *Focus* 39(1):17–19.

Van Abs, Daniel J. 1986. "Regional Environmental Management in the Pinelands National Reserve." Ph.D. dissertation, University Microfilms, Ann Arbor, Mich.

VanKoski, Susan. 1983. "If at First You Don't Secede . . ." *New Jersey Reporter* 13:16–20.

Vidich, Arthur J., and Joseph Bensman. 1968. *Small Town in Mass Society*. Princeton: Princeton University Press.

Vig, Norman J. 1984. "The President and the Environment: Revolution or Retreat?" In *Environmental Policy in the 1980s: Reagan's New Agenda*, edited by Norman J. Vig and Michael E. Kraft,

77–96. Washington, D.C.: CQ Press.

Vig, Norman J., and Michael E. Kraft. 1984a. "Environmental Policy from the Seventies to the Eighties." In *Environmental Policy in the 1980s: Reagan's New Agenda*, edited by Norman J. Vig and Michael E. Kraft, 3–26. Washington, D.C.: CQ Press.

———, eds. 1984b. *Environmental Policy in the 1980s: Reagan's New Agenda*. Washington, D.C.: CQ Press.

Vivian, Eugene. 1979. "Habitat Investigations on Threatened Plant Species in the New Jersey Pine Barrens and Their Implications." In *Natural and Cultural Resources of the New Jersey Pine Barrens: Inputs and Research Needs for Planning. Proceedings and Papers of the First Research Conference on the New Jersey Pine Barrens*, edited by John W. Sinton, 132–145. Pomona, N.J.: Stockton State College Center for Environmental Research.

Wacker, Peter O. 1979. "Human Exploitation of the New Jersey Pine Barrens Before 1900." In *Pine Barrens: Ecosystem and Landscape*, edited by Richard T. T. Forman, 3–23. New York: Academic Press.

Walker, Richard A., and Michael K. Heiman. 1981. "Quiet Revolution for Whom?" *Annals of the Association of American Geographers* 71:67–83.

Warren, Roland L. 1963. *The Community in America*. Chicago: Rand McNally.

Waterfield, Larry. 1986. *Conflict and Crisis in Rural America*. New York: Praeger.

Weaver, Clyde. 1984. *Regional Development and the Local Community: Planning, Politics and Social Context*. Chichester, England: Wiley.

Weissman, Dan. 1980. "Assembly Votes to Uproot Byrne's Power on Pineland's Development." *Star-Ledger* (Newark), June 7.

Wengert, Norman. 1976. "Citizen Participation: Practice in Search of a Theory." *Natural Resources Journal* 16:24–40.

Westcoat, James C., Jr. 1984. *Integrated Water Development: Water Use and Conservation Practice in Western Colorado*. Research Paper 210. Chicago: University of Chicago, Department of Geography.

Weygandt, Cornelius. 1940. *Down Jersey: Folks and Their Jobs, Pine Barrens, Salt Marsh and Sea Islands*. New York: D. Appleton-Century.

White, Gilbert F. 1969. *Strategies of American Water Management*. Ann Arbor: University of Michigan Press.

Williams, Raymond. 1973. *The Country and the City*. New York:

Oxford University Press.

Williams, Rosalind. 1985. Review of *Dwellers in the Land: The Bioregional Vision* by Kirkpatrick Sale. *New York Times*, October 6.

Wilson, Graham. 1978. "Farmers' Organizations in Advanced Societies." In *International Perspectives in Rural Sociology*, edited by Howard Newby, 31–53. Chichester, England: Wiley.

Wirth, Conrad L., Ben H. Thompson, and Roger Thompson. 1967. *A Report on a Proposed Adirondack Mountains National Park*. New York: n.p.

Wolf, Peter. 1981. *Land in America: Its Value, Use, and Control*. New York: Pantheon.

Wood, Colin J. B. 1976. "Conflict in Resource Management and the Use of Threat: The Goldstream Controversy." *Natural Resources Journal* 16:137–158.

Woodland Township. 1976. "Township of Woodland." Official Souvenir Program.

———. 1983. *Master Plan*. Prepared by Townplan Associates and revised by Marc Associates.

Zelinsky, Wilbur. 1973. *The Cultural Geography of the United States*. Englewood Cliffs, N.J.: Prentice-Hall.

INTERVIEWS

Adams, George. Member, Township Committee, Woodland Township. September 13, 1984.

Ammon, Albert. Chair, Woodland Township Planning Board. October 3, 1984.

Applegate, Alberta. Former teacher, Chatsworth School, Woodland Township. November 28, 1984.

Ashmun, Candace. Pinelands commissioner. March 8, 1983.

Backer, Robert. Principal, Chatsworth School, Woodland Township. November 28, 1984.

Barrett, Carol. Former chair, New Jersey Sierra Club (West Jersey). June 15, 1985.

Barringer, Mae. Resident, Woodland Township; member, Pine Barrens Coalition. August 27, 1984.

Batory, Joan. Pinelands commissioner; director, Camden County Environmental Center. August 26, 1982.

Bembridge, Robert. Pinelands Commission Public Programs coordinator. October 26, 1982.

Bird, Arthur. Mayor, Hamilton Township. January 10, 1985.

Bloom, Jane. Attorney, Natural Resources Defense Council. October 18, 1985.

Brady, Barry. Pinelands Commission cultural resources planner. February 22, 1984.

Brower, Ethel and Peter. Director of finances and former mayor (respectively), Woodland Township. November 8, 1984.

Brower, Walter. Dean, School of Education, Rider College. July 11 and July 18, 1985.

Buzby, Katherine. Former proprietor, Buzby's General Store, Woodland Township. August 28, 1984.

Byers, Michelle S. Special Projects coordinator, New Jersey Conservation Foundation. July 12, 1985.

Byrne, Brendan T. Former governor of New Jersey. September 24, 1985.

Carpenter, Betsy. Education Programs coordinator, Pinelands Commission. August 13, 1984.

Carter, Reverend Raymond. Pastor, Chatsworth United Methodist Church, Woodland Township. November 29, 1984.

Catania, Michael. Director, Office of Regulatory Affairs, New Jersey Department of Environmental Protection; former committee aide and executive director, New Jersey Senate. August 28, 1985.

Cedar, Bernard. Director, Burlington County Planning Board. October 19, 1982.

Chadwick, John T., IV. Planning director, E. Eugene Oross Associates. December 4, 1984.

Chamberlain, Thomas. Principal planner, Camden County. August 12, 1982.

Chavooshian, B. Budd. Pinelands commissioner; land use specialist, Rutgers University. April 5 and April 11, 1983.

Coady, Sharon. Chair, Hamilton Township Planning Board. January 24, 1985.

Cobb, Carol. Clerk, Woodland Township. August 14, 1984.

Conover, Kirk. Businessman, consultant, clammer. June 22, 1984.

D'Angelo, Louis. Mayor, Berlin Township. August 25, 1982.

DeGeso, Michael. Chair, Manchester Township Historical Commission. March 7, 1985.

DePetris, Robert and Katherine. Members, Woodland Township

Committee; former proprietors, Buzby's General Store. November 28, 1984.

Dewey, William. Author, numismatist, Manchester Township. March 20, 1985.

Dodd, Frank. Former New Jersey state senator and chair, Senate Energy and Environment Committee. August 21, 1985.

Donahue, Joseph. Reporter, *Atlantic City Press*. January 2, 1985.

Ekelman, David. Mayor, Ocean Township. September 29, 1982.

Eugster, J. Glenn. Chief, Division of Park and Resource Planning, U.S. Department of the Interior, National Park Service, Mid-Atlantic Office. July 29, 1985.

Festa, Mary. Planner, City of Vineland. July 29, 1982.

Fisher, David B. Director of environmental affairs and planning, New Jersey Builders Association. May 30, 1985.

Fiorilli, Patrick. Mayor, City of Vineland. July 29, 1982.

Gandolfi, Edward. Mayor, Folsom Boro. August 6, 1982.

Gillespie, Angus. Associate professor, Department of American Studies, Rutgers University. March 15, 1984.

Gudauskis, Fran. Resident and former proprietor, Buzby's General Store, Woodland Township. December 11, 1984.

Haines, M. Dean. Deputy county clerk, Ocean County. August 5, 1982.

Hauptman, Jack. Superintendent, Fire Island National Seashore; formerly with Heritage Conservation and Recreation Service. October 17, 1985.

Hedge, Thomas. Proprietor, Buzby's General Store, Woodland Township. November 19, 1984.

Hengst, William. Planning consultant. September 29, 1982.

Hoagland, Nancy. Planning Board administrator, Hamilton Township. January 3, 1985.

Hoskins, David. Science associate, Environmental Defense Fund. June 27, 1985.

Jackson, Janet. Chair, Conservation Committee; past president, New Jersey Audubon Society. June 28, 1985.

Jados, John. Environmental officer and chair, Environmental Commission, Hamilton Township. February 6, 1985.

Johnson, Tyree. Former television news reporter. November 30, 1984.

Kent, Rodney. Member, Woodland Township Planning Board. November 18, 1984.

Kessler, Stephen J. Assessor, Winslow Township. November 23, 1982.

Kruysman, Mary. Planning Board secretary, Manchester Township. February 27, 1985.

Kubiac, William C. Dennis Township construction official. January 20, 1983.

Kurtz, George. Chairman, Bass River Township Planning Board. August 19, 1982.

Layton, Katherine. Chair, Hamilton Township Historical Commission. January 23, 1985.

Linky, Donald. Vice-President, New Jersey Business and Industry Association; former chief counsel to Governor Byrne. August 6, 1985.

Little, Charles E. Private consultant. September 20, 1985.

Lynch, Joseph. Mayor, Manchester Township. March 20, 1985.

MacIver, Loren C. Executive director, Manchester Township Municipal Utilities Authority. February 27, 1985.

Manton, Albert E. Administrator, Franklin Township. August 12, 1982.

Marsh, Elizabeth. Chair, Galloway Township Planning Board. January 20, 1983.

Matlack, Marvin. Resident, Woodland Township. October 4, 1984.

Moore, David. Director, New Jersey Conservation Foundation. July 24, 1985.

Moore, Terrence D. Executive director, Pinelands Commission. January 29, 1982.

Morrison, Albert. Schoolteacher, Woodland Township. August 27, 1984.

Nagy, Lewis J. Director, Burlington County Department of Economic Development. October 19, 1982.

Newcomb, Charles E. Pinelands commissioner; assistant planning director, Gloucester County. August 26, 1982.

Nunnenkamp, Ronald C. Clerk, Winslow Township. November 23, 1982.

Palmer, William. Planning consultant. September 29, 1982.

Patermo, Joseph. Planning director, Camden County. August 13, 1982.

Patterson, Gary. Resident, Woodland Township; former Pinelands commissioner. October 26, 1984.

Patton, Aubrey. Member, Parvin State Park. August 12, 1982.

Peary, Margaret. Member, Township Committee, Ocean Township; Barnegat Township Planning Board. September 29, 1982.

Pollock, Steven L. Planning director, Ocean County. September 13, 1982.

Portash, Joseph. Administrator, Manchester Township. February 6, 1985.

Price, Sally Brecht. Executive director, Pinelands Preservation Alliance. May 29, 1991.

Ripley, Elmer. Vice-chair, Hamilton Township Historical Commission. January 23, 1985.

Roberts, Joseph J., Jr. Freeholder director, Camden County. August 13, 1982.

Romick, Charles E. Principal planner, Gloucester County. August 18, 1982.

Rubinstein, Nora. Ph.D. candidate, Environmental Psychology Program, City University of New York. August 24, 1982.

Scangarello, Thomas J. Planning consultant. October 26, 1982.

Schuck, Elaine. Chair, Barnegat Township Planning Board. August 13, 1982.

Scolpino, Robert. Planning director, Gloucester County. August 18, 1982.

Shinn, Robert C. Vice-chair, Pinelands Commission; Burlington County freeholder. October 9, 1982.

Sinton, John. Pinelands commissioner; professor, Environmental Studies, Stockton College. November 16, 1982.

Speer, Lisa. Scientist. Natural Resources Defense Council. August 21, 1985.

Stemmer, Peter. Town clerk and Planning Board secretary, Bass River Township. July 22, 1982.

Stevenson, John and Marcella. Members, Woodland Township Planning Board. December 12, 1984.

Thompson, Mary Ann. Attorney, Vincentown. September 10, 1985.

Tolischius, Peter. Planning consultant, Manchester Township. March 27, 1985.

Vivian, V. Eugene. Director of Research, Conservation and Environmental Studies Center. October 22, 1982.

Walnut, Nancy and Richard. Members, Pine Barrens Coalition Steering Committee. June 23, 1985.

Wells, Sharon. Tax Office, Woodland Township. August 14, 1984.

West, Floyd. Pinelands commissioner; mayor, Bass River Township. August 7, 1982.

Wills, Constance. Planning Board secretary, Woodland Township. September 13, 1984.

Worrell, Stanley. Blueberry farmer, teacher. Woodland Township. November 1, 1984.

Worthington, Charles. Former executive, Atlantic County. June 15, 1984.

Index

Accommodation, of local interests and concerns: regional planning and, 152–153; reversal of trend toward, in Adirondacks, 196. *See also* Communities, case-study

Adams, George, 149

Adirondack Council: compared with Pinelands Preservation Alliance, 123; and wealthy absentee landowners, 192–193

Adirondack Forest Preserve, creation of, 23, 194

Adirondack Local Government Review Board, 40, 43, 80

Adirondack Park, 15, 16; and Adirondack Northway, 27–28; bioregionalism in, 44; compared with Pinelands, 31; conflict over wilderness area designation in, 122; as greenline park, 15; and gubernatorial leadership, 176; leisure home development in, 36; opposition to regional planning in, 31–32, 40, 42–43, 71, 80, 196–197; private land ownership in, 32; public interest in, compared with Pine Barrens, 74; state support for regional land use programs in, 192; as vacation mecca, 74. *See also* Commission on the Adirondacks in the Twenty-First Century

Adirondack Park Agency (APA), 149; compared with Pinelands Commission, 120, 168; creation in 1971, 31–32; opposition to, 196; relationship with Adirondack Council, 123; response to opposition to regional planning, 42–43

Adirondack Park Agency Private Land Use and Development (1973), 30, 31–32; conformance to, compared with Pinelands plan, 169

Adirondackers: as conservationists, 152; opposition to regional planning, 42–43; stereotypes of, 189

Adirondacks, Temporary Study Commission on the Future of, 31

Aesthetic considerations in Pinelands management, 102

Age structure of case-study communities, 138t

Agricultural interests, 129–133; and business interests nationally, 130; characteristics of, 110t; Farm Bureau as representative of, 131–132; influence of, 130; leadership of, 126; opposition to Pinelands planning, 13, 169; and Pinelands decision making, 133; and transfer of development rights program, 130–131; and U.S. Supreme Court decision of 1964, 129. *See also* Farmers

Agricultural lands: in Comprehensive Management Plan, 99; and Quiet Revolution, 36; and Reagan administration, 46; and state laws, 30, 42

Agricultural "readjustment," 24

Agricultural Study Commission, 131–132

241